Social Work Practice in Child Welfare

THEODORE J. STEIN
University of Illinois

Prentice-Hall, Inc., Englewood Cliffs, New Jersey, 07632

Library of Congress Cataloging in Publication Data

Stein, Theodore J
  Social work practice in child welfare.

  Includes bibliographical references and index.
    1. Social work with children—United States.
  2. Social work with children—United States—Case
  studies.   I. Title.
  HV741.S745   362.7′0973   80-20556
  ISBN 0-13-819524-2

HV   4-1-81
741
.S745
c. 1

To Andrew Michael Stannard without whose assistance and support
this book would not have been written

Printed in the United States of America

10 9 8 7 6 5 4 3 2 1

Editorial production/supervision
  and interior design by Cyrus Veeser
Cover design by Infield/D'Astolfo Associates
Manufacturing Buyer: John Hall

Prentice-Hall International, Inc., London
Prentice-Hall of Australia Pty. Limited, Sydney
Prentice-Hall of Canada, Ltd., Toronto
Prentice-Hall of India Private Limited, New Delhi
Prentice-Hall of Japan, Inc., Tokyo
Prentice-Hall of Southeast Asia Pte. Ltd., Singapore
Whitehall Books Limited, Wellington, New Zealand

Contents

3

Protective Services, Foster Care, and Adoption   *58*

4

Issues in Child Welfare Services   *99*

Part 2

PROVIDING SERVICES TO CHILDREN AND FAMILIES   *117*

5

Information   *119*

6

Assessment—The Beginning Phase 149

7

Assessment—The Investigation 184

8

Case Planning 212

Part I

CHILD WELFARE: THE SOCIAL CONTEXT

INTRODUCTION

The subject of this text is child welfare, an area of specialization within the field of social welfare. The concept of welfare is an expression of the value that society places on helping people. In child welfare, this concept is operationalized as a series of activities and programs through which society expresses its special concern for children and its willingness to assume responsibility for some children until they are able to care for themselves.[1] Social work is one of the professions charged with performing the activities through which social welfare objectives are accomplished.

Social work practice in child welfare is not necessarily synonymous with social work practice with children. The following definition of child welfare services may be used as a reference point for understanding the nature of social work practice in child welfare:

Child welfare services have as their objective the *preservation of family life*. As such, the *family* unit rather than the individual is the population of concern. We are concerned specifically with children who are *dependent, neglected* [or abused].[2] [emphasis added]

Three components of this definition are useful for our purposes. These are (1) the problems that give rise to the need for services, (2) the populations that are served, and (3) the objectives of programs. The concepts of dependency, neglect, and abuse are defined with reference to the behaviors of parents and the effects of certain behaviors on children. For example, child abuse often occurs through acts of commission, whereby parental actions cause a child to suffer physical injury. Services are provided to parents and children in order that family life can be restored and preserved. Thus families, not individuals, are the service population, and restoring and preserving family life are service objectives. Social work practice with children is conceptually broader than social work practice in child welfare. Services may be provided to resolve any of the myriad problems of childhood and adolescence, ranging from behavior problems affecting a child's progress in school to severe emotional problems that may limit a youngster's future potential. The child, alone, may be the focus of intervention, and there is no presumption of parental fault. While the family unit may benefit from assistance offered to a child, this is not the primary objective of assistance. The setting in which services are offered provides a further point of distinction. Most child welfare services are provided under the auspices of public welfare agencies. Social work practice with children occurs in diverse settings such as schools, community mental health centers, and family service agencies.

It is possible to argue for alternative approaches to making the distinctions that concern us. Since the concept of child welfare suffers from a lack of shared definition and since one-half of the states differ in the services they classify under the rubric of child welfare, it is clear that different approaches may be used. For our purposes, the definition of child welfare services offered above sets boundaries on the material to be covered in this text. These boundaries and what they include will become clearer in the following pages, in which the objectives of this text and the plan for achieving them are reviewed.

Preface

"Happy families are all alike; every unhappy family is unhappy in its own way,"* begins Leo Tolstoy's trenchant study of family relations, *Anna Karenina*. This famous opening suggests two insights of special interest to child welfare workers: first, that there does exist an ideal of family life, allowing readers of the passage to know what Tolstoy means, and to summon up an image of a healthy, prosperous, loving family; and second, that troubled families do face diverse, seemingly idiosynchratic problems, whose apparent uniqueness hinders their solution by discouraging families from seeking help.

Social workers concerned with children attempt to help troubled families, with their multitude of problems, become more like the "ideal" family as defined in law, literature, and informally by society. Early on, this text examines the "ideal" or autonomous family and considers the implications that this social archetype has for workers in our field.

The quote opening this preface implies the existence of an infinite and irreducible number of family problems. Despite the variety of causes, though, the results are tragically similar, and workers in the field become familiar with the scenario of dependent children suffering from abuse or neglect. It is not surprising, then, that social work practice in child welfare treats the family as the unit in which problems arise, and through which problems can often best be overcome. Social work practice in child welfare differs from social work with children in the treatment of the family as its primary concern.

Social work in child welfare is a profession in the service of an ideal, and this book's organization reflects the dual nature of the field. Part one surveys the concepts and programs most important to workers concerned with children, acquainting the reader with the ideas shaping child welfare theory, while part two offers cases and examples illustrating the nuts and bolts of field work and showing how practice follows

*Count Leo Tolstoy, *Anna Karenina* (New York: The Modern Library Publishers, 1930), p. 3.

theory. The text covers many specific problems that confront child welfare workers and it reviews a variety of activities that workers undertake to serve children and their families through social programs such as protective services, foster care, and adoption.

Social welfare programs demonstrate a society's concern for the well-being of its less priveleged or legally incompetent members. The range and depth of social programs in a nation are an index not only of that country's wealth, but its commitment to realizing ideal social conditions. Social work practice in child welfare is one of the professions charged with nurturing that ideal, and workers in this area owe it to themselves and their clients to know theory as well as practice. This book hopes to guide students to an understanding of both.

OBJECTIVES AND OVERVIEW

This text is divided into two parts. The objective of the first part is to acquaint the reader with the major components of the system within which child welfare practice occurs. The first part of the text provides a conceptual scheme for ordering the elements of the system of child welfare and for understanding the relationships among these elements.

The preservation of family life is the rationale for the existence of the child welfare system. Our perceptions of families—their strengths and weaknesses in coping with the problems that create risks to family stability—shape the content of child welfare programs. In chapter one we will explore some of these perceptions and consider how accurately they reflect family life in the last quarter of the twentieth century. In chapter two the role of federal and state government in providing child welfare services is reviewed. We will concern ourselves with social policy and various legislative and statutory provisions for providing services to families and with the relationship between federal and state government in the operation of child welfare programs. The juvenile court and its role in the delivery of child welfare services is also explored in this chapter. Chapter three describes three major areas of child welfare services: protective services, foster care, and adoption services. We will review the objectives of these services and the structural elements that taken together create a framework that makes service provision possible. Research relevant to understanding the strengths and weaknesses of current knowledge and practice is reviewed here and in chapter four. In the last of the four chapters that make up part one, issues in the provision of child welfare services are explored. Impediments to realizing the objective of finding permanent homes for children are identified, and new supports for attaining the goals of permanency—found in legislative activity, juvenile court activity and innovations in child welfare practice—are reviewed.

The objective of part two is to describe the processes in which child welfare workers engage while providing the services discussed in chapter three, and to illustrate these with case examples taken from practice. Information is the subject of the first of six chapters in part two. The sources on which child welfare workers rely for information are described, and a framework for evaluating this information is presented. We will examine methods of recording information, review the contents of case records, and discuss some of the ways in which child welfare personnel use information. In the next four chapters the processes involved in assessment and investigation, case planning, service delivery and evaluation, case termination and follow-up are covered in detail. In the final chapter, future directions in child welfare are explored.

There are necessary limitations to the material covered in any text. For example, there are in excess of twenty federal programs that affect the well-being of children. Chapter two of part one covers only three of these: Aid to Families with Dependent Children, the Food Stamp Program, and Medicaid. The provisions in federal policy through which these social services are provided are explored. These areas are selected because in combination they have the greatest impact on families-at-risk. Other federal programs—housing assistance, for example—benefit no more than 10 percent of the population served by child welfare workers.[3] The second and perhaps more compelling reason for these limitations is that our objective is to further the reader's understanding of concepts and to provide a conceptual framework for understanding how our society approaches the task of providing assistance to needy families, rather than to detail numerous existing programs, many of which are undergoing significant change.

The decision to cover protective services, foster care, and adoption services follows from the fact that these programs account for over 70 percent of all services child welfare workers provide for children and their families.[4] There are limitations here as well. These services, adoptions in particular, are more extensive in practice than the material covered here will suggest. While the processes that are explored are described in great detail, the overriding concern is to acquaint the student with the ways in which these services interface to provide permanent homes for children. Thus, certain adoption services, such as family planning, are not covered, and certain issues (such as the controversy over whether adoptees should have access to adoption records) are not reviewed.

NOTES

1. *Child Welfare as a Field of Social Work Practice*, 3d. ed. (New York: Child Welfare League of America, 1967), p. 5.

2. Elizabeth A. Ferguson, *Social Work: An Introduction* (Philadelphia: J. B. Lippincott Company, 1975).

3. B. J. Frieden, "Housing," *Encyclopedia of Social Work - Volume I*, eds. John B. Turner and others (Washington, D.C.: National Association of Social Workers, 1977), pp. 639–51.

4. Ann W. Shyne and Anita G. Schroeder, *National Study of Social Services to Children and Their Families* (Washington, D.C.: United States Children's Bureau, DHEW publication No. [OHDS] 78-30150, 1978), p. 62.

1

The Family

Society expresses its concern for family life in statutory law, in social policy, and in funding programs through which services are provided to restore, strengthen, and preserve family life. Social values—our ideals of what family life *should be*, as well as our perceptions of what it *is*—profoundly influence the provisions found in legislation and policy and give direction to program development. Understanding the strengths and weaknesses of the system within which child welfare services are offered proceeds on an understanding of our ideals and perceptions of family life. In this chapter these ideals and perceptions will be identified, and consideration will be given to the question of how accurately they reflect family life in the last quarter of the twentieth century. The implications of these views for families, for the development of programs that serve families, and for direct practice in the field of child welfare are addressed.

THE AMERICAN FAMILY: VALUES AND PERCEPTIONS

The social value having the greatest influence on legislation, policy, and program development is the concept of family sanctity. Sanctity refers in part to matters of privacy. Tradition holds that family privacy should not be violated except where intrusion by an outside authority is necessary to protect the rights of family members or to safeguard their well-being. The concept also expresses the state's interest in preserving the family unit as the basic framework for raising children. The right of parents to raise their children free of outside interference is "considered to be as close to a 'natural right' as the law and society recognize."[1]

Our perceptions of family life are influenced by the information that we have describing the condition of families at any given point in time. Our values, in turn, influence the information that we gather, how we interpret this information, and hence, our perceptions. The following examples of what we know about families highlight their changing character:

- Between 1948 and 1975 the percentage of married women with children aged six to seventeen who were working outside of the home or looking for work doubled from 26 percent to 52 percent. The number of working mothers with children under six tripled in the same period.[2]
- In one-parent families the percentage of working mothers was higher still. Seventy-two percent of those with children six to eleven years of age and 56 percent with children under six were employed. Overall, 80 percent of these women worked full-time.[3]
- The number of children affected by divorce increased 700 percent between the turn of the century and the early 1970s. While the remarriage rate was higher for persons previously married than for single people, it was expected that four out of ten children born in 1970 would spend a part of their childhood in single-parent, female-headed families.[4]
- The percentage of women who were unmarried when their first child was born doubled from 5 percent in the late 1950s to 11 percent in 1971. Approximately one million of these women established their own households with their babies each year.[5]

Other changes in family life, not as easily quantified, have taken place. During the latter part of this century Arlene Skolnick notes the following:

- "Numerous people are involved in relationships and living arrangements that may not be recorded in official statistics—unmarried couples living together, married couples living apart, or practicing 'open' marriages, or in a number of ways trying to alter the traditional terms of married life."
- There is "an atmosphere of increased frankness about sexuality. Formerly taboo subjects are openly discussed, and formerly taboo sexual practices, such as homosexuality, have emerged as defensible ways of life."[6]

One of the ways in which this information is evaluated is seen in the frequently drawn conclusion that the American family is being "destroyed." Why this particular evaluation? Why "destruction" and not simply change? Before this question can be answered, we must identify the reference point against which change is evaluated and consider some of the ramifications of this particular view.

At times of change it is not uncommon for people to become nostalgic for a more secure past. Past images of the family suggest that it consisted of two parents, one of whom (the mother) remained at home while the other (the father) worked. The family was often an extended one that included several generations living under one roof or within close proximity of each other. This family was autonomous, capable of satisfying its own needs through personal initiative, and hence, rarely relied on larger society. How accurate is this picture? No one knows for sure. There is, and always has been, a paucity of data describing the average American family and how this family goes about the business of raising children. We do know that the division of labor between men and women that we have learned to accept as a norm is a phenomenon of recent history. Support for the participation of women in the labor force fluctuates as a function of economic necessity. Thus, labor shortages in the early colonies dictated that all family members, including children as young as six, work together.[7] When the locus of production shifted from home to factory, men remained at home tending farms and small businesses, and women and children labored in factories, comprising 90 percent of the industrial work force in the early nineteenth century.[8] For black children and their families, slavery provided the framework for child labor. During the Civil War and in both world wars, women entered the labor force in large numbers to fill vacancies that were created when men went off to war. When the labor of women was no longer necessary—when jobs were needed for men returning from the war—society devised ways to get women back in the home. Thus concepts such as the "maternal instinct" were glorified in order to make a virtue out of motherhood.[9]

What about the extended and nuclear family? Wolfe summarizes historical information on this topic as follows:

> The nuclear family, composed of a couple and their growing offspring, separated often from close ties with other relatives, was thought to be a modern development of urban, industrial society, brought on by separation from the land and the mobility forced on people by the need to seek work. But the farther historians have pushed into the past, searching for the "golden age" of the family, the more it has seemed to elude them. Studies indicate that even in rural parts of Europe before the seventeenth century the average

household size rarely rose above four or five persons, some of whom were as apt to be servants as relatives. There are, of course, many instances where families of three generations or several siblings lived under one roof, or on the same property, but these usually mark only a period of transition in the life cycle of the family unit. Without overstating the case, it can be said that the most common pattern of family life in western civilization for many centuries has been one of nuclear units with a considerable degree of mobility.[10]

Are families as autonomous as tradition would have us believe? Autonomy is a function of possessing personal and monetary resources that enable independent action. Thus, the self-sufficient family is able to provide for its own needs and to solve its own problems with a minimum of outside assistance. To the extent that help is needed, it is purchased through the private marketplace. This idea, of all of our ideas about family life, has had the strongest impact on the development of child welfare services. Therefore, this issue is addressed in detail.

Our ideas about the *autonomous* family, like those about family life in general, are rooted in early American history. From Colonial times until the Industrial Revolution, families, by and large, gained economic independence through farming and home industries. The home was the locus of formal education and of children's socialization into the world of adults. Home health care prevailed long before the amenities of modern medicine were available.

The conditions permitting this measure of self-sufficiency were modified during the nineteenth century. Industrialization brought with it a dependence on the economic marketplace. Today, the economic stability of families fluctuates in relation to the demand for labor. The Great Depression and the cyclical periods of recession that have occurred since then serve as ready reminders of the vulnerability of all people to the vicissitudes of the economic market. In the twentieth century, education and health-care functions have been turned over to institutions external to the family. While families still play a primary role in socializing children, many related functions are performed by schools, television, and peer group relationships.

New family functions were emphasized as educational and health-care functions declined in importance. The role of family members in meeting each other's emotional needs was stressed, and of particular significance at this point in history is what the Carnegie Council on Children refers to as the "executive function" of parents. This role is made necessary by the multitude of "experts" and the diversity of institutions that are now involved in raising children. It requires that parents "consultate with teachers, find good health care, monitor television watching, and so on."[11] This role is made difficult because parents have little authority over others (teachers, psychiatrists, psychologists, social workers and media personnel) with whom they share child-care responsibilities. In fact, they frequently operate from a position of "inferiority or helplessness" in the face of credentialed experts.[12]

This brief review suggests that American families have undergone cyclical change throughout history and in particular since the mid-nineteenth century. Change may be more a hallmark of family life than constancy.

> Families were never as self-sufficient or as self-contained as the myth made them out to be, but today they are even less so than they used to be. They are extraordinarily *dependent* on "outside" forces and influences, ranging from the nature of the parents' work to the content of television programming, from the structure of local schools to the organization of health care. All families today need and use support in raising children. [To deny this] . . . is to deny the simplest facts of contemporary life.[13]

While the extent of family dependency is recognized in the literature and is no doubt known to state and national legislators, it has yet to make a significant impact on legislation, policy, and programs. We now turn to consider some costs of sustaining the myth of the autonomous family.

FAMILIES-AT-RISK

When we say that someone is at risk, we mean that certain conditions endanger that person or family in identifiable ways. Conditions that prevailed during the depression, which put families-at-risk of losing their income and thereby sliding into poverty, demonstrate this. Our perceptions of family life create some risks for all families and increase the vulnerability of others. In general, sustaining the myth impedes the development of new models for helping families cope with the realities of life in this period of our history. For example, how are parents to manage their "executive function"? The relative lack of control parents have over institutions and individuals that affect the well-being of their children is particularly troublesome because we cling to the view that parents bear sole responsibility for what becomes of their children. This may foster a sense of guilt if parents accept this view but are unable to affect those with whom they share the tasks of

raising their children. The problems confronting families are exacerbated because the helping professions have devoted greater attention to
the "criticism and reform of parents themselves than to the criticism
and reform of the institutions that sap their self-esteem and power."[14]
And for some families these risks are further exacerbated by poverty,
racism, and sexism. In the following pages we will explore the problems created by these three variables.

Poverty

To be poor is to be at risk. Leaving aside, for the moment, a definition of
poverty, let us look at some of these risks and review some factors
associated with them. Poor families are more vulnerable than nonpoor
families to a broad spectrum of problems, ranging from ill health to
being uprooted against their will by urban development. Children are
especially vulnerable. They are the group most likely to live in abject
poverty. Here are some relevant facts:

- In 1977, while 11.6 percent of the general population lived in poverty, 15.8 percent of all children did. Younger children were even more
likely to be poor: 18.3 percent of all those under three; 18.1 percent of all
those from three to five; and 17.5 percent of all those from six to thirteen.
One out of every ten children in this country depends on welfare for
survival.[15]
- The risk of dying in the first year of life is approximately two-thirds
greater for poor children than for those whose families live above the
poverty line.[16]
- Having made it through the first year of life, poor children are four
time more likely than nonpoor children to be in "fair or poor health."[17]
- Children from the lowest socioeconomic strata live in substandard
housing.
- Children from poor families are at a disadvantage when entering
school. They are "most likely to have low cognitive development ... and
are less able in general to cope with school."[18]

How is poverty defined? Is it a fixed or relative condition? The
official standard used to define poverty is called the poverty index. It is
based on the United States Department of Agriculture's estimated cost
of a "temporary, low-budget, nutritious diet." Since food costs are said
to represent one-third of a low-income family's expenses, the budget
figure is multiplied by three to yield a figure that represents the
minimum income needed by families to buy a "subsistence level of
goods and services."[19] The index is adjusted for family size, place of
residence (urban or rural, farm or nonfarm) and for inflation. When

viewed in this manner, poverty is a fixed condition. The number of poor people at any time can be estimated by applying index statistics to census data that describe families by current income, size, and place of residence. In 1977, 24.7 million persons (11.6 percent of the population) lived below the poverty level.[20]

An alternative view sees poverty as a relative condition, defining it in relation to the standard of living enjoyed by the general population. This perspective takes subjective variables into account to view poverty, in part, as a "state of mind." Relativists ask the question: To what extent are the problems of absolute poverty exacerbated by input—from advertising, television dramatizations, films, and direct observation—through which people are informed that the standard of living they enjoy is below that enjoyed by a majority of Americans?

The Advisory Committee on Child Development of the National Academy of Sciences and the Carnegie Council on Children argue that families whose income is at or near the official poverty line are particularly vulnerable to risk.[21] They take the position that the poverty line should be defined relative to the standard of living for a family whose income is at an intermediate level for the country as a whole. They recommend that the poverty level be set at 50 percent of this figure.

In order that the reader may see this issue more clearly, data are presented in Table 1.1 showing the total monthly income of two families of comparable size and how this income might be used by various categories of expense. The income of one of these families is at the poverty level. For the other it is set at an "intermediate" level

TABLE 1.1

Monthly Budget for Poor and Intermediate Income Urban Families of Four–1973

Consumption Item	Poor	Intermediate
Total	$378	$859
Food	126	265
Housing	140	242
Transportation	9	84
Clothing and Personal Care	89	105
Medical Care	—	53
Gifts, Contributions and Life Insurance	—	50
Recreation, Education, Tobacco, and so forth	14	60
Total	$756	$1,718

From Robert Harris and Alair A. Townsend, "Poverty" in *Encyclopedia of Social Work,* Vol. II, eds., John B. Turner and others (Washington, D.C.: National Association of Social Workers, 1977), p. 1031.

defined by the Department of Labor as 75 percent of the national median.

The inadequacy of the poverty-level budget should be readily apparent. "Luxuries" afforded the intermediate-level family—owning an automobile, "dessert after meals, rugs, a bed for each family member, school supplies or an occasional movie"[22]—are not accessible to poverty-level families. And what of necessities? One hundred and forty dollars per month for housing, which includes "rent, utilities, and household operations,"[23] is not apt to be sufficient for anything but substandard accommodations. Unless the poor live in federally subsidized projects or are able to obtain rent subsidies, their housing is likely to be physically inadequate ("lacking indoor plumbing, lacking central heat or built-in heating or in an extreme state of physical disrepair"),[24] or overcrowded, or both. The food budget of the poverty-level family allows for one dollar per person per day. The most skilled meal planner would have difficulty providing a nutritionally balanced diet with this limitation. The family cannot set aside money for medical care and life insurance, and one can only wonder at what "recreation, education, tobacco and so forth," can be purchased for approximately twelve cents per person per day.

Racism

Billingsley defines racism, the next risk factor, as follows:

> Systematic oppression, subjugation and control of one racial group by another dominant or more powerful racial group, made possible by the manner in which the society is structured.[25]

Racism takes two forms. It is manifested at the *individual* level by "attitudes and/or behaviors exhibited by members of the dominant racial group toward members of another racial group which are negative, unfavorable, and detrimental to the well-being of the latter and functional for the well-being of the former."[26] The statement that blacks are "lazy, unwilling to work, and not interested in future achievement" reflects a racist attitude. Racist behaviors proceed on an unquestioned acceptance of stereotypes. Thus, systematic exclusion of blacks from the labor market is explained in terms of their motivation to work; the fact that exclusion benefits the majority groups by eliminating competition for jobs is thereby overlooked. *Institutional* racism "results when a society or its organizations use racist values as the basis for laws or formal policies that affect actions."[27] Ozawa suggests that institutional racism affects the behavior of the state legislators when they are determining the size of AFDC grants.[28] She observes that the percentage of nonwhite people in a state, not the economic capability of the state, influences this decision. The most obvious manifestations of racism are seen in the treatment of black Americans. However, American Indians, Mexican Americans, Asians and other minorities are affected as well.

Because people of color have been systematically excluded from educational and work opportunities, they are far more likely than white families to be poor.

- In 1977, the median income for white families was $16,740; for Hispanic families it was $11,420 and for black families, $9,560.[29]
- In 1977, the poverty line was drawn at approximately $6,191 for a nonfarm family of four. Among all white families, 8.9 percent had incomes below this level, among black families 31.3 percent, and among Hispanic families 22.4 percent.[30]

While the poor generally experience less adequate health care than the nonpoor, the health care available to nonwhites is worse yet.

- In 1976, for every 100,000 live births, nine white mothers died and 26.5 nonwhite mothers died.[31]
- Prenatal care is achieved for 70 percent of all live births in this country, but for only one-half of births to nonwhite mothers.[32]
- In 1975, the infant mortality rate for whites was 14.4 percent per 1,000 live births, for nonwhites, it was 22.9 percent.
- Health care for American nonwhites, using infant mortality as a gauge, was fifteen years behind the care provided for the white population in 1975.

Sexism

Like racism, sexism may exist at both individual and institutional levels. At either level it can be defined by substituting the word "sexism" for "racism" in the above definitions. A sexist *attitude* is reflected by use of the noun "girl" to describe an adult female. The immaturity suggested by use of the former term is translated into sexist behaviors when women are treated as less capable than men and denied access to educational and work opportunities. Sexism becomes institutionalized when the attitude is incorporated into policy that results in the denial of job promotions to women, and salaries lower than those paid to men for similar work. The risks created by sexism are illustrated in the following items:

- In 1975, there were approximately 74.5 million children under the age of eighteen in the United States.[33] Of these, approximately 12.4 million lived in single-parent families, 90 percent of which were female-headed.[34]

• The majority of females that head families are in the labor force: Seventy-two percent of mothers with children six to seventeen years old and 56 percent with children under six. Over 80 percent of these women work full-time.[35]

• In 1974, the average earnings of women working full-time—in all occupational groups and at all levels of education—were only 57.2 percent of what men employed full-time earned.[36]

• Despite the high percentage of working mothers, approximately 67 percent of all female-headed households in 1974 had incomes under $4,000. The proportion with incomes over $15,000 has been less than 2 percent since 1968.[37]

To the extent that sexism is associated with earning differentials, it contributes to the poverty status of a significant number of children.

IMPLICATIONS OF THE MYTH OF FAMILY AUTONOMY FOR CHILD WELFARE PRACTICE

What is the relationship between the three risk factors reviewed and the myth of the autonomous family? And what are the implications of this relationship for social work practice in the field of child welfare? In the following pages I will suggest some answers to the first question and trace out some implications for practice.

I have reported statistics showing that children are disproportionately represented in the population of poor people. The risks created by poverty *alone* are increased by racism or sexism or a combination of the two. The myth of the autonomous family holds up as an ideal the family that is able to satisfy its own needs. Deviations from this pattern, seen for example in the use of publicly supported services by poor and minority families, are viewed as problems peculiar to these population subgroups, rather than as reflections of services needed by families in general need.

I have suggested that families are not, as the myth implies, wholly self-sufficient. However, without data that describe how average middle-class families raise their children and cope with problems of everyday life, the myth is easily perpetuated. There is every reason to believe that middle-class and affluent families purchase services through the private marketplace for many of the same reasons that poor people request services from public agencies. Thus, in order to obtain respite from child-care responsibilities, poor families enroll their children in public day-care programs. More affluent families buy their respite by hiring baby sitters and other providers to care for their children, and by giving them "lessons in music, art, skiing, tennis, pottery, swimming, sailing, woodworking, and dancing."[38] Poor families who require assistance at home must request the services of a homemaker or public health nurse; the middle-class and affluent hire "cleaning women and private nurses."

Almost all of our information describing how parents raise their children has been collected when "circumstances bring children into contact with institutions outside the family."[39] Almost all of these contacts (save for those made through schools, and to a lesser extent through hospitals) are made by poor families. Insofar as the information that we have describes service use by only one segment of the population, we have a skewed picture of the services families need in raising children and how families meet these needs. While the absence of data sets limits to the conclusions we can draw regarding service use by poor and nonpoor families, experience suggests that the latter group does purchase both child-care and home-help services. Viewed in this way, a primary difference between the poor and nonpoor is the availability of economic resources for purchase of services, rather than the relative extent of need for these services. However, since middle-class and affluent families purchase these services—acquire them through their own initiative—their use is not seen as a sign of family failure. When these same services are acquired in the public arena, the need for them is said to be indicative of family problems.

The foregoing describes a two-track system through which services are obtained. On one track we find the middle class and affluent who purchase services through the open market. The poor, who are the major recipients of public services, ride the second track. The structure of this system negatively affects child welfare programs in such a way that their quality is poor.[40] Also, necessary services are not available in a quantity sufficient to meet the public demand.[41] The reasons for this are not difficult to discern. Political support is not strong for programs that serve the poor. Decision making that affects the quality and quantity of programs can be influenced by a legislator's vote-getting behavior, by racist and sexist attitudes, and by the still pervasive Puritan ethic, which dictates that, insofar as the poor are given anything, it should be as little as is needed to assure basic survival. Lacking support, public programs are chronically underfunded and are the first to suffer when government budgets are cut. Public programs bear the stigma that is associated with poverty. Middle-class families can avoid using these services, thus precluding the development of the political power base that is necessary if services are to be upgraded in quality and increased in quantity.

TREATMENT OF CLIENTS

If one uncritically accepts the myth of self-sufficiency—if one thinks that a majority of families raise their children without outside assistance—how can one explain the fact that some families require assistance? There are three trains of thought in this area. The first directs attention to the larger social system to suggest that poverty is a sufficient "cause" of social and family disorganization. This position recognizes that racism and sexism at both individual and institutional levels compound the difficulties created by poverty. An alternative view, and by far the most pervasive line of reasoning in our society, places responsibility squarely on the individual involved.[42] Attention to individual responsibility is deeply rooted in the American pioneer tradition and is reinforced by Freudian theory (a strong influence in clinical practice in this country), which finds the cause of problems "inside" the individual. Thus, attention is directed away from social systems. Character deficits, which parents in a "culture of poverty" are said to pass on to their children, provide yet another perspective from which observed differences between the poor and the nonpoor are viewed. According to this thesis the poor are characterized by such features as inherent laziness, an unwillingness to work, and inability to delay gratification or to plan for the future.

Empirical research does not support the culture of poverty thesis. The poor "struggle to earn as much as they can and to use it as wisely as possible to secure the same kind of life most Americans desire," and they "identify their self-esteem with work as strongly as do the nonpoor."[43] To the extent that work-related behaviors of the poor differ from those of the middle class, experiences in the labor market and certain realities of a poverty existence may be more closely related than personal defects. Evidence gathered on women who participated in the Work Incentives Program (WIN) shows that not obtaining employment —an experience of failing in the work world—negatively influenced the work orientation of the women and made them more likely to accept welfare.[44] Liebow, in his anthropological study of poor and unemployed black men, takes the concept of delayed gratification (impulsivity, spending rather than saving, acting with little regard for the future) are, according to Liebow, realistic responses to the knowledge that dreams will be unrealized and that one's worst fears for the future are well founded.[45]

Direct practice in child welfare proceeds on the assumption that families have problems. The "problem" is not the need for services, per se, but rather some deficiency in members of the family that gives rise to the need. This point is an important one, meriting further exploration.

It has been suggested in the previous paragraphs that middle-class, affluent, and poor families may use similar services for like reasons, but that the absence of data masks service use by the former groups. Once a significant number of people use a given service, its use becomes a norm. Problems exist when all of the people who need a service cannot locate it, or when they cannot afford it. The problem would thus be defined as a deficit in needed resources or as a lack of money, rather than with reference to the individual's need for that service. For example, medical services are in short supply in many rural areas of this country. If we wanted to understand why someone traveled hundreds of miles to request medical care from a hospital in a major city, we would learn little if we said that poor health caused them to travel. The absence of local medical services intervenes between health problems and travel to explain the latter. If local services of good quality were available, we might hypothesize that the individual would have sought assistance as close to home as possible. Some, perhaps, many, of the families that request child-welfare services do have personal problems. Marital difficulties, the absence of child-care skills, emotional problems and so forth may be instrumental to service requests. However, practice proceeds on the assumption that personal problems are invariably instrumental, thus coloring the association between poverty, and resource and monetary deficits, and service requests.

An assumption of personal or familial "pathology" dominates in the helping professions in general and in child welfare services in particular.[46] This orientation often results in the neglect of families' strengths and a preoccupation with identifying the weaknesses that led to requests for services. Moreover, this orientation ignores the social factors that often underlie both service requests and family difficulties. Invariably, pejorative labels such as "neglectful," "abusive," "deviant," "antisocial," or "mentally ill" are assigned to families, and these labels are then presumed to describe why services are needed. Clients are stigmatized by this practice. That is, expectations influence the way people are treated. These expectations in turn are influenced by the labels people wear. Thus, clients may be incorrectly taken to task for requiring assistance. The problems caused by poverty, racism, and sexism are thus exacerbated.

There is an additional way in which our thinking about family autonomy affects the treatment of clients. Child welfare workers are frequently asked to evaluate clients on a number of dimensions related to family life. For example, workers judge whether homes are suitable environments in which to raise children and evaluate the quality of parent-child interaction. In making such evaluations one needs a standard against which the families being evaluated can be measured. From her research of the decision-making behavior of protective service workers (that is, how they make decisions on whether to place children in foster care or provide services to them in their own homes), Boehm reports that workers use a "model family"—for our purposes, the self-sufficient family—as a frame of reference.[47] This implies that families are at risk of being evaluated by a standard of behavior that does not exist in the community-at-large and asked to conform to this ideal.

EVALUATING CHANGE

Now we can return to the question raised earlier and consider why the changes identified at the beginning of this chapter are said to be "destroying family life." The word "destruction" implies complete loss, while the word "change" does not. Coping with change suggests a considered, thoughtful process. Coping with destruction demands a swift response. To say that the family is being destroyed is to signal the demise of a major social institution and the cradle of our most cherished social values. The confounding of the ideas of change and destruction may reflect the need for a "simple manageable set of images that will allow us to make sense out of what would otherwise be too complex, too various, too changeable to understand."[48] This confused response to changes in patterns of family life may be related to the *rapidity* of change, rather than to the fact of it. The simple images that are evoked by television programs such as "The Waltons" and "Family" do more to reinforce our fictions than to provide us with a clear comprehension of reality.[49]

The current concern about family life crystalized in the 1960s, a decade of social ferment, as evidenced in campus unrest, protests against the war in Southeast Asia, disenchantment with government because of that war (reinforced by the events of Watergate) and the ethnic, women's, and gay liberation movements. The events of this period are best understood in juxtaposition to the complacency and apathy that characterized the 1950s.

Toffler makes the point that rapid changes, which individuals may perceive themselves as helpless to control, can have so great an impact on the psyche that one wants to "stop the future" and "regress" to the past.[50] It matters little that the images evoked bear only a slight resemblance to prior realities. What does matter is that these images are comforting. The family of old is only one component of the nostalgia craze of the 1960s and 1970s. We see evidence of it in the "fascination with rural communes," in the sudden value placed on used furniture and clothing styles from a bygone era, and in the resurrection of films from the past.[51]

The fear that is created by change can be used in a political context by those in whose interest it is to maintain the status quo. This can be illustrated by an example from recent history. In 1972 both houses of Congress passed legislation (The Comprehensive Child Development Act) that would have made federal funds available for day-care programs for all children. This legislation was subsequently vetoed by then President Richard M. Nixon. In his veto message, Nixon argued that

> For the federal government to plunge headlong financially into supporting child development would commit the vast moral authority of the national government to the side of communal approaches to child rearing over [and] against the family-centered approach.[52]

Two aspects of this statement are noteworthy. First, by using the word "communal," President Nixon may have created an association between day care and "communism" that was troublesome to many Americans.[53] Second, he pitted day care against the "family-centered approach" to raising children, thus capitalizing on the already pervasive concern that the family was being destroyed.

Reference to communal vs. family approaches to child rearing directs attention to another element that may influence our thinking about changes in the family. Specifically, we lack models of what family life might look like if the observed changes continue. Some changes (for example, "open" marriages and unmarried couples living together) may properly be viewed as experiments which prefigure such models.

What would happen if, instead of evaluating change as destructive, we placed it in a historical context and viewed it as an ongoing adjustment to life in urban, industrialized societies? To adopt such a perspective is to acknowledge that the difficulties confronting families will not vanish by attempts to resurrect the past. Even assuming that lost ideals were accurate reflections of family life, they may not be applicable to the realities that confront families in the twentieth and twenty-first centuries. Thus, we might view current changes as the development of potentially useful mechanisms to help families cope, and we might consider what other mechanisms are needed. The problem, however, centers on issues such as who should develop these mechanisms and what their affect will be on family structure. Some people are concerned that the magnitude of the problem is so vast that necessary mechanisms can be established only by means of increased government intervention. Attention is directed to three possible difficulties. First, the value that we place on family sanctity suggests a "hands off" position when it comes to solving the problems of families. This value admonishes us to stay out of family life and supports the belief that families can solve their own problems. (This is one reason why we have failed to gather descriptive information about how families raise their children and how they cope with adversity.) The second area of concern is that government intervention to assist families will affect other areas of social and economic life. If the government provides day-care services or medical services for all people, how will the private sector react? What will happen to the economic market if the government creates jobs for the unemployed? And what will be the effect if the government substantially increases income supports to raise all families out of absolute poverty? Will there be anything left of the family as we know it today if government intervenes on a large scale to help solve these issues? While economists make efforts to predict the effects of large-scale government intervention in the economic marketplace, we have no seers to predict the effects in family life, save for the doomsayers. Neither can we predict the effects of our current hands-off policy, or whether the difficulties confronting families will escalate to a crisis. It seems reasonably clear that, despite problems, most families do at least a creditable job of raising their children. This observation does not escape the attention of legislators. As we will see in subsequent chapters, the role of the government in family life is significant and it is increasing. It goes well beyond what one might expect, given the presumption of noninterference that follows from the value that we place on family sanctity.

The observed changes in family life and the recognition that families are dependent on a variety of support systems challenge us to define the proper role of government and the types of public service programs needed to restore, strengthen, and preserve family life.

SUMMARY

The concept of family sanctity expresses the value our society places on family privacy and the right of parents to raise their children free from outside intervention.

Family life in the last quarter of the twentieth century is undergoing change. A greater percentage of mothers work outside of the home, and a greater number of children live in single-parent families, due in part to rising divorce rates and the willingness of unmarried women to establish their own households with their children. Change is also evident in life styles and sexual mores.

These changes are frequently interpreted as heralding the destruction of family life. A call to return to the extended, self-sufficient family is heard.

Historical information descriptive of family life is sparse, but there is good reason to question the accuracy of this image.

We persist in our view of autonomous families, able to satisfy their needs with a minimum of outside assistance. We have not taken into account how families are affected by outside forces over which they have no control.

Families are dependent on and influenced by the nature of their work and by the fact that many child-rearing functions have been taken over by external institutions, so that parents must rely on a variety of "experts" with whom they share child-care responsibilities.

Families are at a disadvantage because of the absence of skills needed to "manage the managers" with whom child-care responsibilities are shared. They are vulnerable because they are held accountable for what happens to their children despite the relative lack of control over outside forces that influence child development.

For some families the foregoing problems are compounded by poverty, racism, and sexism—alone or in combination.

Children are more apt to be poor than any other segment of the population.

Children in poor, nonwhite, and female-headed families suffer from substandard health care, live in substandard housing, and enter school at a disad /antage.

In the view of many Americans, these families are personally responsible for their situation. The focus on individual responsibility, deeply rooted in American tradition, is supported by theories of human behavior that locate the source of problems "inside the individual"; this view is reinforced by the myth of the autonomous family.

Middle-class and upper-class families purchase services through the private marketplace. Poor families depend upon the public sector for the same services. The fact that data on private purchase of services have not been compiled leads to the conclusion that the poor have unique service needs.

The result is a two-track system of child-welfare services. Public sector programs for the poor comprise one track, services offered through the private marketplace the other.

Public child welfare programs, because they are used almost exclusively by the poor, lack political support. They are underfunded and have been described as programs of poor quality; they bear the stigma associated with poverty.

The myth of the autonomous family provides an artificial standard against which poor families are evaluated and found wanting.

Evidence suggests that the poor struggle to attain economic self-sufficiency. Institutional racism and institutional sexism, rather than individual fault, may best explain the negative experiences of the poor in the labor market.

The rapidity of change and the absence of alternative models for family life results in a measure of anxiety that increases efforts to maintain the status quo. The suggestion that family life is being destroyed is best viewed as an effort to reduce anxiety by stopping change.

An alternative to the destruction hypothesis is to see change as an on-going process and to direct attention to the need for support systems for all families.

The suggestion that support be provided by governmental action raises the concern that family sanctity will be violated and leaves unanswered questions about how government-sponsored support systems will affect the family unit and the larger economy.

NOTES

1. *Children's Rights Report*, Vol. 1, No. 5 (New York: Juvenile Rights Project of the American Civil Liberties Union Foundation, February 1977), p. 1.

2. Advisory Committee on Child Development, *Toward a National Policy for Children and Families* (Washington, D.C.: National Academy of Sciences, 1976), p. 15.

3. Ibid.

4. Carnegie Council on Children, *All Our Children: The American Family Under Pressure* New York: Harcourt Brace Jovanovich, 1977), p. 4.

5. Ibid., p. 5.

6. Arlene Skolnick, *The Intimate Environment: Exploring Marriage and the Family*, 2d ed. (Boston, Mass.: Little, Brown & Company, 1978), p. 4.

7. Robert H. Bremmer and others, eds. *Children and Youth in America*, Volume 1, *1600–1865* (Cambridge: Harvard University Press, 1970), p. 103.

8. Ibid., p. 146.

9. M. Roman and W. Haddas, "The Case for Joint Custody," *Psychology Today*, Vol. 12, No. 4 (September 1978), pp. 96–105.

10. S. G. Wolf, "Family Portrait," *Bryn Mawr Alumnae Bulletin*, Vol. LIX, No. 1 (Fall, 1977), pp. 2–5.

11. Carnegie Council, *All Our Children*, p. 17.

12. Ibid., p. 18.

13. Ibid., p. 22.

14. Carnegie Council, *All Our Children*, p. 23.

15. United States Bureau of the Census, "Money Income and Poverty Status of Families and Persons in the United States: 1977-Advance Report," *Current Population Reports*, Series P-60, No. 116 (Washington, D.C.: U.S. Government Printing Office, 1978), p. 1; *For the Welfare of Children* (Washington, D.C.: Children's Defense Fund, 1978), p. 7.

16. Carnegie Council, *All Our Children*, p. 32.

17. Ibid.

18. Advisory Committee, *Toward a National Policy*, pp. 45–56.

19. R. Harris and A. A. Townsend, "Poverty" in *Encyclopedia of Social Work: Volume 11*, eds. John B. Turner and others (Washington, D.C.: National Association of Social Workers, 1977), p. 1030.

20. United States Bureau of the Census, "Money Income and Poverty," p. 1.

21. Carnegie Council, *All Our Children*, p. 31; Advisory Committee, *Toward a National Policy*, p. 52.

22. Harris and Townsend, "Poverty," p. 1031.

23. Ibid.

24. B. J. Frieden, "Housing," in *Encyclopedia of Social Work: Volume 1*, p. 640.

25. Andrew Billingsley and Jeanne M. Giovannoni, *Children of the Storm: Black Children and American Child Welfare* (New York: Harcourt Brace Jovanovich, 1972), p. 8.

26. Ibid.

27. Henderson and Kim, cited in Donald Brieland and John Lemmon, *Social Work and the Law* (St. Paul, Minn.: West Publishing Co., 1977), p. 498.

28. M. N. Ozawa, "An Exploration into States' Commitment to AFDC," *Journal of Social Service Research*, Vol. 1, No. 3 (Spring 1978), pp. 245–59.

29. United States Bureau of the Census, "Money Income and Poverty Status of Families and Persons in the United States: 1977-Advance Report," *Current Population Reports P-60*, No. 118 (Washington, D.C.: U.S. Government Printing Office, 1979), p. 1.

30. Ibid., p. 1.

31. United State Bureau of the Census, *Statistical Abstracts of the United States*, 99th edition (Washington, D.C.: U.S. Government Printing Office, 1978) Table No. 106, p. 74.

32. The remaining health-care statistics cited here are from: Carnegie Council, *All Our Children*, p. 156.

33. John B. Turner, *Encyclopedia*, Table 2, p. 1623.

34. Advisory Committee, *Toward a National Policy*, p. 17.

35. Ibid., p. 18.

36. Carnegie Council, *All Our Children*, p. 92.

37. Advisory Committee, *Toward a National Policy*, p. 23.

38. S. H. White, "Socialization and Education—for What and by What Means?" in *Raising Children in Modern America: Problems and Prospective Solutions*, ed. Nathan B. Talbot (Boston: Little, Brown & Company, 1976), p. 143.

39. Advisory Committee, *Toward a National Policy*, p. 15.

40. Alvin L. Schorr, "Poor Care for Poor Children—What Way Out?" *Children and Decent People*, ed. Alvin L. Schorr, (New York: Basic Books, Inc., Publishers, 1974), pp. 186–212.

41. Saad Z. Nagi, *Child Maltreatment in the United States: A Challenge to Social Institutions* (New York: Columbia University Press, 1977), pp. 85–87.

42. *For the Welfare of Children*, p. 11.

43. Advisory Committee, *Toward a National Policy*, p. 46.

44. Ibid.

45. Elliot Liebow, *Tally's Corner* (Boston, Mass.: Little, Brown & Company, 1967), pp. 64–68.

46. M. K. Rosenheim, "Notes on Helping Juvenile Nuisances," in *Pursuing Justice for the Child*, ed. Margaret K. Rosenheim (Chicago, Ill.: University of Chicago Press, 1976), p. 57; Shirley Jenkins and Elaine Norman, *Beyond Placement* (New York: Columbia University Press, 1975), p. 142.

47. B. Boehm, "An Assessment of Family Adequacy in Protective Cases," *Child Welfare*, Vol. 41 (January 1962), p. 10.

48. J. Adelson, "Adolescence and the Generation Gap," *Psychology Today*, Vol. 12, No. 9 (February 1979), pp. 33–37.

49. Ibid.

50. Alvin Toffler, *Future Shock* (New York: Bantam Books, Inc., 1970) Ch. 16.

51. Ibid., p. 360.

52. Gilbert Y. Steiner, *The Children's Cause* (Washington, D.C.: The Brookings Institution, 1976), p. 113.

53. Ibid., p. 114.

2

Government,
the Courts,
and Family Life

At the end of chapter one I said that government involvement in family life is significant and that it is increasing. The fact that American values set a premium on family privacy—the right of parents to raise their children free of outside intervention—was also noted. The reconciliation of what may appear as contradictory positions begins with recognizing that no right is absolute. The state has a vested interest in how children are raised, which is articulated in compulsory education laws, child labor laws, and neglect and dependency statutes. Through these laws the state establishes ground rules for child rearing that constitute an explicit contract between the state and parents whereby the privacy of the latter is contingent upon compliance with minimum standards set down by the former. The juvenile court is a state mechanism through which compliance with the standards set forth in law is enforced. All relationships between the family and the state (and for that matter, between individuals and the state) involve a delicate balance between an individual's or a family's right to privacy and the right of the state to articulate its interest in future generations. The effort to balance the rights of parents against those of the state manifests itself in court decisions. In 1972 the United States Supreme Court reaffirmed a 1944 opinion that illustrates this position. The Court stated:

It is cardinal with us that custody, care and nurture of the child reside *first* in the parents, whose primary function and freedom include preparation for obligations the state can neither supply or hinder.[1] [emphasis added]

This statement is noteworthy in that the court identifies parental rights as a *first* consideration, thereby suggesting that alternative considerations may enter into decision making. The conditions under which the state may entertain alternatives will illustrate the balancing issues. If the state is able to show a "legitimate and important interest [that] overbalances" the rights that evolve from the value we place on family sanctity, then instrusion into family life may be justified.[2] The state has, for example, a clear interest in seeing to it that future generations are educated in a manner deemed consistent with maintaining democratic principles. Thus, the state's right to further this end, through compulsory school attendance laws, overrides parental rights to deprive children of educational opportunities.[3] The state's interest in protecting children from undue harm is expressed in child abuse and neglect laws through which parents can be held accountable for providing child care and through which limits are set on the exercise of parental authority in disciplining children. As we will see in part two, many decisions made by child-care workers hinge on striking an appropriate balance between individuals and the state, and between the individual members of a family.

The relationship between families and the state has evolved slowly throughout American history. Its current status reflects a tension that is a by-product of efforts to safeguard family privacy and to respect family rights. Simultaneously, the state seeks to advance its interest in the social and emotional development of children and to balance this interest with a growing recognition of governmental responsibility to provide assistance to families to help them manage in an increasingly complex society.

The framework for government action involves a partnership between federal and state levels of government, The federal government sets policy and provides funds to the states to establish programs to restore, strengthen, and preserve family life. The administration and daily operation of these programs are state-level activities. The federal government also sets regulations for program operation and monitors state compliance with these regulations.

This chapter begins with a review of federal policy and the provisions in that policy through which assistance is provided to needy families. Several major programs benefiting families-at-risk are described. Following this, recommendations for reforming the welfare system and suggested directions for family policy are considered. In the last part of this chapter, the role of the juvenile court in the operation of child-welfare programs is addressed.

THE SOCIAL SECURITY ACT

The Social Security Act is the United States law which embodies basic policy through which assistance is provided to needy individuals and families. A policy is a "course or plan of action"[4] for attaining certain objectives. Policy is important to practitioners. To a large extent it shapes practice by specifying the populations to be served and by setting boundaries around the services that are available.[5] The objectives of the act with regard to dependent children are:

> [to] encourage [their] care in their own homes or in the homes of relatives ... to help maintain and strengthen family life and to help such parents or relatives to attain or retain capability for the maximum self-support and personal independence consistent with the maintenance of continuity, parental care, and protection.[6]

Tenets in the act contribute to attaining these objectives in three ways. First, by providing financial assistance which involves the direct transfer of cash from the public treasury to needy families. Aid to Families with Dependent Children (AFDC), Title IV-A of the act, is the major financial program in this group. The second type of provision encompasses what are called "in-kind" programs. Instead of the transfer of cash, which gives the recipient discretionary purchasing power, in-kind programs afford a specific type of service, such as the medical services provided through the Medicaid program. The third mechanism includes social services such as casework counseling, job training and day-care programs, which are available under Title XX of the act.

The act does not provide a comprehensive system of welfare benefits to all needy individuals. Rather it designates certain categories of need. Eligibility for assistance is contingent upon membership in one of these categories. Three of the original groups covered are unemployed (Unemployment Insurance), the elderly (Old Age Survivors and Disability Insurance), and children in need as a result of parental death, desertion or physical or mental disability (Aid to Dependent Children, or ADC). These and other categorical programs, such as Workmen's Compensation, Veteran's Benefits and Supplemental Security Income, are collectively known as "public assistance programs." Aid provided through any of these may benefit children. A child living in a family supported by unemployment insurance is an example. However, AFDC is the only program with the single, expressed purpose of benefitting children. Other forms of public assistance were developed to provide aid to adults.

AFDC

In February 1978 there were approximately 11 million recipients of AFDC. About 70 percent were children and the remainder represented adult members of their families.[7] Aggregate monthly payments equaled $834 million.[8] The program has grown considerably in the past forty years, increasing from a low of 1.22 million beneficiaries in 1940 to the 1978 figure reported above. Dollar costs have increased from over 149 million in 1945 to over 10 billion in 1978.[9] Despite this growth, AFDC "represents only 5 percent of all federal, state and local spending for cash assistance and only 3.3 percent of all welfare spending."[10] In 1975 the percentage of black and white families in the program was almost equal: Blacks comprised slightly more than 44 percent; whites slightly more than 50 percent. The remaining recipients were "other ethnic groups."[11] In 1973, women headed roughly three-quarters of all recipient families.[12] Federal regulations permit the states, at their option, to provide assistance to two-parent families with an unemployed father (AFDC-UF). Twenty-eight states have exercised the option to do so. In general, two-parent families with fathers who work more than 100 hours per month are ineligible for aid regardless of need.[13]

Operation of the AFDC program represents a partnership between federal and state governments. The federal government provides funds to the states to help defray the costs of providing assistance; they establish regulations with which the states must comply to receive funds; and they monitor compliance with regulations by checking plans the states submit to the Department of Health, Education and Welfare in which the mechanisms established for complying with regulations are described.[14]

The states have a great deal of latitude in operating AFDC programs. Each determines the size of an AFDC grant by establishing a "need standard" which is an estimate of the amount of money necessary to meet a family's basic needs within that state. However, states are not required to pay the full amount of the standard. In 1976 only twenty-five states were doing so.[15] Because of the latitude states have in setting payment rates, the amount of money received by a family of four ranged from $514 per month in Hawaii (100 percent of its need standard) to $60 per month in Mississippi (21 percent of its need standard).[16]

Eligibility for assistance is determined by using one of two models. The first—the self-declaration model—requires an eligibility worker to check information provided by the client for internal consistencies (for example, a worker would check to see whether the income reported by an applicant is sufficient to cover reported expenses). If the application "passes muster" the grant is approved without further verification.[17] The second approach requires that the information provided by clients be verified. Procedural requirements may include visits to the client's home and verification of income and expense records, as well as of documents such as birth, marriage, and death certificates.[18] Additionally, states decide whether to provide emergency assistance to families in crisis situations, whether to aid families with an unemployed father in the home, and whether to continue payments for youngsters aged eighteen to twenty-one who are attending school, college, or vocational training schools. Each state decides how much of the cost of the program will be assumed at the state level and the amount to be borne by local units of government. The federal share is calculated by a complex formula. In general, approximately 55 percent of the total is paid by the federal government, the states assuming responsibility for the remaining 45 percent.[19]

Medicaid

In 1965 the Social Security Act was amended to allow for the provision of federal monies to the states in order to

> Furnish medical assistance on behalf of families with dependent children and of aged, blind, and disabled individuals whose income and resources are insufficient to meet the costs of necessary medical services.[20]

Medicaid, Title XIX of the act, is the largest of the "patchwork" of programs through which the federal government provides medical care for more than 20 million poor children.[21]

AFDC recipients are automatically eligible for Medicaid. At state option, coverage can be provided for "medically needy" persons— those whose incomes disqualify them from cash assistance programs, but whose medical expenses reduce their incomes below the level of eligibility for medical aid.[22] One-half of the states exercise this option.[23] The costs of Medicaid include payments to physicians, hospitals, nursing homes, and pharmacists, as well as administrative costs. In the fiscal year 1975 program costs amounted to $12.7 billion.[24]

Operation of the Medicaid program is similar to that of the AFDC program as far as federal participation is concerned. The federal government provides funds, establishes regulations, and monitors compliance. Each state pays a part of program costs. The cost-sharing formula and eligibility requirements are the same as for AFDC.

In order to receive federal funds states must provide certain coverage, such as inpatient hospital care, outpatient hospital services, and skilled nursing home services to individuals aged 21 and older.[25] However, each state determines the number of inpatient hospital days for which they will pay. And, at state option, "almost complete coverage of all medical, dental, and pharmaceutical costs" can be provided.[26]

THE FOOD STAMP ACT

Under the Food Stamp Act of 1964, eligible individuals and families may purchase food vouchers with face value well in excess of their purchase price.[34] The food stamp program is administered by the Department of Agriculture. While it is not part of the Social Security Act, it is nonetheless an important social welfare program because food stamps can increase family income. The average income supplement in 1977 was $80 per month for a family of four.[35]

Recipients

The Food Stamp program is the only public assistance program providing coverage solely on the basis of need.[36] Food stamps are available to "all low-income households without regard to age, disability, work status or presence of children."[37] Eligibility is contingent on income and family size and not on the availability of income from relatives and former spouses, as in the AFDC program. As a result, families whose income is above the poverty level may receive assistance. In 1976 more than one-half of the nation's 18.5 million food stamp recipients were not welfare recipients.[38] In 1977 the cost of the program to federal, state, and local governments was approximately 6 billion dollars.[39] It was becoming the most rapidly growing component of public assistance.

Operation

Federal regulations mandate the existence of Food Stamp programs in all counties. The cost of the program is borne by the federal government except for administrative expenses, which are shared with the states. Prior to 1977 AFDC recipients were automatically eligible for stamps. The passage of Public Law 95-113 in 1977 changed that so that AFDC families had to meet the eligibility requirements set for all recipients. Also, prior to passage of this law, participants were required to pay a set amount of money in exchange for stamps, the value of which exceeded the recipient's cash outlay. For example, in 1972, a family of four with a monthly income under $100 paid $25 for stamps worth $108.[40]

The purchase requirement was said to discriminate against the poorest groups, who could not afford the cash outlay, and was viewed as a major drawback to this program. It was estimated that 6 million Americans who earned less than $3,000 per year either did not know that they were eligible or could not afford to purchase stamps.[41] For this reason the purchase requirement was eliminated under Public Law 95-113. Thereafter, recipients received the bonus amount only. The family of four who had received $108 worth of stamps for a $25 payment received $83 worth of stamps under the new provision.

The social welfare programs reviewed thus far contribute to the maintenance of family life by enabling recipients to acquire basic necessities through the provision of cash assistance, food stamps, and medical services. The Social Security Act allows for the use of federal monies to establish programs to enable welfare recipients to become self-supporting, thereby strengthening and improving the quality of family life. Attaining the goal of self-support would have the added benefit of reducing the size of the welfare rolls.

SOCIAL CASEWORK SERVICES

In 1956 and again in 1962 Congress amended the act, permitting the federal government to reimburse the states three dollars for every dollar spent to provide *social casework* services.[42] As we will see in subsequent chapters, the concept of casework services embraces a variety of activities that workers engage in on behalf of clients. In the late 1950s and early 1960s, however, the term casework was almost wholly synonomous with counseling.

The emphasis on counseling services to reduce dependency rested on assumptions that poverty was caused by personal inadequacies of a psychological nature. In short, people were to be counseled out of poverty. Confidence in casework services was so great that eligibility for financial assistance was made contingent upon their acceptance.[43] Yet the services did not have the intended effect. Welfare rolls increased each year, so that by 1967, four years after passage of the amendments, 5 million persons were receiving AFDC benefits compared to slightly over 3 million in 1960.[44]

The fact that there was no reduction in the poverty rolls led to disenchantment with casework services, made evident in the 1967 amendments to the act. The concept of services took on a new and expanded definition. "Soft services, which included casework counseling, were deemed 'less valuable' than 'hard services' such as day-care, drug treatment programs and work training programs."[45] The latter, exemplified in the Work Incentive Program (WIN), were seen as particularly important: the primary vehicle through which clients would attain self-support and through which family life would be strengthened.[46]

The 1967 amendments did not require AFDC mothers to work or to accept work training. Mechanisms for work programs and for day-care services which would free mothers to work were established.

Work programs, like the counseling programs that preceded them, have not been successful in reducing economic dependency.[47] Why did they fail to produce the expected results? Surely one of the reasons is that both proceeded on the simplistic assumption that there was a direct relationship between personal inadequacies and economic dependency.[48] The inadequacies were different: In 1956 and again in 1962 the assumption was that psychological problems maintained economic dependency. In 1967 skill deficits and presumed negative attitudes towards work were viewed as causal.[49] Thus, work programs proceeded on the premise that training and motivating people to work were sufficient to reduce welfare rolls. Scant attention was paid to the availability of jobs.[50]

The preoccupation with individual inadequacies as causal to economic dependency is supported by the American view of welfare as a residual institution. In this view, welfare is a secondary social institution that exists to provide support when there is a breakdown in the major, ongoing institutions of the economic market and the family.[51] The institution never ceases to exist, yet the role played by welfare programs fluctuates, increasing or decreasing in relation to the strength of other, primary institutions.[52] Whenever the provision of welfare increases, the residual model directs attention to identifying and solving those problems that caused the increase in order that equilibrium may be restored and the primary institutions may take over the welfare function. An alternative view is provided by an institutional model, which sees welfare as a permanent social institution, one that is "integrated into society, providing services outside the marketplace and family."[53] Rather than a temporary problem-solving mechanism, welfare is seen as a by-product of modern, industrialized society that is made necessary by "inherent limitations in institutions and by the effects of rapid social change on both institutions, individuals and families."[54]

The American experience has, save for the depression and cyclical periods of recession, been one of relative affluence for most of the population, or of upward mobility for those not experiencing affluence. The idea of America as the "land of opportunity" is more than a cliché. It does refer to certain realities of the American experience. Therefore, it should not be surprising that we have sought explanations for "poverty amidst plenty" by focusing on the individual and sought to reduce economic dependency by reforming the individual.

Through a combination of events, such as the failure to reduce dependency through counseling and work programs, and pressure from women and ethnic minorities, we have been forced to recognize that our attitudes and behaviors—specifically, individual and institutional racism and sexism—have played a role in limiting access to the labor market and have thus contributed to maintaining economic dependency.

Title XX

In 1975 the social service efforts of the federal government moved in a new direction with the passage of the Title XX amendments to the Social Security Act. Social services that had been funded under other titles of the act were incorporated into the new amendment, making it the greatest source of social service funds.[27] Title XX differs significantly from prior amendments. In 1962 and again in 1967 services were defined by the federal government. Under Title XX, the content of services is defined by the states, each of which is required to present its Title XX programs in a publicly available document (a Comprehensive Annual Service Program) and to hold public hearings to elicit community response to the programs. In contrast to the relatively limited range of services that were available under prior amendments, a 1975 tabulation by the Department of Health, Education and Welfare reported forty-one *categories* of service. These range from day-care to homemaker services with a total of fifty-one different services listed in the category of services for the developmentally disabled.

Funding

Between 1963 and 1971 federal expenditures for social services increased threefold. It was estimated that by 1973 they would reach 4.7

billion dollars.[28] This prompted Congress to set a ceiling of 2.5 billion dollars on federal social service expenditures under Title XX. In late 1978 Congress increased the funding to 2.9 billion dollars for a one-year period.[29] After the 1962 amendments federal funding for social services was "open-ended," meaning that the government would pay 75 percent of the service costs of *whatever* social service programs each state decided to offer. Under Title XX the maximum amount of federal money *available* to each state is determined by state population. The actual amount *expended* is a function of the state's "willingness and ability to match federal funds by paying 25 percent of the total service bill."[30]

Service Recipients

Prior to Title XX, federal regulations required that 90 percent of all service funds be used for the benefit of public assistance recipients. The remaining 10 percent could be used to provide services to former or potential recipients (individuals and families who would be eligible for financial assistance if they applied).[31] This formula has been relaxed in an effort to make services available to greater numbers of people. Title XX provisions stipulate that at least 50 percent of each state's funds be allocated to current recipients of public assistance. The remaining 50 percent may be used for nonrecipients with annual incomes as high as $16,000.[32] The relaxation in eligibility requirements expands the population of potential service recipients. In 1976 it was projected that two-thirds of the population in eight states and 50 percent of the population in eighteen states would be potential beneficiaries who would not have to meet public assistance eligibility tests.[33]

This review of the Social Security and Food Stamp Acts and social casework services shows that our current approaches to assisting needy families reflect the American view of welfare as a residual institution and are, therefore, inimical to realizing the multiple objectives of restoring, strengthening, and preserving family life. In the following pages we shall consider two suggested approaches to remedying this situation.

WELFARE REFORM

Reforming the welfare system is one way to reduce or eliminate the inequities created by state variations in the size of AFDC grants. Reform measures call for standardizing benefit payments by having the federal government set an "income floor" that would apply nationally. (Conceptually, an income floor is similar to a need standard.) The income floor for a family of four would serve as a reference point for determining the amount of aid to be provided to individuals and family groups of varying size. Benefits would increase or decrease according to the number of persons involved. Cash and food stamp benefits would be incorporated into a single transfer payment. Eligibility would be contingent on demographic characteristics of the recipients, not on proof of poverty, as is currently the case.[55]

Recommendations for welfare reform incorporate work incentives. For example, under one proposal a worker may earn as much as $3,800 without any reduction in benefits. Above that amount, cash benefits would be reduced $0.50 for each dollar of earned income until a point is reached at which benefits would stop.[56]

In addition to reducing systematic inequities, welfare reform also seeks to reduce the bureaucratic complexity that characterizes the administration of welfare programs. This could be accomplished by combining the AFDC and Food Stamp programs, by administering programs at the federal level, and by distributing benefits through the current income tax structure. The phrase *Negative Income Tax* (NIT) refers to the latter approach, through which individuals and families whose income falls below the income floor would receive money from, rather than pay money to, the federal government. The amount received would be the difference between family income, if any, as reported on annual income tax returns, and the income floor. Major impediments to the adoption of a welfare reform program focus on the costs of the program and on who will be required to work.

A COMPREHENSIVE NATIONAL FAMILY POLICY

Welfare reform addresses the importance of changing our current system of providing financial assistance for dependent children and their families. While important, the changes are not sufficient to meet the multiple objectives of restoring, strengthening, and preserving family life. There is growing consensus that if these ends are to be realized we must have a comprehensive national policy for families and children.[57] The concept of a national policy can best be understood by highlighting some of the difficulties in current policy and using these as reference points for clarification.

Our current *categorical approach* has resulted in a plethora of governmental committees, agencies, and programs. Rather than representing a diversity of programs designed to meet the most pressing needs of families-at-risk, these programs constitute a bureaucratic nightmare. They serve overlapping populations, have conflicting goals, and set confusing eligibility standards. Each has its own constituency, in whose interest it competes for limited financial resources. This competition, which has always existed, is reinforced by the 2.9 billion dollar ceiling on Title XX services. The poor in general and children (because they lack political "clout") in particular are at a disadvantage in this competitive marketplace.

Also, funding by categories reinforces compartmentalized thinking that is reflected in the objectives of existing policy. These are often in conflict with, rather than supportive of, each other, resulting in costs to families-at-risk. Consider the following: Maintaining and strengthening family life is one objective set forth in the Social Security Act. However, in the states that have not adopted the AFDC-UF program, eligibility for aid is contingent upon the father being out of the home. If an unemployed male cannot find work and is not eligible for unemployment insurance, his family will benefit financially if he leaves the home. Thus, the program has built into it an incentive for breakup of the family.[58] Similarly, the AFDC-Foster Care program provides for unlimited federal reimbursement to states for maintaining children out of the home, but provides only limited funds for services to prevent placement, thus conflicting with the objective of maintaining family life.[59] In effect, many social welfare policies of government focus on individuals by category, suggesting an insufficient concern with supporting the family as a social unit.

The effects of nonwelfare policy on families must also be considered. For example, family life may be disrupted by urban renewal policies that dictate the destruction of old neighborhoods, effectively displacing family units and separating them from neighborhood support systems.

There are advantages to a categorical approach. The planning, organization, and operation of programs is simplified by development of a single purpose. A categorical approach may open up opportunities for particular children. Special problems can often become rallying points that "facilitate the passage of legislation and organize the efforts of individuals."[60] However, when these advantages are weighed against the costs described above, there is reason to question continuation of a categorical approach. A desire to eliminate current policy shortcomings, thereby reinforcing our commitment to family life, gives impetus to the movement for a comprehensive national family policy. Let us look at this alternative and see how it differs from what we have just reviewed.

A comprehensive national family policy must begin with a statement of society's objectives for all families. Coverage should be universal, not just for those whose need is defined by income deficiencies. Services necessary to realize policy objectives must be identified, the relationships between areas of service must be considered, and an acceptable division of responsibility between federal and state government has to be struck. Three conditions affecting families can be discerned from the objective of restoring, strengthening, and preserving family life. The first is family *breakup*, caused by separation or divorce, or when children are removed from their parent's home and placed in substitute care. The second condition involves a *breakdown* in family life and directs attention to families at risk of breaking up. The final situation may be viewed as a *norm*. The family unit, while stable, is nevertheless vulnerable to the exigencies of life in modern society. The overall goal of social policy should be to move families from the least stable situation (breakup) along a continuum to the most stable (preservation) and to prevent backsliding. Some of the social services necessary to support this goal are applicable only to certain family situations. Some are meaningful under all three conditions. For example, substitute care services (foster home or institutional care) are brought to bear when children cannot be maintained in their own homes. These are meant to protect youngsters and to provide parents with a temporary respite from ongoing child-care responsibilities. Counseling services or parent education classes may be provided to help restore family life, thereby moving them along the continuum to a point where services can be offered to strengthen what has been restored. To prevent breakup, protective services are offered to intact families. They are brought to bear to safeguard children who have suffered abuse or neglect or who are in danger of being maltreated. Services such as counseling and parent education are used to restore family life and also to strengthen it. When the difficulties that lead to breakup or breakdown are worked out, continual service provision may be withdrawn and the situation defined as one of maintaining family life. At this point, services should be available so that families can initiate their use when problems arise and before they escalate to a point of seriously threatening family stability.

It is critical to recognize that policies impact on each other, to identify the relationship between policies, and to be sure that goals are harmonious. For example, work programs that are designed to reduce dependency on income maintenance programs cannot be developed in isolation from monetary policies. These govern the interest rate charged by the federal government, which in turn affects the availability of money at any time. The availability of money affects capital investment by business and hence, work opportunities. Likewise, work policy must be developed along with day-care policy, since single parents cannot be expected to maintain employment without adequate provisions for child care.

Recommendations for national family policy raise many questions to which there are no simple answers: What services are necessary to accomplish the objectives of family policy? What will these services cost? What is the proper division of responsibility between state and federal levels of government?

The question of what services are necessary to accomplish the objectives of family policy can be approached in two ways: (1) by having the federal government identify the needs of all families and structure an array of services to meet these needs (for example, income maintenance programs that provide more than a subsistence level of aid can raise some families out of poverty and prevent others from sliding into it); (2) by allowing the communities being served to decide what services are necessary. The latter is a position that capitalizes on the community involvement provisions in Title XX.

Program costs are difficult to estimate because there is little data to serve as a reference point for predicting how many families would use services that are made available through a national policy. It is reasonable to suggest that money would be saved if current funding practices were made more consistent with policy objectives. For instance, despite the fact that maintaining the family unit is a goal of existing policy, the lion's share of funds is spent on child welfare services that are directed to out-of-home placement of children.[61] Studies have shown that extensive savings can be realized when children are cared for in their own homes.[62] Also, if employment increased through training and incentives for individuals and businesses, the increase in tax revenues could be an added source of funds. And, employed service recipients could pay a fee based on a sliding scale. A graduated income tax and the elimination of tax "loopholes" that benefit the wealthy could be additional sources of money.

In the early stages of a national policy for families, programs may have to be given selective priorities and implemented in an incremental manner. Those that might be expected to reduce the greatest risks confronting families should come first. If program costs force restrictions on who will receive services, populations could also be ranked, with those in greatest need having primary access to services. There is little argument that income programs, health-care services, and day care are top priorities. Other program priorities should be set after research identifies areas that create the greatest risk for families. While

less desirable than full-scale implementation, a staggered introduction would at least set a precedent for national family policy. To avoid reinforcing current inequities, we must remain cognizant of the fact that an incremental approach represents only an approximation to the final objective of providing a full array of services for all families.

To some people the suggestion that the federal government take leadership in family policy smacks of "creeping socialism" and represents a radical departure from our free enterprise system. It is important to recognize that government intervention has increased significantly since the depression—the point in history when the federal government assumed a major role in the provision of welfare—while our economic system has nevertheless remained viable.

The movement toward federal control of welfare programs is clear. Of the original public assistance programs created by the Social Security Act, only AFDC "remains on a joint, federal-state framework."[63] Federal action in 1972 consolidated three former state-administered programs—Old Age Assistance (OAA), Aid to the Blind (AB), and Aid to the Permanently and Totally Disabled (APTD)—into one federally operated program entitled Supplemental Security Income (SSI).

The changing conditions of the American family, outlined in chapter one, are not likely to be reversed, and policies that "ignore or attempt to reverse them are not apt to be successful and will run a grave risk of failing many of the children they were designed to help."[64] The continued growth of federal involvement seems inevitable. The evidence suggests that it is necessary to achieve equity and attain the objectives of restoring, strengthening, and preserving family life. We must take stock of the real situation of significant numbers of families and formulate policy and provide funds in a manner consistent with our expressed concern for the concept of family sanctity.

THE JUVENILE COURT

The juvenile court, or family court as it is called in some states, plays an important role in the provision of child welfare services. It is a state institution whose actions affect both the administration of child welfare programs and the provision of direct services. In this section we will look at the purpose of the court, review the statutory laws which legitimize court action on behalf of children, and discuss court operation as it relates to social work practice in child welfare.

The purpose of the juvenile court is to protect children. Unlike criminal court, where the objective is to establish the guilt or innocence of a person accused of committing a crime, the juvenile court is con-

cerned with prescribing treatment, not ascribing guilt. Hence, the approach is "clinical"; the focus, rehabilitation. The justification for a protective role is found in the English Common Law doctrine of *parens patriae*, under which the sovereign, acting in the role of father, "protected subjects unable to care for themselves."[65] In its modern application it is used to give jurisdiction to the state to "act when a child's best interests are involved." Thus, a juvenile court judge is expected to put himself or herself in the role of a "wise, affectionate and caring parent,"[66] whose task it is to take action to further the well-being of children.

The court has jurisdiction over three classes of children: those who are in need of supervision; those who are said to be delinquent; and those who are dependent or neglected. Children in the first category, referred to as Persons in Need of Supervision (PINS), behave in a manner that would not be of concern to the court if they were adults. These behaviors range from infractions of school rules (such as truancy or disruptive classroom behavior) to problems involving parent-child relationships (such as disobedience or running away from home). Delinquent youngsters engage in acts of commission such as theft or vandalism. Dependent and neglected children, our concern in this text, are youngsters whose parents either cannot or will not care for them. The laws covering this group of youngsters direct attention to parental acts of commission (abuse) or omission (neglect).

The Statutory Authority
to Intervene in Family Life

All states have legislation describing the conditions under which intervention in parent-child relationships may occur. These conditions are set forth in neglect and dependency statutes, which also cover child abuse. Dependency exists when parents, for reasons of poverty, are unable to provide for a child.

The statutes of most states define neglect with reference to "chronic failure of adults" to protect children from physical danger.[67] Many are now being expanded to include "failure to provide for the positive social and psychological development of the child."[68] Whereas dependency statutes do not explicitly point to parental fault, neglect statutes direct attention to parental failure to provide proper care, control, or guardianship of a child (and abuse laws to actions that result in physical or emotional harm to children).[69] Statutes differ state by state, limiting the generalizations that can be made about specific elements in law. For these one must refer to the legal code of the individual state.

Operation of the juvenile court as it relates to dependent and neglected children is depicted in the flow chart in Figure 2.1. Court operations may differ for delinquent and PINS children, and they may vary by state.

Caseworker contact with the court generally begins with the filing of a *petition*. A petition "requests a particular finding from the court."[70] In neglect and dependency cases it is that the court, using evidence that has been gathered by child welfare workers and collaborating professionals, finds the allegation that a child is dependent, neglected, or abused to be correct. In some states workers are legally required to file a petition anytime such evidence is found, whereas in others a worker may decide to petition the court only if parents will not cooperate and the worker needs the authority of the court to intervene to protect a child. At the time a petition is filed, a child may be at home or in a substitute care setting.

After a petition has been filed, a court hearing takes place. Juvenile court proceedings are separated into fact finding (jurisdictional) and decision making (dispositional) stages. At the jurisdictional hearing, a

FIGURE 2.1   Juvenile Court Operation

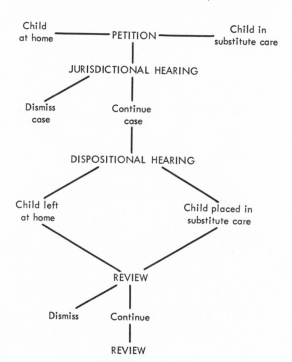

judge must determine whether the facts presented in a petition provide grounds for state intervention. The question of concern is: Do the conditions described and the supporting facts suggest that the child fits the statutory definition of a neglected or abused child? If they do not, the case is dismissed. If they do, a second hearing (dispositional) is held, at which time the judge must decide where the child will live for the immediate future. The options are to leave the child in the home of biological parents under supervision by the child welfare agency or to place the child in a substitute care setting.

The court assumes the authority to make legally binding decisions for children who are declared dependents. Thus the court not only determines where the child will live, but may make certain demands of parents (such as their cooperation with child welfare workers in formulating case plans in which methods for resolving the difficulties that necessitated the court action are spelled out).

Some states have procedures for periodic *review* of cases that are under court jurisdiction. At review hearings, workers present evidence describing a family's progress in solving problems and the child's progress if the child is in out-of-home care. Workers also make recommendations for case disposition. Such recommendations might be: to continue the case in its current status while ongoing services are provided; to alter the status by dismissing protective services; or to return a child from foster care to the home of biological parents. When cases are continued, a date for the next review hearing is set.

The juvenile court is concerned with rehabilitation rather than punishment. Because all its actions are directed at enhancing the well-being of children, the standard for decision making is less stringent here than it is in criminal proceedings. However, the court's decision has far-reaching consequences for the families involved. It is important therefore that we look at the decision-making standard used in juvenile court and some of the consequences of using this standard.

The Juvenile Court Standard for Decision Making

The laws of most states direct juvenile court judges to make decisions that "promote the *best interests of the child*."[71] Katz observes that the decision-making standard embodies a set of shared social values about what is desirable "for the adjustment of children in society."[72] He expresses these values as a series of expectations for children:

> ... we expect our children to be physically and emotionally secure; to become responsible citizens in their community and to become economically independent; to acquire an education and

develop skills; to respect people of different races, religions, and national, social and economic backgrounds; to become socially responsible and honorable, and to have a sense of family loyalty.[73]

The standard comes into play when judges make decisions that affect a child's living arrangements. In making such determinations members of the bench predict whether the child's best interests will be furthered in the home of his parents or in a substitute care situation, or whether children already in substitute care should be returned to their parents or freed for adoption.

PREDICTING OUTCOMES OF DECISIONS

To predict is to hypothesize the outcome of a certain course of action. For example, the decision to place a child in a foster home, rather than leaving the child in the home of biological parents, involves an explicit or implicit prediction that the youngster's well-being will be enhanced by such a move. The process of making predictions requires that a set of facts be weighed in the context of current knowledge. By balancing the facts of a specific case against a more general level of information, predictions about likely outcomes are made. For instance, if we know that the probabilities of abuse are increased when a single parent is unemployed and has no assistance with child care, temporary out-of-home placement may be called for (if respite care services such as homemakers are not available) to give the parent time to find work and arrange for part-time child care. This is an example of a short-term prediction—one in which the decision maker is hypothesizing that the child may suffer harm in the immediate future because of the situation of the parent. The other side of this coin is the prediction that the child will be protected in a substitute care situation. There is no doubt that short-term predictions of this nature must be made. However, many of our efforts to predict concern themselves with the long-range consequences of certain patterns of parenting. The critical issue for child welfare is whether we are able to make these long-range predictions called for by the best interest standard. The evidence that concerns us comes from longitudinal studies of child development. These investigations begin with a series of hypotheses, deduced from theory or induced form clinical practice, that suggest relationships between certain childhood experiences and subsequent adult adjustment. Jean MacFarlane and her colleagues at the Institute of Human Development at the University of California at Berkeley conducted one such study. Beginning in 1929 with a group of 166 infants, she and her associates tested and later interviewed these subjects over a period of thirty years. "The purpose was to observe physical, mental and emotional growth in average people."[74] Based on early data, children's homes were classified as "troubled or untroubled." The predictions the researchers made were straightforward: Children coming from troubled homes would become troubled adults; those from untroubled homes, untroubled adults. What of the predictions? Well, they were wrong in two-thirds of the cases! In MacFarlane's words:

> Many of the most outstandingly mature adults in our entire group, many who are well integrated, highly competent, and/or creative, who are clear about their values, who are understanding and accepting of self and others, are recruited from those who were confronted with very difficult situations and whose characteristic responses during childhood and adolescence seemed to us to compound their problems.[75]

Discussing the children who came from untroubled homes, she reports that those who had "enjoyed admiration, success and approval as children failed to live up to the expectations that the researchers, along with everybody else, held for them. As adults they seemed strained and dissatisfied, wondering what went wrong and longing for the good old days."[76]

Investigations by others highlight our limited ability to make long-range predictions.[77] They also challenge our assumptions that adult behavior is "determined by specific techniques of child rearing in the first five years of life."[78]

There are several reasons why our efforts to predict have proved so fruitless. First, because we assume that early childhood experiences, particularly those occurring in the first five years of life, shape, and perhaps determine, adult adjustment, we fail to take into account the modifying effects of later experiences. Thus, the extent to which children can be influenced by television programming and by ongoing and changing interaction with peers, with teachers, and with other adults is ignored. Also, we have not given due consideration to the child's perception of events and the fact that evaluations that follow from these perceptions can affect future development.[79]

It is also important to note that major support for our hypotheses about the relationships between childhood experiences and adult adjustment come from clinical studies where troubled individuals describe their childhood experiences to therapists or researchers. Data that is gathered from people who come to the attention of professional therapists cannot be presumed to reflect the experiences of the population-at-large or the population of persons with a given problem, because the individuals interviewed have asked for help or been referred for it. Thus, they may differ in significant ways from others who have similar problems but do not receive assistance.

Many of the studies from which child development hypotheses are drawn rely on verbal reports as their main source of information. The reliability of information gathered in this way is suspect because a client's verbal report can be strongly influenced by differential reinforcement from a therapist.[80] If a therapist pays strict attention to a patient when he or she is discussing the past, and minimal attention when the patient is discussing the present, the probabilities are good that the frequency with which past events are reviewed will increase, while the frequency with which the present is considered will decrease. Additionally, these studies accept ex post facto accounts as accurate reflections of the past. The difficulty concerns selective memory and the recognition that in recalling the past, all of us forget information that, if accessible, could lead to conclusions other than those drawn from what is remembered. Freud recognized this problem long ago. He wrote:

> So long as we trace a development from its final outcome backwards the chain of events appears continuous, and we feel we have gained an insight which is completely satisfactory or even exhaustive. But if we proceed the reverse way, if we start from the premises inferred from the analysis and try to follow these up to the final result, then we no longer get the impression of an inevitable sequence of events... We notice at once that there might have been another result, and that we might have been just as well able to understand and explain the latter.[81]

AN ALTERNATIVE STANDARD
FOR STATE INTERVENTION

Critics of the best interest test call for a new standard for state intervention.[82] They argue that removing a child from the parents' home results in the deprivation of certain rights—those of parents to raise their children according to their own conscience, as well as those of a child to be raised by its own parents. In American society justification for depriving an individual of his or her rights rests on showing that the larger society benefits by such action. The benefits in child welfare practice derive from a concern that is common to all societies. It is to direct the development of future generations in ways most conducive to maintaining social values. Since we consider the family unit to be the main force for socializing children, concern develops when we identify families whose behavior seems inimical to this end. However, opponents of the best interest test argue that insofar as our predictive abilities are limited, we must limit intervention to a narrow range of situations where we can clearly show that a child is in danger or is at risk of harm.[83] Reinforcing our commitment to parent-child rights is not the only reason for taking this position. As Schur reminds us, in doing something for a child—because of what he or she needs—we are also doing something to the child.[84] The "something" in this case draws our attention to what happens to some youngsters and to their parents once separation occurs.

It is reasonable to expect that when children are removed from their own homes, they will be placed in settings where their well-being will be enhanced. It is also reasonable to expect that rehabilitative services will be provided to natural parents so that family difficulties can be resolved and parents resume full-time care of their children. Critics argue that we fail many children on both counts.

Supportive data come from a number of studies that have looked at the environments in which children are placed, at what happens to youngsters in these environments, and at rehabilitative services that are offered to natural parents.[85] The environmental issue asks the question: Is the setting in which a child is placed appropriate for his or her needs? For example, if a youngster has academic or behavior problems that contribute to family difficulties and lead to the decision to place the youngster in out-of-home care, we would expect the new environment to include facilities and professional help to remediate these problems. That this does not always occur is clear from data reported by a number of states[86] and illustrated by findings in the State of California which showed that 50 percent of children placed in psychiatric facilities were not mentally ill, but had types of academic or behavior problems not treated in these facilities.[87]

In addition to inappropriate settings, a large number of children are placed in facilities outside their home states, effectively cutting them off from contact with biological families. Others are placed in unlicensed institutions. Abuse and neglect of children in foster homes and institutional settings has been documented.[88] In addition, rehabilitative services for natural parents is the exception, not the rule.[89] Finally, despite the fact that out-of-home placement is intended to be temporary, the median length of time that children spend in substitute care is two and one-half years.[90]

There are many reasons why these difficulties exist. A lack of sufficient placement resources precludes locating the appropriate situation for each child. Monetary concerns may take precedence over a child's need. For instance, it is sometimes less expensive to place a child in an out-of-state institution than one near the home of natural parents, even though we know that the greater the geographic distance between a child and parents, the less the chances that the parents will continue to maintain contact with their child. Hence, the likelihood of the child returning home is reduced. Child welfare workers operate under severe time constraints, due to high caseloads and excessive paper work. This may reduce the chance that they will get to know a child well enough to assess his or her particular placement needs. And this contributes to the lack of services to natural parents.

An alternative explanation for the situation of these children and their families draws attention to what might be termed a hidden agenda in juvenile court decision making. It has been suggested that punishing parents for antisocial behavior, rather than protecting children from specific harms, is an issue behind these decisions. More states have statutes regulating moral conduct than physical neglect,[91] and they are frequently invoked to control behaviors defined by the community as "deviant."[92]

The situations reported above do not apply to all children receiving child welfare services. Many are in appropriate settings, and many parents receive rehabilitative services. However, the social neglect described presents a compelling argument supporting those critics who suggest that we are not serving the best interest of all children.

The assignment of pejorative lables to clients who come in contact with the court raises further questions about state objectives. In order for the court to assume jurisdiction over a youngster, parents must be "alleged to have done something wrong."[93] Thus parents are labeled "abusive," "neglectful," or "mentally ill." Many observers of juvenile court practices take this practice to task for several reasons. First, labels are not descriptive. Suggesting that parents are neglectful, for instance, says nothing about the specific behaviors of the parents vis a vis a child. Most state laws require that the problems that necessitated intervention be resolved before children are returned to the care of their parents. However, the use of general labels does little to inform workers of the changes that must occur, and their use creates an antitherapeutic atmosphere harmful to the rehabilitative objective of child welfare services.[94] For these reasons, the Juvenile Justice Standards Project of the American Bar Association recommends that labels not be used in juvenile court proceedings or reports. Rather, information descriptive of what has been observed should be used at the time a label would routinely be applied.[95]

The difficulties reviewed thus far support the argument that a new standard for juvenile court intervention is needed. If such a standard is to effectively redress the problems created by use of the best interest test, it must take the following into account. First, recognizing that we are unable to make long-range predictions, coercive intervention should be sanctioned only when the danger to the child is identifiable in the present or near future. It should not be dependent on hypotheses about long-range effects. When evidence shows that a child has suffered harm, or where there is a "substantial likelihood that the child imminently will suffer . . . harm," intervention would be appropriate.[96] Intervention decisions should be concerned with the well-being of children, not solely with parental behavior. Thus, it would no longer be appropriate to intervene because parents are mentally ill unless we can show how this affects the child. If, due to emotional difficulties, a parent is not feeding a child or is leaving a young child unsupervised in dangerous situations, intervention would proceed because the child is suffering from malnutrition or is in identifiable danger as a result of not being supervised. Finally, decisions to remove children from their parent's homes and to place them in substitute care should require showing that the child cannot be protected in the home of natural parents from the specific harm that justified intervention.

Efforts to act in the best interests of children are praiseworthy, evidencing as they do society's concern for the well-being of all youngsters. However, when we move beyond the intention of these efforts and take the outcomes into account, we are left with a less than satisfactory picture of goal attainment for significant numbers of children and their families. Since a majority of the clients of child welfare agencies are poor and minority families, it appears that a small segment of the population is being asked to bear the weight of larger society's good intentions.

Changing the decision-making standard is only one step toward resolving the difficulties reviewed. It is an important step, however, insofar as social neglect has been shown to be one consequence of applying the best interest test. There is no question that use of a new standard will also result in errors. Intervention may not occur when it should, and some children will suffer the consequences of this. Either way, there are risks involved.

SUMMARY

The Social Security Act is the basic public policy through which assistance is provided to needy individuals and families.

Its provisions permit the federal government, in cooperation with state governments, to provide cash assistance (AFDC) and in-kind aid (Medicaid) to families-at-risk. These programs, together with food stamps and social services such as casework counseling and job training, are the means by which government seeks to restore, strengthen, and preserve family life.

There are inequities in the system. The AFDC benefit level in one-half the states is less than the minimum necessary to meet a family's basic needs within those states. Benefit levels vary widely from state to state; yet they are in excess of what one might expect, given differences in the cost of living.

Welfare in America is seen as serving a residual function, the importance of which fluctuates in relation to the viability of two more permanent institutions: the economic marketplace and the family unit. When welfare rolls grow, this model directs us to identify and remove the causes of the increase so that primary institutions can take over and restore equilibrium.

This model accepts the viability of the economic marketplace as a given, which helps to explain why our efforts to reduce economic dependency have focused on individual reform and not taken into account larger social forces that contribute to economic dependency.

Reforming the welfare system might reduce inequities. Reform calls for: standardizing benefit programs through federalization of the AFDC program; basing eligibility on demographic characteristics of recipients; consolidating the AFDC and Food Stamp programs; and distributing benefits through the current income tax structure.

We do not have a comprehensive national family policy. Rather, we have numerous programs that serve specific categories of individuals, which increases competition for limited resources. The poor, given their relative lack of political power, are at a disadvantage in this competition.

Current policy goals often conflict, detracting from, rather than contributing to, the overall objectives of restoring, strengthening, and preserving family life.

A comprehensive national policy, with services to reduce risk to all families, is one approach to reinforcing our commitment to family life.

The juvenile court is a state-level institution sanctioned by society to protect and rehabilitate children, not to adjudicate blame or to punish.

The statutes of each state give the court authority over delinquent children, children in need of supervision, and dependent, neglected and abused youngsters.

Dependency results from poverty; neglect, from acts of omission; and abuse, from acts of commission.

Juvenile court operation, as regards neglected and dependent children, involves four steps: Workers file a petition asking the court to declare a child a dependent. The court, in a two-stage process, must first determine whether the child is a dependent child as defined by state law. If so, the court must decide where the child will live. Review of case progress, which may result in dismissal or continuance of a case, is the fourth and last stage.

Most state laws admonish juvenile court judges to make decisions in the best interests of the child. Doing so requires that judges predict and weigh the costs of leaving children in their own homes against the benefits of removing children.

While it is possible to make short-term predictions, given knowledge of current parenting behaviors, evidence from longitudinal studies shows that our ability to make long-range predictions is severely limited.

Data show that, once removed from the home of their parents, many children experience social neglect. Some children are placed in inappropriate settings; rehabilitative services to reunite families are in short supply; and certain of our practices—labeling parents, for example—may exacerbate initial problems.

For these reasons, a new standard for state intervention has been recommended. Such a standard would require that we identify the specific harm to the child with a focus on present and short-term dangers, that we de-emphasize our preoccupation with parental behaviors unless the negative effects on children are established, and that removal be justified only after evidence shows that a child cannot be protected in his own home.

This position is taken because intervention does not invariably result in benefits that outweigh the cost of deprivation of rights. We must reinforce our commitment to parental rights and family privacy by allowing parents to raise their children free of outside intervention unless evidence indicates that children are endangered because parents are unwilling to provide minimum levels of care.

NOTES

1. Gilbert Y. Steiner, *The Children's Cause* (Washington, D.C.: The Brookings Institution, 1976), p. 5.

2. *Law and Behavior: Quarterly Analysis of Legal Developments Affecting Professionals in the Human Services*, Vol. 2, No. 1 (Champaign, Ill.: Research Press Co., Winter 1977), p. 4.

3. Exceptions to this can occur when the religious preferences of parents contain educational directives that conflict with state law. See, Wisconsin vs. Yoder, 406 U.S. 205 (1972).

4. Neil Gilbert and Harry Specht, *Dimensions of Social Welfare Policy* (Englewood Cliffs, N.J.: Prentice-Hall, Inc., 1974), p. 4.

5. Ibid., p. 1.

6. United States Senate, Committee on Finance, *The Social Security Act as Amended through January 4, 1975, and Related Laws*, 94th Congress, 1st session (Washington, D.C.: U.S. Governmental Printing Office, February 1975), p. 206.

7. *Social Security Bulletin*, Vol. 1, No. 8 (Washington, D.C.: U.S. Dept. of Health, Education and Welfare, Social Security Administration, August 1978), p. 58.

8. Ibid.

9. *Social Security Bulletin*, Vol. 42, No. 6 (Washington, D.C.: U.S. Dept. of Health, Education and Welfare, Social Security Administration, June 1979), p. 56.

10. Kenneth Kenniston and the Carnegie Council on Children, *All Our Children: the American Family Under Pressure* (New York: Harcourt Brace Jovanovich, 1977), p. 100.

11. United States Bureau of the Census, *Statistical Abstracts of the United States—99th edition* (Washington, D.C.: U.S. Government Printing Office, 1978) Table No. 106, p. 361.

12. E. T. Weaver, "Public Assistance and Supplemental Security Income," *Encyclopedia of Social Work: Volume II*, eds. John B. Turner and others (Washington, D.C.: National Association of Social Workers, 1977), p. 1125.

13. James R. Storey and others, *The Better Jobs and Income Plan: A Guide to President Carter's Welfare Reform Proposal and Major Issues* (Washington, D.C.: The Urban Institute, January 1978), p. 91.

14. In October of 1979, President Carter signed a bill creating a separate Department of Education. Health, Education and Welfare became the Department of Health and Human Services.

15. *Social Security Bulletin, Vol. 40, No. 10* (Washington, D.C.: U.S. Dept. of Health, Education and Welfare, Social Security Administration, October 1977), p. 21.

16. Ibid.

17. M. Cunningham, "Eligibility Procedures for AFDC," *Social Work*, Vol. 22, No. 1 (January 1977), p. 21.

18. Ibid., p. 22.

19. Sharon P. Krefetz, *Welfare Policy Making and City Politics* (New York: Holt, Rinehart, & Winston, 1976), p. 93.

20. Committee on Finance, *The Social Security Act*, p. 497.

21. Advisory Committee on Child Development, *Toward a National Policy for Children and Families* (Washington, D.C.: National Academy of Sciences, 1976), p. 59.

22. James R. Storey and others, *The Better Jobs and Income Plan: A Guide to President Carter's Welfare Reform Proposal and Major Issues* (Washington, D.C.: The Urban Institute, January 1978), p. 93.

23. R. F. Boaz, "Health Care System," *Encyclopedia of Social Work: Volume 1*, (1977), p. 554.

24. Weaver, "Public Assistance," p. 1131.

25. Robert Harris, *Federal Assumption of Welfare and Medicaid Costs: Issues and Budgetary Impacts* (Washington, D.C.: The Urban Institute, March 1977), p. 3.

26. Ibid.

27. N. Gilbert, "Transformation of Social Services," *Social Service Review*, Vol. 51, No. 4 (December 1977), p. 625.

28. Candace Mueller, *Pocket Guide to Title XX: Social Services to Children and Youth* (New York: Child Welfare League of America, 1976), p. 2.

29. Jane Knitzer, Mary Lee Allen and Brenda McGowan, *Children Without Homes: An Examination of Public Responsibility to Children in Out-of-Home Care* (Washington, D.C.: The Children's Defense Fund, 1978), p. 111.

30. H. Levin, "Voluntary Organizations in Social Welfare," *Encyclopedia of Social Work: Volume II* (1977), p. 1578.

31. *Final Report—Alameda County Pilot Project on Human Services Planning* (n.p.: Arthur Young and Company, 1976), p. A-2.

32. This was made possible by the addition of an "Income eligible" category which includes people earning up to 115 percent of the state's median income. Free services may be provided to those whose incomes do not exceed 80 percent of the state median. For those earning 80 to 115 percent of state median income, services may be offered on a subsidized basis for reasonable, income-related fees. Some Title XX services—information and referral and protective services, for example—are made available regardless of income. M. Rein, "Social Services as a Work Strategy," *Social Service Review*, Vol. 49 (December 1975), p. 627.

33. Gilbert, "Transformation of Social Services," p. 627.

34. Gilbert Y. Steiner, *The State of Welfare* (Washington, D.C.: The Brookings Institution, 1971), p. 191.

35. Toby H. Campbell and Marc Benedick, Jr., *A Public Assistance Data Book* (Washington, D.C.: The Urban Institute, October 1977), p. 106.

36. Robert Harris, *Welfare Reform and Social Insurance: Program Issues and Budget Impacts* (Washington, D.C.: The Urban Institute, May 1977), p. 14.

37. Margaret B. Sulvetta, *The Impact of Welfare Reform on Benefits for the Poor* (Washington, D.C.: The Urban Institute, April 1978), p. 16.

38. M. Rein, "Equality and Social Policy," *Social Service Review*, Vol. 51. No. 4 (December 1977), p. 574.

39. Harris, "Welfare Reform and Social Insurance," p. 15.

40. M. MacDonald, "Food Stamps: An Analytical History," *Social Service Review*, Vol. 51, No. 4 (December 1977), pp. 642–58.

41. J. W. Polier, "External and Internal Roadblocks to Effective Child Advocacy," *Child Welfare*, Vol. LVI, No. 8 (September/October 1977), p. 498.

42. Rein, "Social Services as a Work Strategy, p. 516.

43. This changed in 1969 when D.H.E.W. separated services from assistance, so that more effective services could be provided if one worker was not responsible for both tasks. After this, aid ceased to be conditional on acceptance of services.

44. The suggestion that counseling could reduce economic dependency rested on weak evidence culled from demonstration projects which presumably showed such a relationship. Even had the projects been more adequate in design, the casework component of the 1962 amendments never received a fair test. There were not enough trained workers to fill the vacancies created by the availability of federal money. Also, it is questionable whether the intensive services that characterized counseling in these projects could be provided in a public welfare setting. Extensive paper work and high caseloads pose time constraints on workers militating against the provision of such services. The fact that services were imposed on clients rather than being optional may have limited their effectiveness. For a thorough discussion of this issue, see Steiner, *State of Welfare*, Ch. 6.

45. Gilbert, "Transformation of Social Services," p. 630.

46. Rein, "Social Services," p. 518.

47. G. Hoshino, "Public Assistance and Supplemental Security Income: Social Services," in *Encyclopedia of Social Work: Volume II*, p. 1152.

48. An added assumption underlying work programs and work requirements is that persons who receive welfare remain on the rolls for long periods of time, that they constitute a "welfare class." Data reported by Rein and Rainwater dispute this assumption. According to their report only 9 percent of the recipient population constitute such a class; the remainder moving on and off the welfare rolls. Earnings from employment are one factor permitting such movement. Cyclical periods of unemployment contribute to their reentry to the welfare rolls. See, M. Rein and L. Rainwater. "Patterns of Welfare Use," *Social Service Review*, Vol. 52, No. 4 (December 1978), pp. 511–34.

49. Gilbert and Specht, *Dimensions of Social Welfare Policy*, p. 48.

50. Additionally, limited fiscal appropriations prevented all interested persons from enrolling in programs. And they limited the availability of day care, an essential component of such programs if single parents are expected to work outside of the home.

51. Richard M. Titmuss, *Social Policy*, 2nd edition (London: George Allen and Unwin Ltd., 1977), pp. 30–31.

52. Gilbert and Specht, *Dimensions of Social Welfare Policy*, p. 6.

53. Titmus, *Social Policy*, p. 31.

54. Gilbert and Specht, *Dimensions of Social Welfare Policy*, p. 7.

55. The demographic or "demogrant" approach to eligibility provides a set payment to anyone in the population who possesses certain characteristics, regardless of income. For example, these may be related to age (children or the elderly) or to physical disabilities. Eligibility requirements uniformly applied to the population should reduce discrimination, for instance, against two-parent families and the "working poor." See, M. N. Ozawa, "Issues in Welfare Reform," *Social Service Review*, Vol. 52, No. 1, pp. 37–55.

56. Margaret B. Sulvetta, *The Impact of Welfare Reform on Benefits for the Poor* (Washington, D.C.: The Urban Institute, April 1978), p. 26.

57. See, Dennis R. Young and Richard R. Nelson, *Public Policy and Day Care of Young Children* (Lexington, Mass.: D.C. Heath & Co., 1973); Nicholas Hobbs, *The Futures of Children* (San Francisco: Jossey-Bass, Inc., Publishers, 1976); Robert M. Rice, *American Family Policy: Content and Context* (New York: Family Service Association of America, 1977); Advisory Committee on Child Development, *Toward a National Policy for Children and Families* (Washington, D.C.: National Academy of Sciences, 1976); Kenniston, *All Our Children* (New York: Harcourt Brace Jovanovich, 1977).

58. See, Rice, *American Family Policy*, p. 59; "A Statement by Senator Walter F. Mondale," *Harvard Educational Review*, Reprint Series No. 9, 2nd printing (1977), p. 51. The presumed relationship between eligibility requirements and family breakup has also been cited by Presidents Nixon and Carter in support of their arguments for welfare reform. Recent evidence from experimental income maintenance programs in Seattle and Denver, in which benefits were made available to two-parent families, suggests that this relationship may not be as direct as previously thought. Both programs report a higher rate of marital breakup for experimental families than for those whose eligibility was determined under traditional rules. See, A. Cherlin, "Divorcing Welfare from Marriage," *Psychology Today*, Vol. 13, No. 2 (July 1979), p. 92.

59. Knitzer, *Children Without Homes*, p. 123.

60. Hobbs, *The Futures of Children*, p. 13.

61. Knitzer, *Children Without Homes*, p. 123.

62. David Fanshel and Eugene B. Shinn, *Dollars and Sense in the Foster Care of Children: A Look at Cost Factors* (New York: Child Welfare League of America, 1972); *Why Can't I Have A Home? A Report on Foster Care and Adoption in North Carolina* (Raleigh, N.C.: Governor's Advocacy Council on Children and Youth, 1978); for a review of other studies, see Knitzer, *Children Without Homes*, Ch. 6.

63. Arthur B. LaFrance, *Welfare Law: Structure and Entitlement* (St. Paul, Minn.: West Publishing Co., 1978), p. 22.

64. Advisory Committee, *Toward a National Policy*, p. 12.

65. Sanford N. Katz, *When Parents Fail: The Law's Response to Family Breakdown* (Boston, Mass.: Beacon Press, 1971), p. 17, 17n.

66. Donald Brieland and John Lemmon, *Social Work and the Law*, (St. Paul, Minn.: West Publishing Co., 1977), p. 175.

67. Sanford N. Katz and others, "Child Neglect Laws in America," *Family Law Quarterly*, Vol. IX No. 1 (1975), p. 4.

68. Ibid., p. 5.

69. *Abuse and Neglect: A Comparative Analysis of Standards and State Practices: Volume VI of IX* (Washington, D.C.: National Institute for Juvenile Justice and Delinquency Prevention, Law Enforcement Assistance Administration, U.S. Dept. of Justice, 1977), p. 56.

70. Brieland, *Social Work and the Law*, p. 140.

71. M. S. Wald, "State Intervention on Behalf of 'Neglected' Children: Standards for Removal of Children from Their Homes, Monitoring and Status of Children in Foster Care, and Termination of Parental Rights," *Stanford Law Review*, Vol. 28, No. 4 (April 1976), p. 649.

72. Katz, *When Parents Fail*, p. xiii.

73. Ibid., p. xv, fn2.

74. Arlene Skolnick, *The Intimate Environment: Exploring Marriage and the Family*, 2nd ed. (Boston, Mass.: Little, Brown & Company, 1978), p. 353.

75. Ibid., p. 354.

76. Ibid.

77. See M. Pines, "Superkids," *Psychology Today*, Vol. 12, No. 8 (January 1979), pp. 53–63; N. Garmezy, "Vulnerable and Invulnerable Children: Theory, Research & Intervention" (Washington, D.C.: American Psychological Association, Journal Supplement Abstract Service-Document MS 1337); D. C. McClelland and others, "Making It To Maturity," *Psychology Today*, Vol. 12, No. 1 (June 1978), pp. 42–53, 114; Sheldon H. White and others, *Federal Programs for Young Children: Review and Recommendations: Volume 1: Goals and Standards of Public Programs for Children* (Washington, D.C.: Superintendent of Documents, 1973), p. 130; Joseph Goldstein, Anna Freud & Albert J. Solnit, *Beyond the Best Interests of the Child* (New York: The Free Press, 1973), p. 6; J. Kagan, "The Parental Love Trap," *Psychology Today*, Vol. 12, No. 3 (August 1978), pp. 54–61, 91.

78. McClelland, "Making It To Maturity," p. 45.

79. Kagan, "The Parental Love Trap," pp. 54–61, 91.

80. For a review of this subject, see Albert Bandura, *Principles of Behavior Modification* (New York: Holt, Rinehart & Winston, Inc., 1969), Ch. 9.

81. Sigmund Freud, "The Psychogenesis of a Case of Homosexuality in a Woman," in *Collected Papers: Volume II*, ed. Ernest Jones (New York: Basic Books, Inc., Publishers, 1959), p. 226.

82. Goldstein, *Beyond the Best Interests;* Wald, "State Intervention," (1976); R. H. Mnookin, "Child Custody Adjudication: Judicial Functions in the Face of Indeterminacy," *Children and the Law*, Vol. 39, No. 3 (Summer 1975).

83. Wald, "State Intervention," (1976); R. H. Mnookin, "Foster Care—In Whose Best Interest?" *Harvard Educational Review*, Vol. 45 (1973), pp. 559–63.

84. Edwin M. Schur, *Radical Non-Intervention: Rethinking the Delinquency Problem* (Englewood Cliffs, N.J.: Prentice-Hall, Inc., 1973), p. 128.

85. Extensive reviews of these issues can be found in; Knitzer, *Children Without Homes;* Ann W. Shyne and Anita G. Schroeder, *National Study of Social Services to Children and Their Families* (Washington, D.C.: U.S. Dept. of Health, Education & Welfare, DHEW publication No. (OHDS) 78-30150, 1978); *Who Knows? Who Cares? Forgotten Children in Foster Care* (New York: The National Commission on Children in Need of Parents. Available from The Child Welfare League of America, New York, 1978).

86. Knitzer, *Children Without Homes*, Ch. 2.

87. Ibid., p. 39.

88. Alan R. Gruber, *Children in Foster Care: Destitute, Neglected, . . . Betrayed* (New York: Human Sciences Press, 1978), p. 67.; Kenneth Wooden, *Weeping in the Playtime of Others: America's Incarcerated Children* (New York: McGraw-Hill Book Company, 1976); *Child Abuse and Neglect in Residential Institutions: Selected Readings on Prevention, Investigation and Correction* (Washington, D.C.: National Center on Child Abuse and Neglect, U.S. Dept. of Health, Education and Welfare, DHEW publication No. (OHDS) 78-30160, 1978).

89. For a review of studies of this subject, see, Theodore J. Stein, Eileen D. Gambrill and Kermit T. Wiltse, *Children in Foster Homes: Achieving Continuity of Care* (New York: Holt, Rinehart & Winston, 1978), pp. 13,106.

90. Shyne, *National Study*, p. 120; Knitzer, *Children Without Homes*, p. 6.

91. M. Wald, "State Intervention on Behalf of "Neglected" Children: A Search for Realistic Standards," *Stanford Law Review*, Vol. 27 (April 1975), p. 1033.

92. Courts have removed children because "they disapprove of a parent's lifestyle or childrearing practices. Children have been removed because parents are not married, because a mother frequents taverns, or had men visitors overnight, because the parents adhered to extreme religious practices, or lived in a communal setting, or because the parent was a lesbian or homosexual, or the mother of an illegitimate child." Wald, ibid.

93. Stein, *Children in Foster Homes*, p. 112.

94. Shirley Jenkins and Elaine Norman, *Beyond Placement: Mothers View Foster Care* (New York: Columbia University Press, 1975), p. 142.

95. *Standards Relating to Juvenile Records and Information Systems—Tentative Draft*, The Institute of Judicial Administration of the American Bar Association: Juvenile Justice Standards Project (Cambridge, Mass.: Ballinger Publishing Co., 1977), pp. 11–12.

96. Wald, "State Intervention," (1976), p. 642.

3

Protective Services, Foster Care, and Adoption

Child welfare services may be defined at both a general and a specific level. At a general level the definition includes all public systems with responsibility for children, such as the public education, health-care, and public welfare systems. At a more specific level, reference is made to services and professional practices that place children in out-of-home care, that protect children at risk of placement, and that find permanent homes for children whose parents cannot or will not provide ongoing care.[1]

The mechanisms that society has created for attaining these goals are found in protective services—foster care and adoption services—the subject of this chapter. Each of these services can be described in terms of structure and process. The structure of a service consists of its elements which, taken together, provide a framework that makes the provision of services possible. Process refers to the day-to-day activities in which workers engage when providing services. Structure comes from official sanctions that authorize the provision of services. Sanctions are found in social policy, professional standards, and statutory law by which service objectives are delineated, service boundaries are established, and mechanisms for attaining objectives are created. For instance, protective services are governed by a legal structure, the elements of which require persons with knowledge of neglect or abuse to report these conditions. A system for accepting and responding to reports has been created in all states. The law *mandates* protective service intervention to safeguard children whether or not parents want assistance, and it identifies mechanisms for intervening in family life if parents are not cooperative. The law limits the population to be served by identifying conditions that constitute abuse and neglect. Thus, a structure is created within which the social objective of protecting children can be realized. In a similar manner, structures have been created through which society offers substitute parenting for a limited period of time for children whose natural parents cannot, or will not, provide ongoing care. Structures also exist that make it possible to provide permanent adoptive homes for children who cannot be raised by their biological parents. The elements of these structures are explored in this chapter. The process of providing services is described in part two.

CHARACTERISTICS OF THE CHILDREN RECEIVING SERVICES

From the results of a 1978 national survey of public child welfare agencies, we learn the following: The largest percentage of children receiving child welfare services were white, comprising 62 percent of the total population, followed by black youngsters who accounted for 28 percent. Seven percent of the children were of Hispanic descent, and 1 percent each were Alaskan-Indian and Asian-Pacific. Two percent of all children served were of other origins. The median age of the children, in hierarchical order, was 8 years for blacks, 9.9 years for whites and 10.1 years for Hispanic youngsters. The median for children whose racial or ethnic background was not identified was 8.4 years. Overall, 52 percent of the children were boys, and 48 percent, girls.[2]

We begin this chapter by looking at the incidence of child abuse and neglect in the United States. Next, we will review the state of knowledge as to the causes of these phenomena and describe the structural elements of the service areas that concern us.

Incidence of Abuse and Neglect

In order to allocate resources to combat abuse and neglect we must have reliable information on the incidence of maltreatment (since the number of workers in a protective service unit should be determined on the basis of the number of cases requiring services). Incidence rates vary widely, however, so the exact number of maltreated children is not known. Estimates range from 30,000 cases to 1.5 million.[3]

Our knowledge of this subject is inexact because official statistics, from which most estimates are derived, are viewed as unreliable.[4] States differ with regard to the conditions that must be reported (some, for example, include emotional abuse and neglect, whereas others do not), and some record incidents of both abuse and neglect, while others record abuse only. It is also unclear whether states systematically expunge unproven cases or count these when compiling statistics. Thus, the comparability of data across states is questionable. Statistics from any one state may vary over time as a function of concerted efforts to enforce reporting laws. In Florida, for instance, the number of reported cases increased from just over 19,000 in 1971, to between 25,000 and 30,000 by 1974.[5] Thus, official statistics may reflect overestimates (if unverified cases are not expunged), or they may reflect underestimates if reporting is not enforced. Therefore, caution must be exercised in accepting these data as accurate. The suggestions that maltreatment is increasing should also be viewed with skepticism. We lack historical incidence data to serve as a basis for drawing conclusions about increases in these phenomena.

Etiology of Maltreatment

Incidence data are important in determining the quantity of services needed in any community. The exact type of services (such as drug treatment programs, marital counseling or day care services) to reduce and eliminate maltreatment is partly determined by the presumed causes of these phenomena. In the following pages current knowledge in this area is reviewed.

Both abuse and neglect have been explained with reference to *psychodynamic traits of the parents*. Based on information in case records and in newspaper reports, Kempe and others conclude that (abuse is caused by personality disorders, behavioral disorders, and emotional problems of parents.[6] These conclusions are not supported by the work of others. Steele and Pollock, using information provided by psychiatrists, psychologists, and social workers, concluded that less than 10 percent of the parents studied were seriously mentally ill. They note that child abusers do not appear to be different from a random sample of people selected from a downtown street. Young concluded that there were no essential differences between a random sample of nonabusing families whom she compared with a sample of families who came to a child welfare agency following a complaint of abuse or neglect.[7]

A number of investigators have suggested that abusive and neglectful behaviors reflect intergenerational patterns of child rearing.

Steele reports that a history of neglect or deprivation, "with or without physical abuse," is the most common element in the lives of parents who neglect or abuse their children. He notes that this finding is "more nearly universal in the population of parents who maltreat their babies than any other single factor such as socioeconomic status, living conditions, race, religion, education, psychiatric state, cultural milieu or family situation."[8]

An opposite conclusion was reached by Giovannoni and Billingsley, who report no significant differences in the background characteristics of neglectful compared to nonneglectful mothers. They report that stress, created by the environmental and situational conditions under which many low income families live, and the absence of resources and supports for coping with these stresses, contribute significantly to child neglect.[9] Likewise, Shapiro informs us that only 16 percent of the 171 abusive and neglectful mothers in her study reported "frequent and severe physical punishment in childhood."[10] Her findings are supported by other investigations.[11]

Demographic Characteristics

Some investigators report that nonwhite families are overrepresented in samples of abuse families, whereas others have not found this to be so.[12] Data regarding a child's age and its relationship to abuse are also equivocal. Statistics from clinical studies suggest that infants and younger children are more likely to be abused than are adolescents, whereas survey data indicate that abuse is distributed across age groups.[13] According to Gelles, the relationship between age and abuse is bimodal, with children aged three to five and fifteen to seventeen being most vulnerable.[14]

Evidence suggests that more boys than girls are abused. However, when age and sex are viewed jointly, a different picture emerges. Gil reports that abused boys under twelve outnumber girls; however, the pattern shifts for adolescents, where we find that 63 percent of the victims are girls, and approximately 37 percent boys.[15] Others have reported similar differences when both age and sex are considered. Mothers are said to be perpetrators of abuse more often than fathers, and stepfathers more frequently than stepmothers.[16] The relationship between the age of parents and the likelihood of abuse is unclear. Gelles reports that younger parents are more likely to abuse their children than older parents; Gil's findings do not support this conclusion.[17]

While abuse is found in families of all income levels, it is reported to occur with greater frequency in those with the lowest incomes. Education, occupation, and unemployment have also been linked to acts of maltreatment. Manual workers are reported to be more abusive towards their children than white collar workers, and abuse is more likely to occur in families where the father is either unemployed or employed part time than in families where the father is working full time.[18] Family size is yet another factor that is said to be related to abuse, with the probabilities of maltreatment being higher in families with four or more children.[19]

The Interaction of Parent and Child

In 1966, Milowe was the first to suggest that children may contribute to their own abuse. He noted that some characteristics of the child might affect the parent so as to "trigger" an abusive act. Helfer concurs with this opinion, noting that the abused child is a special kind of child whose behavior or condition (such as birth defect) violates parental expectations, thereby facilitating an act of maltreatment.[20]

Gil reports that children who are abused deviate in general functioning, in social functioning, and in physical functioning more than do children who are not abused. Mentally retarded children are said to be at greater risk of abuse than are children with average IQ's.[21]

Role reversal, a pattern of interaction wherein a parent demands that a child assume the role of adult and satisfy his or her unmet parenting needs, is also viewed as contributing to abusive acts.[22]

There is a general consensus that abuse is caused by the *interaction of multiple variables*. Simon and Down, using data from New York's central registry, report that a "strikingly high proportion of the reported cases came from multiproblem families, where the interplay of mental, physical, and environmental stresses could not be ignored as etiologic factors, and where the abusive acts appeared chiefly as late indicators of serious family difficulties.[23] These findings are supported by similar investigations in other states.

Recognizing that abuse and neglect have multiple causes, efforts have been made to develop *profiles* of abusive families in which the variables most characteristic of parents likely to maltreat their children are depicted. If such descriptors could be isolated, it would be possible to predict the likelihood of abuse given knowledge of family characteristics. To date, such efforts have not been successful, reinforcing the conclusion that abusing families do not possess characteristics that readily distinguish them from nonabusing families. Of those variables showing some relationship to abuse, a cluster of three—unemployment, large families, and social isolation—seem most descriptive.[24] These findings lend support to the hypothesis that stress, resulting from income deficiencies, family size, and so on, is causally related to abuse.[25]

The possibility that child abuse is an extension of our *cultural acceptance of violence* provides one of the more unsettling explanations of the phenomenon. It is estimated that 84 percent to 97 percent of all parents use physical methods of punishment with their children at some time.[26] Both Gelles and Straus suggest that physical abuse of children is related to a more general level of family violence. They found that "the rate of severe violence toward children was 129 percent greater in homes where husbands and wives had used violence on each other than in homes where this did not occur.[27] Along these lines, Gil notes that abusive acts are perpetrated by "normal individuals who are acting in a manner approved by their culture while disciplining children in their care. The undesirable outcome of their actions may be due to chance factors, but the dynamic source underlying their behavior is a culturally determined attitude."[28]

Variations in Etiological Findings

To a great extent, researchers seeking to identify the causes of maltreatment have relied on information contained in clinical records and public documents for their investigations. These data sources both direct and restrict the range of findings. They direct in the sense that data in clinical documents will, by definition, describe a population that is most likely to evidence personality disorders. The focus on personality disorders is, in turn, influenced by psychoanalytic thought, which directs attention to individual pathology rather than environmental variables. Therefore, it is not surprising that a majority of these investigations have found "defects in the character of parents as of prime importance."[29] Clinical studies are also subject to the methodological problems discussed in the review of longitudinal studies in chapter two. Sheff offers another perspective for the focus on pathology. He suggests that all of us find it necessary to explain bizarre behavior (and child abuse can certainly be characterized as such). However, our "vocabulary of motives" is limited when the observed behavior gets beyond the bounds of culturally prescribed norms. When objective causes cannot be isolated, we tend to characterize people as mentally ill. Thus, at one and the same time, we increase our comfort in what is an otherwise uncomfortable situation, and we think that we have explained the behavior of concern.[30] As Gil has observed, the "illness as cause" hypothesis soothes society's conscience, detracting from viewing social causes as related factors.

Data compiled from public records are subject to the range of problems reviewed in discussing inaccuracies in incidence data. Public documents are restrictive in that the population that uses public resources is generally limited to the poor. Families who can afford to purchase services in the private sector are not commonly described in such records. Adding to the likelihood that the middle and upper classes are under-represented in offical statistics is the possibility that physicians do not report cases of maltreatment involving private patients.

A further limitation of clinical records is that they often "restrict the age of the sample studied" or they rely on data from pediatric services that exclude older children. Thus, it is not surprising that clinical reports find that abuse is most likely to involve infants and young children. When the data base is expanded, as it is when survey methodology is used, the picture that emerges differs, informing us that abuse occurs across age categories. Likewise, comparative studies such as those conducted by Young and Giovannoni and Billingsley yield different explanations than do clinical records or public documents.

Definitive conclusions regarding the etiology of child maltreatment cannot be drawn. The suggestion that abuse and neglect may be learned behaviors and that they are frequently precipitated by stress resulting from a combination of socioeconomic and personal factors has been reported with greater consistency than have other findings. We cannot however conclude that there is a direct cause-and-effect relationship between these variables and the phenomenon of child maltreatment. It is entirely possible that many parents with problematic learning histories and many who are subject to ongoing stress do not abuse their children. Whether this is correct cannot be known unless we have a random sample of abusive and nonabusive families or data on the entire population. When these are on hand, we may learn that certain of the relationships suggested in the literature are quite direct or that other as yet unidentified variables intervene to increase the probabilities that children will be neglected or abused.

THE SERVICES

Child welfare services are initiated when clients request assistance for themselves or when they are referred by others. Referrals contain a suggestion (that a particular type of help is needed) and a request (that the child welfare worker confirm the need for assistance and that it be offered). They are made because a specific type of service (such as foster care or protective service) is not provided by the referring agency, or because the referring source knows of or suspects that a child is being maltreated and wants to initiate an investigation. Referrals from professionals are instrumental in intiating services in 53 percent of child welfare cases; referrals by lay persons for an additional

16 percent; and self-referrals for 27 percent. The referral source for the remaining 4 percent is unknown.[31] Referrals may result in the granting or the denial of services, depending upon the child welfare worker's assessment of the appropriateness of the request. Workers, in turn, refer clients to other community agencies. The percentage of cases referred ranges from a low of 1 percent (for services such as foster care and protective services that are commonly offered by public child welfare agencies) to a high of 26 percent for health services and 38 percent for mental health services.[32]

Some cases open and close having experienced only one type of service, while others move across areas of service. An example of the former is when a child who has entered foster home placement following a parental request for this service is reunited with her biological family after difficulties are resolved. The latter may occur when a protective service worker recommends that a child be placed in foster care following a period during which the child was receiving services in his or her own home. After placement occurs, services to reunite the family may prove unsuccessful and a decision made to terminate parental rights in order to free the child for adoptive placement.

Now let us examine the structural elements of protective services—foster care services and adoption.

PROTECTIVE SERVICES

Protective services seek to safeguard the physical and emotional well-being of children who have been, or who are in danger of being, neglected or abused. In 1977 protective services were provided to a greater percentage of children than any other child welfare service, accounting for 33 percent of the assistance given to the 1.5 million children for whom service data were available.[33] Services are provided to the child and family in the family home. Two categories of social work services to children in their own homes can be identified. In one (generally referred to as "services to children in their own homes," as distinct from protective services) assistance is usually initiated by the parents, and there is no imputation of neglect or abuse. Protective services, in contrast, are usually initiated by a third party referral specifically because of suspected or proven maltreatment. It is not difficult to discriminate between these areas of service in these terms. However, in moving beyond definitions, one encounters conceptual problems. First, as the Child Welfare League of America observes, services to children in their own homes are not within the exclusive purview of social workers. Others in the community—public health personnel, probation officers, and psychologists, for example—also provide assistance to families in their own homes, making it difficult for the profession to lay claim to this as a distinct area of social work practice. An even more serious difficulty is encountered when one tries to state objectives that distinguish these areas of service. The protective service mandate is broad, as are the conditions that constitute neglect and abuse. Services to safeguard the well-being of children range from interventions to eliminate safety hazards in a home (such as faulty electrical wiring that presents a fire hazard), to eliminating substance abuse that prevents a parent from providing full-time care for a child, to teaching parents noncorporal methods of disciplining children. Since neglect or abuse may result from any of a number of difficulties (for example, financial problems that may, at first, appear to necessitate services for parents rather than to the entire family unit) it is very difficult to identify goals for at-home services that do not overlap with those of protective services. This discussion will focus on protective services, the distinguishing characteristics of which are:

- They focus on family problems that result in the neglect, abuse, or exploitation of children.
- They are sanctioned by law. Most state statutes require protective services investigations and interventions to safeguard children whether or not the parents desire services.
- They are generally initiated following a third party report, rarely by the parents involved, that a child has been maltreated.
- Because child abuse is a medical, legal, and social problem, protective service workers invariably operate in conjunction with court, medical, and law enforcement personnel, as well as with persons from other agencies in the community.[34]

There is little doubt that child abuse is as old as recorded history. As a social problem of major proportions, it was "discovered" in the early 1960s. At that time the work of Helfer and Kempe directed public attention to the phenomenon they labeled the "battered child syndrome," which was defined as a "condition in children of severe physical abuse."[35] Today the more inclusive phrase "child abuse and neglect" is used, reflecting concern for a broader range of conditions that affect the well-being of youngsters. The concern expressed in Helfer and Kempe's work was echoed by other professionals and reinforced by widespread media attention to the phenomenon of maltreatment. Concern over the magnitude and severity of this problem was reflected in the 1962 and the 1967 amendments to the Social Security Act which required that protective services be provided to all neglected and abused children in families receiving AFDC, and to nonrecipient families if the states chose to use money in this way.[36] Under Title XX, protective services must be available for all families regardless of income.

Reporting Child Abuse

In 1962, prompted by a concern that physicians would not report suspected cases of child abuse because they did not want to become involved in legal proceedings or because they did not want to implicate well-to-do private patients, or because they wanted to avoid civil liability that might result from "making accusations that later proved to be unfounded," the Department of Health, Education and Welfare published a "model act," for the reporting of child abuse.[37] In 1974, Public Law 93-247, known as the Child Abuse Prevention and Treatment Act, was passed by Congress. Under the provisions of this law, federal assistance is available to the states for the prevention, identification, and treatment of child abuse and neglect.[38] Today, all fifty states and the District of Columbia have enacted some statutory provision for the "mandatory reporting of nonaccidental injury and neglect of children." The elements of these statutes are reviewed next.

The laws of most states identify *five conditions that must be reported.* Nonaccidental physical injury, including burns, broken bones, and bruises, is included by all states. Forty-seven states and the District of Columbia include neglect which is generally defined as failure to provide basic necessities such as food, clothing, shelter, and medical attention. A number of states require that sexual molestation and emotional or mental injury be reported. Unfortunately, these conditions are not defined. Thus, those persons required to report are not offered guidance in discriminating reportable from nonreportable conditions. Emotional or mental injuries are generally inferred as secondary effects (it is assumed that children who have suffered physical or sexual abuse will have experienced emotional trauma). Eighteen states require that threatened abuse or neglect be reported.

The *categories of persons who are required to make reports* have been expanded beyond the original focus on physicians. Today most states require any person in the helping professions (educators, social service workers, law enforcement officers, and hospital personnel, for instance) to make reports. In twenty-two states, "any person" with knowledge of abuse or neglect must file a report. Failure to do so is subject to criminal penalties in thirty-six states, to civil penalties in six, and to a fine in three. All states provide immunity from prosecution for reporters.

Receipt of Reports

When reporting laws were first enacted, law enforcement agencies were the locus for making reports. Then, as the social ramifications of maltreatment were recognized, what had been defined as a law enforcement problem was redefined in social terms. Thus, the locus for reporting began to shift from police departments to child protection agencies. At present, both child protection units and police units are designated to receive reports, depending upon individual state practices. In a number of cities, telephone "hot lines" have been established. Some exist mainly to receive reports of abuse or neglect. Others serve the added function of offering crisis intervention services.[39] A crisis hotline offers parents the opportunity to talk to a person who is trained to offer supportive counseling and to make referrals for needed services. The law in thirty-five states and the District of Columbia require that oral reports be made *immediately* upon knowledge of reportable conditions. Other states require that they be made *promptly*.

CENTRAL REGISTRY. This is a file containing information on reported cases of maltreatment. The purpose in maintaining a registry is to have a single repository of information on the phenomena of concern. Registries range from sophisticated computerized systems to three by five card files stored in a shoe box.[40] Data from a 1977 survey shows that thirty-five states maintain registries for reports of abuse and neglect and six for abuse only. Seven states do not maintain a registry and two did not respond to the survey.[41] States differ in regard to the items of information they catalog. Most record data on the age and sex of the child. Four-fifths compile statistics on race, on the identity of the alleged abuser, the nature of the injuries, and the source of the report. Some also contain details of a child's medical history and information describing past services provided to families. Less than one-half of all states store follow-up information. This is a matter of concern since, without such information, it is likely that unsubstantiated reports are not expunged.

USES OF REGISTRY INFORMATION. Registries, depending upon the information they contain, serve different purposes. If all reports were recorded, if unsubstantiated ones were removed, and distinctions made between different types of neglect and abuse (physical abuse as compared to sexual abuse) their utility for compiling incidence data would be markedly improved. When information on a child's medical history is maintained, registries are viewed as serving a diagnostic function for doctors. The importance of this function can be seen in the suggestion that parents who have abused their children "shop" among different hospitals and doctors in order to avoid detection. This reduces the likelihood that any one physician will have historical information on the child. Lacking such data, physicians may be reluctant to diagnose an injury as abuse. Since most cases of maltreatment are not extreme, the question of whether an injury is or is not abuse may not be wholly answerable from a medical examination. Thus prior information may be essential to a diagnosis. Protective service workers may use registry information in a similar manner. For example, it is not always clear, particularly when reports are received from lay members of the community, whether an investigation is warranted. In certain situations a decision may hinge on whether there are prior reports in the registry. A final use of information in registries is for planning purposes. If accurate information is contained in files, trends can be monitored and planning priorities shifted or maintained.

The diagnostic function of registries poses two possible difficulties. First, without a medical history, a doctor may be reluctant to report when abuse has actually occurred. Or, the doctor may be unduly influenced by prior reports, thus diagnosing abuse when it does not exist. The question is whether the diagnostic value of registries is overshadowed by the undue influence of past information.

Forty-six states require that data in the registry be kept confidential. Access to information is usually limited to social service personnel, physicians, a child's guardian, court personnel, and researchers. Provisions may exist for expunging unfounded reports as well as for sealing or expunging records after a specified period of time.

Additional features of reporting laws are the abrogation of traditional privileges under which a person may claim the right to refuse to answer questions in a court of law. For instance, privileged communication between doctor and patient and between husband and wife are abrogated in thirty-three states. A commitment to public education as well as to the education of professionals who are required to make reports is written into the laws of fifteen states. In twenty-seven, a child may be removed from the home when there is imminent danger. Some but not all states require that workers petition the juvenile court if allegations of maltreatment are substantiated.

FOSTER CARE

The majority of American children are raised by their biological parents. There are situations, however, when parents cannot or will not provide necessary care. When this occurs, society intervenes to protect youngsters by placing them in a substitute living arrangement. In 1977 there were approximately 500,000 children living in foster family homes, group homes, or institutions in the United States.[42] This is a dramatic increase from the early 1960s, when the number of children in out-of-home care was approximately 277,000.[43] Substitute care is meant to be short-term; it is assumed that a child will be returned to the home of natural parents once the difficulties that necessitated placement are resolved. If family reunification is not possible, permanent homes can be provided through adoption or legal guardianship. In recent years there has been an increased acceptance of planned long-term foster care, until a youngster reaches the age of majority, as an adequate solution for some children.[44]

Entry Into Foster Care

Children enter out-of-home placement in one of two ways. Their parents may place them on a voluntary basis. This may occur during a family crisis—for example, when a single parent has to be hospitalized and there is no person to provide care for the child at home. Some youngsters are placed through an order of the juvenile court (involuntary placements). A protective service worker may petition the court to place a child in a substitute home if there is evidence that the child cannot be protected in his own home. There are no national statistics showing the number of children placed in either way.

A review of the literature shows that children are placed in substitute care because of *parental behavior* such as neglect or abuse, or because of the *child's behavior*, such as repeated truancy or running away from home. *Conditions* of a parent or of a child, such as substance abuse, mental retardation, or mental illness, are other factors. In addition, *circumstances of the parent* (in need of hospitalization or incarcerated in prison) and *circumstances of the family* (financial hardship or inadequate housing) may enter into placement decisions. The categories do not provide wholly satisfactory explanations of why children enter foster care, for the following reasons.

First, there are no universally accepted typologies for classifying the problems or reasons why child welfare services are sought or why they are provided. The reporting categories used differ from study to study, reflecting variations across states as well as within states. For example, mental illness of a parent is cited as the reason why 23 percent of the children in foster care in the state of Massachusetts entered placement.[45] A report from Nashville, Tennessee, contains no such category, but informs us that twelve children entered substitute care as a result of a parent's emotional difficulties.[46] One New York report tells us that 18 percent of the children in placement entered care because of their personality or emotional problems.[47] Yet a California report shows no comparable category.[48] What we do not know is whether the problems referred to as mental illness in Massachusetts are similar to those referred to as emotional problems in Tennessee. If they are different, are we to assume that mental illness is not a precipitating factor in the placement of children in the latter state? Likewise, are we to assume that personality and emotional problems of children do not enter into out-of-home placement decisions in California? An example of within-state variations is found in two New York City reports, one of which contains the category of drug addiction and alcoholism as reasons for placement of children, while the other does not include these categories.[49]

According to the Massachusetts report referred to above, 13 percent of the children in foster homes were placed because of "neglect, abuse, or inadequate home." No distinction is made between these problem areas. By contrast, in Nebraska, 9 percent of the children in care were placed because of abuse and approximately 45 percent because of neglect.[50] Eleven percent of the children who were the subject of a report from New York City entered foster homes because of "severe abuse or neglect."[51] Another report from the same city does not preface the category with any indication of severity.[52] These discrepancies, rather than reflecting actual differences in the reasons for placement, are probably more indicative of different typologies used by agencies or created by researchers. Problems also arise because there are no commonly accepted definitions of concepts such as mental illness, neglect, and abuse. Thus, even when similar categories are reported, we must question whether the data is comparable. For example, when neglect or abuse are not evidenced in an extreme form, a case may be assigned to either category, depending upon worker predilection or agency policy.

A final source of difficulty stems from what might be described as an inappropriate conceptualization of problems. For instance, in reviewing the hypothetical causes of neglect and abuse I noted that mental illness has been cited as causal to child abuse. If mental illness is a cause, and abuse an effect, does it make sense to say that both are causal to placing children in foster homes? Stated otherwise, what is the distinction between these categories? What are the conditions under which the reason for placement would be cited as mental illness, rather than abuse, or vice versa? One answer may lie in whether the child enters care under voluntary or involuntary conditions. Fifty-four percent of the 130 children studied by Fanshel and Shinn who entered placement through the New York Court had abuse or neglect cited as the reason for placement.[53] By contrast, this reason was reported for only 15 percent of the total sample of 624 children. The suggestion here is that because statutory law gives the courts jurisdiction over neglected and abused children, and because these categories are vague and subject to broad interpretation, it may be easier to have a petition sustained when the reasons for it are general. For the more specific charge of mental illness, confirming evidence is not as readily attainable. Other factors may enter into the use of differential reporting categories. Theoretical training, for instance, can influence assessment such that the difficulties identified by a professional working within a behavior modification framework might differ from those cited by a person working within a more psychodynamic framework. Also, there is evidence that minority persons are more likely to be assigned a pejorative label, such as mental illness, than are nonminority persons.[54]

Bearing in mind the limitations just reviewed, information gathered during the 1977 survey mentioned previously informs us that the majority of children in placement entered care because of parental neglect (30 percent) followed closely by those who were placed due to emotional problems of their parents (29 percent). Financial difficulties accounted for 22 percent of the placements, followed by parent-child conflicts which tied with emotional problems of the child, each accounting for 19 percent of the placements. An almost equal percentage of the children entered care because of their behavior at home (17 percent) or because of their behavior at school (14 percent). Abuse and parental unwillingness to care for a child each accounted for 12 percent of the placements.[55]

Efforts to discern the exact reasons why children enter out-of-home care are more than an academic exercise. They are important for the same reasons that data identifying the causes of abuse and neglect are important. Resources to assist families-at-risk should be developed in relation to the types of problems creating risk. For example, knowledge that large numbers of children enter out-of-home care because of the financial problems of their parents would direct us to one line of attack, whereas knowledge that alcohol or drug abuse precipitates many placements would lead us to another.

Where Are the Children Placed?

The majority of children in out-of-home placement are in foster family homes (394,000 out of 503,000, or 79 percent). Fourteen percent (75,000 children) are in institutions and 7 percent (34,000) in group homes.[56]

Four types of *foster family homes* can be identified. These are: regular foster homes where two adults provide care for one to four children; specialized homes where care is provided for physically and emotionally handicapped youngsters; emergency shelters which offer short-term care during crisis situations; and long-term care homes where children are placed for an indefinite period of time.

INSTITUTIONS.   Service institutions can be classified by size, location, or purpose. Large-scale institutions frequently house twenty-five to one hundred children in several buildings on a single "campus."[57] Such facilities are generally located at great distances from metropolitan areas. Residential treatment centers are small institutions. Whereas some large-scale facilities may be primarily custodial in nature, residential treatment centers offer therapeutic services. Like their larger counterparts, they are often located outside of urban areas. Group residences are institutions located in urban centers. They house a smaller number of children than large-scale institutions and a greater number than group homes. Their urban location distinguishes them from centers. Care is usually provided for thirteen to twenty-five children. Whereas youngsters in group homes are generally close in age and have similar types of problems, those in group residences may vary in both dimensions.

GROUP HOMES.   These are urban facilities in which approximately twelve children receive care. They can be classified as family-owned group homes, agency-owned homes, and specialized homes. Family-owned group homes differ from foster homes in that they seek to provide four to six children with peer group experiences. Agency-owned homes are staffed either by a married couple hired by the agency, or by counselors who create a therapeutic milieu for the children. If the adults who own and operate a family home decide to move or cease to provide care, the children must be moved to a new facility. In an agency-run home, if the caretaking adults leave, the children remain in the home and new caretakers are hired. Specialized group homes, like specialized foster homes and residential treatment centers, provide care for handicapped youngsters. Unlike foster homes, care is given to larger numbers of children, generally four to twelve.

Preferred Type of Placement

The history of substitute care reflects cyclical shifts from placing children in family homes to placing them in institutional settings.[58] Here we will look at some of the issues that affect decisions to use either type of facility.

It has been reported that many institutions provide little more than custodial care,[59] despite the fact that youngsters are generally institutionalized because of specific treatment needs that cannot be met in foster family homes. In recent years there have been a number of successful law suits on behalf of children whose "right to treatment" has been abrogated by being placed in custodial facilities.[60] In discussing the purpose of the juvenile court I noted that treatment and rehabilitation, not punishment, are its goals. The rehabilitative function is cited as justification for depriving youngsters of due process rights at juvenile court hearings, as well as justification for losing the right to remain in the community and to be raised by their parents. The courts, in deciding law suits in favor of the youngsters, have specifically stated that there is no justification for the deprivation of civil liberties unless treatment services are provided.[61]

A far more serious problem than the issue of custodial care vs. treatment has come to light in recent years and directs attention to the accumulated evidence of institutional abuse of children.[62] Tying children to their beds at night, placing them in solitary confinement for up to thirty days, and overmedication of youngsters are some of the types of institutional abuse that have been documented.[63] Also, children in institutions are invariably labeled in some manner said to be descriptive of their problems. The categories in which children are placed are often "repugnant to larger society," limiting the child's future potential.[64] Because the majority of children in institutions are from minority backgrounds, other discriminatory practices are reinforced.

The geographic isolation of institutions creates a host of difficulties. Children are denied normal learning experiences, such as how to interact with members of a larger community, how to make purchases in stores, how to use public transportation, and how to behave in opposite sex relationships, making the transition back into the community problematic. Even if such experiences were provided, there is no reason to believe that children would move easily from institution to community unless opportunities were built into programs giving them the chance to practice these skills outside institutional settings. In short, youngsters in these situations stand a chance of becoming estranged from ordinary life. Geographic isolation reduces the chances that parents will visit with their children. Transportation may not be available, and, remembering that a majority of these children come from poor families, it may be unaffordable even if available. Children in institutions tend to be older than those placed in family homes. Thus they are cut off from continuous contact with their parents, with whom they may have formed strong emotional attachments. The fact that institutions rarely include parents in treatment programs not only reinforces estrangement, but gives rise to serious doubt that parents will be able to assist in maintaining behavior changes if the children are returned to their homes. Nor do these programs take into account the chances that the conditions which maintain problem behaviors are to be found in patterns of family and community interaction.

These are only some of the reasons that have given impetus to a movement known as "deinstitutionalization." This is accomplished by moving children out of institutional settings into community-based care facilities or by reducing the number of children placed in institutions, or both. Group home placement is viewed as a viable alternative to care in large-scale institutions. The movement to deinstitutionalize has been gaining momentum since the early 1960s and has widespread support, despite the lack of evidence for the superiority of group homes.[65] Current thinking on this issue is summed up in the following:

> Large congregate institutions characterized by control and not offering educational, treatment, or wholesome socializing experiences, should be replaced by a diversity of facilities, including foster homes, small group homes, and small residential institutions located and programmed so that children may continue to participate in family, school, and community life as much as possible. Residential programs should have liaison services with the child's family, school, and community.[66]

Since the pendulum of preference for foster family homes vs. institutional care has swung back and forth, the lesson of history suggests caution by reminding us that cycles may repeat themselves. While large congregate institutions are presently at the bottom of a hierarchy of preferred placement facilities, they may reach the top again. This could be facilitated by increasing concern over "law and order" issues and a prevailing "get tough" policy with juveniles. Even should institutional disenchantment prevail, such placement facilities will no doubt continue to be used for the most severely handicapped youngsters. It is important to bear in mind that we are proceeding with deinstitutionalization without information that alternative facilities are effective in overcoming the problems identified for institutions. Community based care is appealing to common sense. However, proceeding without evidence—expecting more from group care than we may have a right to expect—opens the door for disenchantment when and if group homes do not meet expectations. Cross-cultural research provides evidence that institutional care of children can be effective.[67] It is possible that the concept will be redefined, as we learn from and possibly model institutions after those in other countries.

Who Cares for The Children?

The majority of children in out-of-home care live in foster family homes. In the following pages we will look at a profile of the "typical" foster parent, explore the process of recruiting and licensing foster homes, view the financial and service relationship between foster parents and child-caring agencies, and review current issues in this area.

PROFILE OF FOSTER PARENTS.   The majority of foster parents in a single age group are forty-five to fifty-nine years of age (45 percent) followed closely by persons twenty-five to forty-four years of age (40 percent). They are likely to have less than a high school education and to earn slightly less than the national median. The majority of fathers are in semiskilled occupations (40 percent). The majority of mothers are unskilled (44 percent).[68]

RECRUITMENT AND LICENSING.   Recruitment refers to the process of searching for foster homes; licensing to the process of certifying homes as suitable placement facilities. Families who are currently licensed foster parents are the single greatest source for recruiting new foster parents. The process begins when an application is made to a state or local agency. It proceeds with an investigation of the home that results in granting or denying a license. Licensing regulations vary state by state, precluding generalizations. In general, prospective homes must meet certain physical requirements; for example, adequate bedroom space in relation to the number of children in the home, as well as satisfying health and safety standards. The location of a home—its proximity to schools, health-care facilities, churches, and recreation areas—may also be an important factor. The age of the adults, their motivation to become foster parents, their expectations of having a foster child, their attitude towards adults whose children are in placement, and their willingness to permit a child's natural parents to visit with the child may all be considered. If foster parents have children of their own, there may be an opportunity for a licensing worker to assess their child-care skills through direct observation and to ask the children how they feel about having a foster child in the home. Once a home is approved, the responsibilities of the agency and the child-caring persons may be delineated in a contract. Contracts identify the boundaries of the tripartite relationship between foster parent, child, and agency. Foster parents, for example, agree to notify the agency of any changes in their life that may affect the child, and they acknowledge that primary responsibility for legal and medical decisions that affect the child remains with the agency, as does the decision regarding the length of time the child will remain in the home.[69] The child-placing agency agrees to provide services to the child and the foster parent. Agency responsibilities are carried out by the child welfare worker who interprets agency policy and who communicates the needs of foster parents and children to the agency.

Foster homes are in short supply, particularly those with adults of diverse ethnic backgrounds and homes that can provide specialized care for handicapped children. Recruitment efforts are hindered by shortages in agency personnel. Changing social conditions, such as greater job opportunities for women outside of the home and the increased importance given to leisure time activities, are factors that contribute to the reduction in the number of potential foster homes. In addition to recruiting difficulties, there are problems in retaining homes. The average length of time that foster parents continue to provide this service is two to six years.[70]

New approaches to recruitment and the use of incentive systems to retain foster parents are suggested remedies. Rather than continuing to rely on present foster homes as a major source of recruitment, education for people in the community with regard to the need for homes is recommended. Expanding the universe of potential foster parents by considering single parents and public assistance recipients as possible sources is another suggestion. Incentives might include foster parent dinners, awards for outstanding service, and professional support of foster parent organizations. The American Public Welfare Association and others suggest that the foster parent role be professionalized. Career ladders for foster parents that would include a salary scale with payment based on "length of service, training, and type of child served are recommended."[71] There is some evidence that training for foster parents can help to resolve some of the difficulties noted above. Boyd and Remy, reporting the results of a two-year followup study of fifty-five foster families who received training, observed that when these families were compared to a control group of 113 untrained families, there was evidence that training reduced the number of placements that "failed" (situations where children had to be moved to new homes). Training increased the probabilities of desirable placement outcomes, as well as the likelihood of foster parents remaining licensed.[72] Four states now mandate that foster parents receive training as a condition for obtaining a license.[73]

FINANCIAL ASSISTANCE TO FOSTER PARENTS. Foster parents are provided with financial assistance to raise the youngsters in their care. In general, assistance is provided for basic necessities such as food, clothing, educational, and medical expenses. Payments may cover recreational costs and certain luxuries, such as bicycles and camp. Extra costs incurred in caring for handicapped children may be paid. Minimum monthly payments range from $80 in New Mexico and Louisiana to $206 in Alaska. Some states vary payments by the age of the child, and some do not. New Mexico and Louisiana, for example, pay the same amount of money for seven-year-olds as they do for a child thirteen years of age. In contrast, Alaska pays $248 for a seven-year-old and $281 for a thirteen-year-old. One-time payments for clothing, school supplies, physical examinations, and "special needs of the child at the time of placement" are provided by some states.[74] It has been suggested that payments made to foster parents rarely cover all of the costs of raising a child. Thus, out-of-pocket expenses for housing, schooling, education, meals taken out of the home, orthopedic shoes, and bedroom furniture have been reported in some studies.[75]

SERVICES TO THE CHILD AND FOSTER PARENTS. Child welfare workers are expected to prepare children for entry into a foster home and to prepare foster parents prior to placing the child. They may also bear responsibility for providing or arranging for services to resolve any problems that occur in the foster home that directly relate to the child.

Preparatory tasks may include a series of introductory visits to ease the child into the setting, sharing information with foster parents that is descriptive of the child's background, and interpreting agency policy. Evidence suggests that preplacement visits do not always occur, that agencies do not make clear their expectations of foster parents, and that foster parents are sometimes not apprised of a child's special needs. This situation is "... unfair to the foster parents (and) to the foster child ... unless the child's special need is quite visible, it means that he simply will not receive the proper services."[76] Once children are in placement, however, the available evidence suggests that foster parents, rather than the child's natural parents, receive the bulk of attention from child welfare workers.

ADOPTION

The purpose of adoption is to allow children "who would not otherwise have a home and who can benefit by family life, to become members of a family."[77] It is probably the most well known of the social services because it is used by people of all socioeconomic classes. When a child is adopted, all rights and responsibilities that existed between the child and natural parents are terminated and transferred to the adoptive parents. Thus, the legal relationship becomes similar to that between a child and biological parents.

Changes in the Field of Adoption

There is agreement that the field of adoption is changing. However, since data are not collected systematically, the nature and magnitude of all changes cannot be specified. Some of what we know is described next.

The total number of adopted children decreased from a high of 175,000 in 1970, the "peak year for adoptions," to 149,000 in 1973. The number of homes approved for adoption decreased by more than 55 percent between 1971 and 1975.[78] Children born out of wedlock have always been the major source of children available for adoption. Although the greatest percentage who are adopted by unrelated adults still comes from this group, the overall percentage has declined. The majority of children placed for adoption have characteristically been white, nonhandicapped, and less than one year of age. In 1977 children under one year of age represented the smallest group, accounting for only 9 percent of children available for adoption. More than 55 percent were seven years of age or older. White children still represent the majority who are freed for adoption (62 percent). Black youngsters comprise the next largest group, representing 27 percent of this population, followed by Hispanic children who account for 3 percent. Two percent of the children are American Indian/Alaskan, 1 percent of Asian/Pacific origins, and 4 percent of "other" ethnic origins.[79]

Population changes can be attributed to several factors. The total number of births is affected by the availability of abortion and improved methods of birth control. Changing social values place less emphasis on having children, provide support for women to seek alternative careers to homemaking, and support the movement for zero population growth. Also, growing acceptance of unwed motherhood increases the chances that women may keep, rather than relinquish, their children.

While our concern here is with adoption as a route to permanency for children in foster care, the issues to be reviewed apply to the field in general. As children who are born out of wedlock cease to be the major source of adoptees, those in out-of-home care who cannot be reunited with their parents become a primary resource. In many ways, the universe of adoptable children is becoming synonomous with the universe of children in foster placement. These youngsters have historically been considered *hard-to-place*. This category includes children from ethnic minority backgrounds, older children (five to six years of age is "old" by adoption standards), youngsters who are physically or emotionally handicapped, and those who are members of sibling groups for whom one adoptive home is desired. In the following pages issues related to the adoption of hard-to-place children are reviewed, efforts to increase the numbers for whom permanent homes are found are described, and suggestions for placing more of these children in adoptive homes considered. We begin by looking at different types of adoption.

Types of Adoption

Adoption can be classified as regular, independent, and black market. Regular adoptions are arranged by public or voluntary social service agencies. They are characterized by the provision of services to natural parents (to help them decide whether to relinquish a child, for example); to the adoptive parents (by helping them find an appropriate child and by providing assistance in completing the adoption process); and to the child (by placing him in an adoptive home that is most suitable to his needs). Postadoption services, to assist adoptive parents and child through the process of adjustment, may also be offered. An independent adoption is an adoption that is "completed without the help or aegis of a licensed social service agency."[80] A natural parent may place a child directly with the adoptive parents, or the placement may be arranged by a third party—an attorney or physician, for example. Agencies may, if the court requests it, conduct a *home study* which is an evaluation of the adoptive home as a suitable placement resource. Independent adoptions are frowned upon by professionals because of the lack of social services. Black market adoptions are independent adoptions where a sum of money is paid—to a physician or lawyer, for example—who, in turn, contracts with a pregnant woman to "turn her child over to an unknown couple following birth."[81] Because money changes hands, this practice has been referred to as "baby selling." Independent adoptions may also include the payment of fees to cover a woman's medical expenses.

Who May Adopt

Agency policies regarding who may adopt have reflected what the Child Welfare League of American calls a search for the "ideal" parents. Requirements have been rigid, restricting adoptions to relatively young, two-parent families. Frequently home ownership, separate bedroom space for each child, a "modest" bank account and proof of infertility were requirements.[82] Matching of children and parents, particularly with regard to religious preferences, has also been a practice.

Policies have changed due to the need to increase the pool of potential adoptive homes. Older applicants, single parents, unwed mothers, and parents with marginal incomes are now considered as possible adoptive parents. The emphasis on religious matching has diminished in importance.

Recruitment of Adoptive Parents

Recruitment is an out-reach process by which agencies seek to increase the pool of adoptive homes. Since agency policies have excluded certain applicant groups, information describing changes must be disseminated. Community education takes many forms. It includes media advertising, the distribution of newsletters, brochures, and flyers, as well as door-to-door recruitment campaigns. Community meetings using speakers and videotapes to inform the public of the need for adoptive homes and to describe the adoptive process have been used, and advice has been sought from community residents as to the best ways to reach potential applicants.[83] Adults who have adopted hard-to-place children are a valuable resource for disseminating information, as well as for assisting new adoptive parents in dealing with difficulties they may encounter. Because of the potential for conflict between foster parents and adoptive parents, the former have not been viewed as a major source for recruitment. This too is changing, and foster parents are now considered a prime resource. Data suggest that recruitment efforts such as these have been successful in increasing the pool of applicant homes.[84] Active recruitment may have diminishing returns over time. Once these efforts reduce the universe of applicant homes, new approaches may have to be developed.

Adoption Subsidies

The costs incurred in raising hard-to-place children can be a barrier to their adoption, particularly when recruitment efforts are directed at families with modest incomes and when the children are handicapped. Foster parents, since they stand to lose the funds they receive for raising a foster child, may be discouraged from adopting. Thus, monetary incentives to offset child-rearing costs may be a determinant in whether permanent homes can be found for hard-to-place children.

Adoption subsidies, which provide for ongoing payments to adoptive parents, are a way of overcoming this barrier. As of late 1976, forty-two states had enacted subsidy programs.[85] The provisions in these programs vary. While almost all states earmark funds for the hard-to-place child, some limit the amount of the subsidy to 75 percent of the cost of caring for a child in foster placement; others pay an amount equal to foster care rates. Some set annual limits of $6,000 to $10,000, while others do not specify limits.[86]

Data highlight the value of subsidies in the adoption of hard-to-place children. From the results of the 1977 survey previously mentioned, we learn that the importance of subsidies increases with the child's age. They were required for 8 percent of the children under one year of age, for 20 percent of those one to three years of age, and for 30 percent of those four to six years of age. They were necessary for almost one-half of all adopted adolescents. While subsidies were important factors in the adoption of 33 percent of all children, they were of particular importance in the adoption of black children, 52 percent of whom were placed in subsidized homes; as well as for Hispanic youngsters, 49 percent of whom were placed in subsidized settings. They were instrumental to the adoption of 30 percent of the children of American Indian/Alaskan heritage, for 28 percent of the white children, and for 10 percent of those of Asian/Pacific origins.[87]

From the point of view of a prospective adoptive parent, subsidies may have two drawbacks. First, some states base eligibility on the adoptive parent's income, not the child's need.[88] Thus some families may be ineligible, even though expenses for a child's special education or medical needs are very high. Limits on the duration of subsidies are a second drawback. California and Texas, for example, restrict payments to three years, with the possibility of a single two-year extension. Hence, some families who cannot foresee managing without assistance may be unwilling to risk adoption.

It has been suggested that subsidies are underutilized, either because workers are not trained in their use or because agency administrators do not encourage their use. Administrative support is viewed as necessary to increasing the numbers of children who move from foster placements into adoptive homes.[89]

Adoption Exchanges

Adoption exchanges are another tool for increasing the chances of finding homes for hard-to-place children. An exchange compiles information on youngsters available for adoption for whom homes cannot be found, as well as information describing adoptive applicants for whom children cannot be located. The utility of this data lies in matching available children with available applicants. The Adoption Resource Exchange of North America (ARENA), developed in 1967 by the Child Welfare League of America, is a prototype of an exchange system. One or more agencies in all fifty states, the District of Columbia, and seven Canadian provinces were registered with ARENA in 1973.[90] The exchange is credited with facilitating the adoptions of 1,760 children between 1967 and 1976.[91] A majority of these children were considered hard-to-place due to age, race, or physical or emotional handicaps.

There is some evidence suggesting that exchanges have not fulfilled their potential. The New York Exchange, which is mandated by law, is credited with placing fewer than 100 children in the first three years of its operation. Grossman and others, in evaluating this exchange, point to the importance of ongoing recruitment to maximize the potential for placing children. Regardless of the number of listings, there is no guarantee of a "fit" between applicants and children.[92] Exchanges that provide national coverage can facilitate the adoption of children across state lines. There are difficulties with *interstate adoptions*, however, that are highlighted in a Child Welfare League report.

The League notes that the procedures used to terminate parental rights in one state may not satisfy the legal requirements in other states. Also, some states reserve the right to consent to adoptions to agencies within the state, therefore raising the possibility that consent by an out-of-state agency will not be recognized. State policies that do not allow for "expenditures on behalf of children outside of the state's borders" result in confusion as to who is responsible for meeting expenses and create another barrier to interstate adoptions.[93] In general, it can be said that the laws of most states have been geared to block, rather than to facilitate, the movement of children across state lines in order to protect their well-being.

Overcoming such limitations and increasing a child's opportunities for adoption is one objective of the American Public Welfare Association's Interstate Compact on the Placement of Children. The intent of this measure is to establish a "constitutionally recognized means of extending a court's jurisdiction across state boundaries."[94] The American Bar Association's Uniform Child Custody Jurisdiction Act is another effort to extend court jurisdiction by making a child custody decree enforceable in states other than the one where it was issued.[95]

Terminating Parental Rights

Termination is a legal process whereby the ties between natural parents and their children are severed so that a child can be freed for adoption. Such action is necessary if permanent homes are to be found in cases where parents will not relinquish their children, but cannot or will not resume full-time child-care responsibilities.

Laws that permit termination exist in all but three states. The importance of such legislation is seen in that over half of the states either "enacted new termination statutes or substantially amended existing ones," in the mid-1970s.[96] The grounds for termination action vary across states. Most contain a time requirement, specifying, for example, a minimum period of time that must pass before parents can be said to have abandoned a child. Some states permit termination action if there is evidence that parents are mentally ill, or that a parent habitually uses drugs or alcohol. Physical or sexual abuse, neglect, and failure to supervise or control children are grounds in over one-half of the states.[97] In 1977 termination of parental rights ranked second only to voluntary relinquishment (34 percent, compared to 52 percent) in explaining why children were available to be adopted.[98] Several demonstration projects have shown that the numbers of children placed in permanent homes can be increased through use of state termination statutes.[99]

Transracial Adoption

Children from minority backgrounds have long been considered hard to place. In the late 1960s, 71 percent of the eligible white children were placed in adoptive homes; the comparable figure for nonwhite children was 31 percent.[100] At that time there were 116 applicant families for every 100 white children, but only thirty-nine for every 100 nonwhite children. In an effort to increase the numbers of minority youngsters placed in permanent homes, transracial adoptions were used. A transracial adoption is one where the race of the adoptive parent differs from that of the child. For the most part, children adopted in this manner have been black, their adoptive parents white.

The practice of transracial adoptions has stirred a great deal of controversy, centering mostly on questions relative to the development of the black child's identity.[101] Chestang expresses this concern by asking whether white parents can "equip a black child for the inevitable assaults on his personality from a society that considers his color to be reason enough to reject him."[102]

Concern over the ability (and perhaps the willingness) of whites to provide experiences that would support a positive identity follows from an awareness of racist practices in society and from recognition of how this has affected generations of black people. It is not surprising that the black movement of the 1960s and 1970s, with its focus on increasing racial consciousness and pride, would center attention on questions of identity in cases of transracial adoption.[103]

Concern regarding the development of the black child's identity in a white home is not shared by all black professionals. According to Ladner, the psychiatrists that she interviewed for her study on transracially adopted children think that it "is possible for some white parents to rear emotionally healthy black children." Quoting Curtis, Ladner reports that "it has been demonstrated endlessly that a similar racial group membership alone cannot serve as a reliable guarantee of a successful marriage, family or home."

One of the unfortunate aspects of this controversy is that the basic issue of finding permanent homes for children has become obscured in a "power struggle." Ladner succinctly captures this problem by noting that the "interests of warring adults—adoptive parents, agencies and black social workers—have been served to the detriment of the child's welfare." She expresses her own preference for every child's right to a permanent home.[104] And Madison and Schapiro question whether good adoptive homes for all black children who need them will be found in the next decade.[105]

Given our history of racism, the concern voiced about transracial adoptions is understandable. However, historical arguments should be tempered with consideration of the possibility that today's children are growing up in a society that is different from the one in which today's adults grew up. We cannot predict the future form of race relations, nor can we describe the coping skills that future generations will need. And our ability to predict the long-range consequences of various patterns of child rearing is very limited.

The practice of transracial adoptions "peaked" in the early 1970s and has been decreasing since that time. An estimated 15,000 black children were adopted by white parents between 1961 and 1975.[106] Data describing how these children have been affected by being reared in white homes are sparse. The evidence suggests that the children and their adoptive parents are adjusting quite well.[107] The data are limited, of course, in that the many adoptees are still quite young. It is possible that they have yet to confront situations in which identity is important. If they have had negative experiences, the effects may not be measurable at this time.

Definitive information can only be produced by longitudinal studies. One such investigation is underway in Illinois. In its fourth year at the time of this writing, the investigation plans to follow up three groups of black children (one group of children adopted by single parents; another, transracial adoptees; and the third, children adopted by parents of the same race) for sixteen more years.[108]

Experience in trying to find adoptive homes for hard-to-place children has shown that "contrary to long standing agency assumptions, many families will adopt these youngsters."[109] However, unlike the past, when adoptive applicants exceeded the number of children available and where the process was initiated by an applicant approaching an agency, new tools—such as subsidies, exchanges, community outreach programs, and revisions in statutory law—play an important role today. Modifications in agency requirements, such as those giving consideration to populations who have not been viewed as likely candidates to adopt, are important. Available information indicates that transracial adoptions, like adoptions in general, are successful ventures for a majority of the children and their new parents.[110]

GUARDIANSHIP

Some children in out-of-home placement cannot be reunited with their families. Parents may be unwilling or unable to resume full-time care. Adoption may not be possible, either because parents will not relinquish their children, or because there are no statutory grounds for terminating parental rights. And adoption is not always desirable. Some children in the continuous care of one set of foster parents have formed good relationships with their caretakers, who may be unable or unwilling to adopt, and the agency may deem removal of the child to a preadoptive home inappropriate. For children who cannot be restored to their parents or adopted, guardianship provides a third route to achieving continuity.

Types of Guardianship

There are five types of guardianship. Natural parents are *natural guardians* of their children unless they relinquish them for adoption or have their guardianship status revoked by court order. They are responsible for day-to-day decision making and long-range planning for their children and for continuing support and education. Natural parents have the right to claim their children's earnings, and children have the right to inherit from their parents. Natural parents may designate a person to act as guardian in the event of their death. *Testamentary* guardianship, as this is called, is accomplished by nominating a person in a will. The court must approve the nominee, who is then subject to ongoing court supervision.

A *guardian ad litem* is a person who is designated by the court to represent the child's interests in a court preceeding—for example, in a custody dispute between natural parents, or in a hearing to terminate parental rights. A *guardian of a child's estate* is appointed by the court to manage a youngster's inheritance. Persons occupying this position do not acquire legal title to the property, nor may they commingle it with their own; and guardians may not profit by managing the child's estate. Natural parents do not automatically assume this latter role. They must be appointed to it by the court. A *guardian of the person* assumes responsibility for the child's care and nurturance. A person acting in this capacity may or may not have physical custody of the child. A guardian of the person has the rights and responsibilities of a parent with two exceptions. He or she is not responsible for supporting a child (except from the child's own estate), and there are no reciprocal rights of inheritance.

Unless parental rights have been terminated, court appointment of a guardian does not abrogate all of their rights or responsibilities. They retain the right to visit, to determine their child's religious affiliation, and they may consent, or refuse to consent, to their child's adoption. Parents may petition the court to terminate a guardianship and have the child returned to their care, and they are responsible for ongoing support. Likewise, a guardian may petition the court to dissolve his or her relationship with the child.

Guardianship overlaps with, but can be distinguished from, child custody. Custody refers to physical possession of a child. It includes day-to-day responsibility for care, supervision, guidance, and discipline. Guardianship involves greater rights and responsibilities, as delineated above. When a child is in the care of natural parents, guardianship and custody are synonomous. If a child is removed from home, parents lose day-to-day custody, but may retain guardianship. The two are not necessarily vested in the same person.

Guardianship as Distinct From Adoption

Adoption creates the same legal relationship between a child and adoptive parents as existed between a child and natural parents. Guardianship differs in several ways. Guardians are not responsible for support or for education beyond minimum state requirements. A guardian does not have any rights to the earnings of a ward, nor are there reciprocal rights of inheritance. While a guardian can exercise discretion as to where the child lives, he or she cannot remove a youngster from the area of the court's jurisdiction without its approval.

Guardianship as Distinct From Long-Term Care

The relationship between children and long-term care foster parents is tenuous. There are no legal safeguards, and so it is vulnerable to disruption. Technically a youngster may be removed from a foster home by the placing agency, regardless of how long the child has been there, with only a minimum amount of notice. While this is unlikely to occur if the child has been in continuous care, it is nevertheless possible.

In long-term foster care arrangements, decisions related to a child's schooling, medical treatment, and vacation plans remain in agency control (although in practice many foster parents make major decisions concerning the children in their care). Yet the relationship is tenuous because authority is not legally vested in the foster parents. Guardianship, by contrast, invests decision-making responsibility in the person assuming that role. If foster care is of brief duration, agency control over decisions is appropriate. However, if the relationship becomes long-term, the likelihood of foster parents and children making a reciprocal commitment may be lessened because each knows that the placement is vulnerable to disruption. The importance of such a commitment between children and caretaking parents makes guardianship a significant option for youngsters who cannot be reunited with their birth parents and who cannot be adopted.[111]

Agency Guardianship

For substantial numbers of children guardianship is vested in administrative officers or other staff persons of state departments of public welfare or other agencies. This practice has been defended on the grounds that agencies need the authority of guardianship to carry out plans for the care and treatment of children. It has been criticized because it lacks the personal quality of social guardianship and because the children are functionally wards of the state.

The Child Welfare League has the following to say about this agency practice:

> Appointment of private persons employed by or associated with an agency holding legal custody of the child, such as the social worker or a board member, may deprive the child of potential family or community ties, and may involve a conflict between the official duties imposed upon such individuals as a member of the agency and the loyalties involved in serving as a guardian of the child or youth.[112]

Deprivation of family ties may result if alternatives such as adoption or guardianship with child-caring adults is not pursued because guardianship is already vested in an agency person. Conflicting loyalties may occur when, in order to fulfill the responsibilities of guardian, the worker is "pitted" against the agency. Guardians are charged to advocate the interests of their wards. In pursuing these interests, a social worker-guardian may be in the untenable position of having to confront a supervisor or an agency administrator who disagrees with the worker's interpretation of the child's need. Such a confrontation is difficult enough, but the problem is compounded when the advocate is employed by the agency on which she or he is making demands. A further disadvantage to the worker-guardian concept is that a personal relationship based on an ongoing commitment between child and guardian is not likely to occur. Workers rarely have the time to develop such relationships, given other responsibilities, and worker turnover in public agencies is high, further reducing the chances for an ongoing relationship. The Child Welfare League suggests that agency guardianship may be appropriate when

> ... a child will be in placement until he reaches his legal majority and significant adults such as relatives (or long-term care foster parents) are not available for the responsibilities of guardianship.[113]

Impediments to the Use of Guardianship

There is a paucity of data on the use of guardianship. It is not mentioned as a case plan in the national survey previously referred to.

There are several reasons for the infrequent use of this planning option. First, there are no subsidies for guardians. Without financial aid, foster parents who cannot afford child-care expenses may be unwilling to accept the responsibilities of this role. Agencies may lack expertise in the use of guardianship. Unlike foster care and adoptions, it is not an area of specialization in child welfare. Lacking the support of tradition, a framework within which agencies can commit themselves to this alternative has not been developed. Agency personnel may be unaware of this option or of its advantages, or they may be unclear as to how to secure guardianship for a child, and administrative support may be lacking. Guardianship also suffers from an overemphasis on its legal advantages, with insufficient attention paid to the social gains for children in placement. An added difficulty is that the courts rarely monitor guardianship arrangements, although they are supposed to do so. Since child-care agencies frequently close cases following the appointment of a guardian, there may be a concern that there is no authority to safeguard the child's interests.

SUMMARY

The exact incidence of abuse and neglect is not known. Statistical variations occur when data are compared across states because of differences (1) in the conditions that must be reported, (2) in whether abuse and neglect, or abuse only, is documented, (3) in whether states systematically expunge unproven cases, and (4) in whether recent enforcement efforts may have had the effect of increasing the number of reported cases.

The etiology of maltreatment has been explained with reference to parental pathology, parental experiences in growing up, demographic characteristics of families, parent-child interaction, and cultural acceptance of violence.

We have little definitive knowledge, because data sources both direct and restrict the range of possible explanations, and methodological problems limit possible conclusions.

The most consistent findings are that patterns of abuse can be learned in early childhood and that abusive acts may be triggered by social and economic stress.

Since learning patterns and stress factors may be found in nonabusive families, these variables are best viewed as correlates, not causes, of maltreatment.

Definitive information must wait on data gathered from a random sample of abusive and nonabusive families or on information descriptive of the population-at-large.

Safeguarding the physical and emotional well-being of children in their own homes is the objective of protective services.

Protective service intervention is sanctioned by law. It is required following a report of abuse or neglect whether or not parents want it.

All fifty states and the District of Columbia have statutes requiring that suspected or proven maltreatment be reported to a designated agency.

States differ on conditions that must be reported, persons required to report, and agencies identified as reporting centers.

Data compiled in central registries vary across the states, ranging from simple demographic information to medical histories and information about services provided to families.

Professionals use registry information to make intervention decisions, particularly in grey area cases. Information describing the prior provision of services contributes to case-planning decisions.

Foster home care is meant as a short-term service to provide substitute parenting for children whose own parents cannot or will not provide ongoing care.

Children should be reunited with their biological parents once the difficulties that necessitated placement are resolved. When this is not possible, permanency can be achieved through adoption, guardianship, or planned long-term care arrangements.

Knowledge of the reasons that children enter care is limited by the absence of universally accepted typologies for classifying problems. The most common reasons for placing children out of their homes are: neglect, emotional problems of parents, financial difficulties, parent-child conflict and emotional problems of children, behavior problems of children at home and at school, abuse, and parental unwillingness to provide ongoing care.

The majority of children receive substitute care in foster family homes, followed by those in institutions and lastly by those in group homes.

The history of substitute care reflects cyclical shifts form placing children in family homes to placing them in institutional settings.

Disenchantment with institutional care is caused by the absence of rehabilitative programs, by documented cases of child abuse, and by concern that institutions impede, rather than facilitate, a child's return to the community. For these reasons, a movement known as "deinstitutionalization" is underway. Deinstitutionalization means reducing the number of institutional placements, moving children from these settings to community based group homes, or both.

This movement is proceeding without data showing that group home care is superior. So it is possible that disenchantment with the outcomes of such placements could lead to institutional care once again being favored.

The states license foster family homes as suitable child-care facilities. Licensing standards differ across the states. Requirements may focus on the size, location and physical safety of the home, the age of prospective foster parents, their motivation, and their expectations for a foster child.

Agreements between foster parents and the child-placing agency delineate the responsibilities of each. Major decisions affecting the well-being of children remain in agency control.

Recruitment, the process of locating new foster homes, is important because there is a shortage of homes for children of diverse ethnic and racial backgrounds and because the total number of applicants has decreased due, in part, to the changing roles of women.

To retain foster homes, the use of incentives, including professionalization of the foster parent role and awards for foster parents, is recommended.

Foster parents are given financial assistance to help raise children in their care. Evidence indicates, however, that payments are not sufficient to meet expenses; so foster parents may incur out-of-pocket costs.

Child welfare workers bear responsibility for providing services to the child and foster parents. These include informing parents of a child's special needs, preparing the child and substitute parents for placement, and offering services to resolve postplacement difficulties.

Adoption can provide permanent homes for children whose natural parents cannot or will not provide ongoing care.

When a child is adopted, all rights and responsibilities that existed between the child and birth parents transfer to the adoptive parents.

The population of children available for adoption is decreasing due to improved methods of birth control, the availability of abortions, growing growing acceptance of unwed motherhood, and changes in women's roles.

As the number of white infants available for adoption decreases, attention turns to children considered hard-to-place due to age, ethnicity and physical or emotional handicaps.

Methods to expand the pool of adoptive applicants include modifying requirements as to who may adopt, recruitment drives to inform people of the need for adoptive homes, and financial subsidies to help defray the costs of raising hard-to-place children.

Methods to increase the likelihood of adoption for children without permanent homes include the development of adoption exchanges and the expansion or modification of state laws which allow the rights of natural parents to be terminated in order to free children for adoptive placement.

The numbers of adoptive homes and adopted children have increased through recruitment efforts, subsidies, and aggressive action to terminate parental ties.

When children cannot be returned to their biological parents and adoption is not possible, guardianship offers a third route for attaining permanency.

A guardian of the person may be appointed by the court to provide care and nurturance for a child when there is no adult to assume these responsibilities.

Unless ties are severed, natural parents retain the right to visit their children, to determine their religious affiliation, and to consent, or refuse to consent, to their adoption.

Unlike adoptive parents, guardians are not responsible for providing ongoing financial support, and there are no reciprocal rights of inheritance. Guardians remain subject to ongoing court supervision.

The increased decision-making responsibility vested in a guardian and the fact that the guardian-ward relationship is legally sanctioned makes this alternative more stable than planned long-term care which, without legal safeguards, is subject to disruption.

The presence of legal safeguards may increase the likelihood of a reciprocal commitment between foster parents and children.

Guardianship can be vested in an employee of a child-care agency. The desirability of this alternative is questionable because of conflicts that can result when one person attempts to fill the dual role of employee and child advocate. Time constraints and staff turnover may limit the chances that an ongoing personal relationship will be formed.

The lack of financial subsidies, the fact that guardianship is not an established area of specialization in child welfare, and an emphasis on the legal, rather than the social, gains for children are factors accounting for the limited use of this option.

NOTES

1. Jane Knitzer, Mary Lee Allen and Brenda McGowan, *Children Without Homes: An Examination of Public Responsibility to Children in Out-of-Home Care* (Washington, D.C.: The Children's Defense Fund, 1978), p. 3, fn5.

2. Ann W. Shyne and Anita G. Schroeder, *National Study of Social Services to Children and Their Families* (Washington, D.C.: U.S. Dept. of Health, Education and Welfare, D.H.E.W. publication No. (OHDS) 78-30150, 1978), Ch. 2.

3. Richard J. Gelles, "A Profile of Violence Toward Children in the United States," paper presented at the Annenberg School of Communications Conference on Child Abuse, Philadelphia (November 1978), p. 6.

4. Richard J. Light, "Abused and Neglected Children in America: A Study of Alternative Policies," *Harvard Educational Review*, Vol. 43, No. 4 (November 1973), pp. 202–13; Projections from survey data are an alternative approach to estimating the incidence of maltreatment. This is the method used by Gil, see David C. Gil, *Violence Against Children: Physical Child Abuse in the United States* (Cambridge, Mass.: Harvard University Press, 1973).

5. Saad Z. Nagi, *Child Maltreatment in the United States: A Challenge to Social Institutions* (New York: Columbia University Press, 1977), p. 2.

6. C. H. Kempe and others, "The Battered Child Syndrome," *Journal of the American Medical Association*, Vol. 181, No. 7 (July 1962), pp. 107–12; J. Densen-Gerber, M. Weiner and R. Hochstedler, "Sexual Behavior, Abortion and Birth Control in Heroin Addicts: Legal and Psychiatric Considerations," paper presented at the Annual Meeting of the American Academy of Forensic Sci-

ences, New York (1972); H. D. Bryant and others, "Physical Abuse of Children: An Agency Study," *Child Welfare*, Vol. 42 (March 1963), pp. 125–30; R. Gladston, "Observations of Children who have been Physically Abused by Their Parents," *American Journal of Psychiatry*, Vol. 122, No. 4 (1965), pp. 440–43; S. Minuchin and others, *Families of the Slums* (New York: Basic Books, Inc., Publishers, 1967).

7. Leontine Young, *Wednesday's Children: A Study of Child Neglect and Abuse* (New York: McGraw-Hill Book Company, 1964), p. 113.

8. C. H. Kempe, "Child Abuse and Neglect," *Raising Children in Modern America*, ed. Nathan B. Talbot (Boston, Mass.: Little, Brown & Company, 1974), p. 175; B. F. Steele, "Violence Within the Family," *Child Abuse and Neglect: The Family and the Community*, eds. Ray E. Helfer and C. Henry Kempe (Cambridge, Mass.: Ballinger Publishing Co., 1976), pp. 13–14; J. Spinetta and D. Rigler, "The Child Abusing Parent: A Psychological Review," *Psychological Bulletin*, Vol. 77 (1972), pp. 296–304; for a review of studies related specifically to neglect, see Norman A. Polansky, Carolyn Hally and Nancy F. Polansky, *Profile of Neglect: A Survey of the State of Knowledge of Child Neglect* (Washington, D.C.: U.S. Dept. of Health, Education and Welfare, Social and Rehabilitation Service, 1973), p. 12.

9. J. M. Giovannoni and A. Billingsley, "Child Neglect Among the Poor: A Study of Parental Adequacy in Families of Three Ethnic Groups," *Child Welfare*, Vol. XLIX, No. 4 (April 1970), pp. 203–5.

10. Deborah Shapiro, *Parents and Protectors: A Study in Child Abuse and Neglect* (New York: Child Welfare League of America, 1979), p. 34.

11. Shapiro cites two studies where the percentage of parents who were abused as children ranged from a low of 11 percent (Jean M. Baker, *Parents Anonymous Self-Help for Child Abusing Parents Project*, Behavior Associates, Inc., p. 69) to a high of 14 percent (Gil). As she notes, there is a "lack of convincing evidence to support the intergenerational hypothesis." (Ibid., p. 39, fn6).

12. Studies in support of this finding include: E. M. Thomson, and others, *Child Abuse: A Community Challenge* (East Aurora, N.Y.: Henry Skeward, 1971), p. 169; C. L. Johnson, *Child Abuse in the Southeast: An Analysis of 1172 Reported Cases* (Athens, Ga.: Georgia University Welfare Research, 1974); Gil, *Violence Against Children*; Studies where the data do not support this finding include; Gelles "A Profile of Violence"; B. Lauer, "Battered Child Syndrome: Review of 130 Patients With Controls," *Pediatrics*, Vol. 54, No. 1 (1974), pp. 67–70; H. Martin and others, "The Development of Abused Children," *Advances in Pediatrics*, Vol. 21 (1974), pp. 25–73.

13. J. A. Baldwin and J. E. Oliver, "Epidemiology and Family Characteristics of Severely Abused Children," *British Journal of Preventive Social Medicine*, Vol. 29, No. 4 (1975), pp. 205–21; J. R. B. Currie, "A Psychiatric Assessment of the Battered Child Syndrome," *South African Medical Journal* (1970), pp. 635–39; Kempe and others, "The Battered Child Syndrome"; Gil, *Violence Against Children*; David M. Ferguson, John Fleming and David O'Neill, *Child Abuse in New Zealand* (Wellington, New Zealand: Research Division, Department of Social Work, 1972).

14. Gelles, "A Profile of Violence," p. 11.

15. Gil, *Violence Against Children*, p. 104.

16. Gelles, "A Profile of Violence," p. 11; Light, "Abused and Neglected Children," p. 232.

17. Gelles, ibid., reports that parents 30 years of age and younger "were more than five times more violent than individuals over fifty and 62 percent more so than those thirty-one to fifty," p. 16. Gil's data is reported in *Violence Against Children*, p. 110.

18. Gelles, "A Profile of Violence," p. 19.

19. Gil, *Violence Against Children*, p. 110.

20. R. Helfer, "The Etiology of Child Abuse," *Pediatrics*, Vol. 51 (1973) pp. 777–79; R. Helfer, *The Diagnostic Process and Treatment Programs* (Washington, D.C.: Office of Child Development, 1975).

21. E. Elmer and G. Gregg, "Developmental Characteristics of Abused Children," *Pediatrics*, Vol. 40 (1967), pp. 596–602; A. Sandgrund, R. W. Gaines, and A. H. Green, "Child Abuse and Mental Retardation: A Problem of Cause and Effect," *American Journal of Mental Deficiency*, Vol. 79, No. 3 (1974), pp. 261–68.

22. S. Antler, "Child Abuse: An Emerging Social Priority," *Social Work*, Vol. 23, No. 1 (January 1978), pp. 58–61; Gil, *Violence Against Children*, pp. 23–24.

23. B. Simons and others, "Child Abuse—Epidemiologic Study of Medically Reported Cases," *New York Journal of Medicine*, Vol. 66 (1966), pp. 2783–88.

24. Light, "Abused and Neglected Children," p. 230.

25. Ibid.; Gelles, "A Profile of Violence," p. 21; Gil, *Violence Against Children*, Ch. 6.

26. Gelles, ibid., p. 5.

27. Ibid., p. 26.

28. Gil, *Violence Against Children*, p. 13.

29. Spinetta and Rigler, "The Child Abusing Parent," pp. 296–304.

30. T. J. Scheff, "On Reason and Sanity: Some Political Implications of Psychiatric Thought," in *Labeling Madness*, ed. Thomas J. Scheff (Englewood Cliffs, N.J.: Prentice-Hall, Inc., 1975), pp. 12–20.

31. Shyne, *National Study*, p. 46.

32. Ibid., pp. 68–69.

33. Ibid., p. 62.

34. *Standards for Child Protective Services* (New York: Child Welfare League of America, 1973, revised), Ch. 1.

35. Kempe, "Child Abuse and Neglect," p. 174.

36. *Standards for Protective Services*, p. 9.

37. *Children's Rights Report*, Vol. 1, No. 7 (New York: Juvenile Rights Project of the American Civil Liberties Union Foundation, April 1977), p. 1.

38. Unless otherwise noted, information describing the elements of reporting laws can be found in: *Trends in Child Protection Laws-1977* (Denver Col.: Education Commission of the States, 1978).

39. *The Community Team: An Approach to Case Management and Prevention, Child Abuse and Neglect: The Problem and Its Management: Volume 3*

(Washington, D.C.: U.S. Dept. of Health, Education and Welfare, DHEW publication No. [OHD] 75-30075, 1975), pp. 37–39.

40. Ibid., p. 13.

41. M. Gibelman and S. Grant, "The Uses and Misuses of Central Registries in Child Protective Services," *Child Welfare*, Vol. LVII, No. 7 (July/August 1977), p. 407.

42. Knitzer, *Children Without Homes*, p. 1.

43. Shyne, *National Study*, p. 33.

44. B. Q. Madison, "Changing Directions in Child Welfare Services," in *Changing Roles in Social Work Practice*, ed. Francine Sobey (Philadelphia: Temple University Press 1977), pp. 53–57.

45. Alan R. Gruber, *Children in Foster Care: Destitute, Neglected . . . Betrayed* (New York: Human Sciences Press, 1978), pp. 40–41.

46. Marvin R. Burt and Ralph R. Balyeat, *A Comprehensive Emergency Services System for Neglected and Abused Children* (New York: Vantage Press, 1977), p. 34.

47. Shirley Jenkins and Mignon Sauber, *Paths to Child Placement: Family Situations Prior to Foster Care* (New York: Community Council of Greater New York, 1966), p. 64.

48. Theodore J. Stein, Eileen D. Gambrill, and Kermit T. Wiltse, *Children in Foster Homes: Achieving Continuity of Care* (New York: Holt, Rinehart & Winston, 1978), p. 48.

49. Deborah Shapiro, *Agencies and Foster Children* (New York: Columbia University Press, 1976), p. 27; Jenkins, *Paths*, Ch. 4.

50. *Where Are the Children?* (n.p.: Nebraska Department of Public Welfare, 1976), p. 17.

51. Jenkins, *Paths*, p. 64.

52. Shapiro, *Agencies*, p. 27.

53. David Fanshel and Eugene B. Shinn, *Children in Foster Care: A Longitudinal Investigation* (New York: Columbia University Press, 1978), p. 47.

54. Arnold P. Goldstein, *Structured Learning Therapy* (New York: Academic Press, Inc., 1973), pp. 8–14.

55. Shyne, *National Study*, p. 27. Percentages exceed 100 percent because of cases where two reasons for placement were noted.

56. Ibid., p. 34.

57. Jeffrey Koshel, *Deinstitutionalization-Dependent and Neglected Children* (Washington, D.C.: The Urban Institute, 1973), pp. 6–9.

58. For an excellent review of this subject, see: Martin Wolins and Irving Piliavin, *Institution or Foster Family Care: A Century of Debate* (New York: Child Welfare League of America, 1964). Group homes were not developed until the early 1960s.

59. Advisory Committee, *Toward a National Policy*, p. 89.

60. Carol M. Rose, *Some Emerging Issues in Legal Liability of Children's Agencies* (New York: Child Welfare League of America, 1978), pp. 18–19.

61. S. N. Katz, "Introduction," in *The Youngest Minority: Lawyers in Defense of Children*, ed. Sanford N. Katz (Washington, D.C.: American Bar Association Press, 1974), pp. 17–19.

62. *Child Abuse and Neglect in Residential Institutions: Selected Readings on Prevention, Investigation and Correction* (Washington, D.C.: National Center on Child Abuse and Neglect, Children's Bureau, DHEW publication No. [OHDS] 78-30160, 1978).

63. Ibid., p. 2; *Children's Rights Report*, Vol. II, No. 9 (June 1978); Kenneth Wooden, *Weeping in the Playtime of Others* (New York: McGraw-Hill Book Company, 1976).

64. *Abuse and Neglect in Residential Institutions*, p. 13.

65. Koshel, *Deinstitutionalization*; Advisory Committee, *Toward a National Policy*, pp. 34–89.

66. Advisory Committee, *Toward a National Policy*, p. 89.

67. M. Wolins and Y. Wozner, "Deinstitutionalization and the Benevolent Asylum," *Social Service Review*, Vol. 51, No. 4 (December 1977), pp. 604–23.

68. James D. Cully, Barbara H. Settles, and Judith B. Van Name, *Understanding and Measuring the Cost of Foster Care* (Newark, Del.: Bureau of Economic and Business Research, University of Delaware, 1977), Ch. 6.

69. *Legal Issues in Foster Care* (Raleigh, N.C.: National Association of Attorneys General, Committee on the Office of Attorney General 1976), p. 21.

70. A. Kadushin, "Child Welfare: Adoption and Foster Care," in *Encyclopedia of Social Work: Volume 1*, eds. John B. Turner and others (Washington, D.C.: National Association of Social Workers, 1977), p. 118.

71. *Standards for Foster Family Service Systems* (Washington, D.C.: American Public Welfare Association March 1975), pp. 43–57.

72. L. H. Boyd, Jr. and L. L. Remy, "Is Foster Parent Training Worthwhile?" *Social Service Review*, Vol. 52, No. 2 (June 1978), pp. 275–96.

73. "Nota Bene," *Child Welfare*, Vol. LVII, No. 1 (January 1978), p. 59.

74. Culley, *Understanding and Measuring*, Ch. 7.

75. Gruber, *Children in Foster Care*, pp. 171–72. The State of North Carolina reports that foster parents subsidize the state by $10 million a year through direct, out-of-pocket expenses, see: *Why Can't I Have a Home?: A Report on Adoptions and Foster Care in North Carolina* (Raleigh, N.C.: Governor's Advocacy Council on Children and Youth, 1978), p. vi.

76. Sally E. Palmer, *Children in Long-Term Care—Their Experiences and Progress* (n.p.: Welfare Grants Directorate of the National Department of Health and Welfare, 2nd edition, 1976), p. 89; Madison, "Changing Directions," pp. 41, 56; Gruber, *Children in Foster Care*, p. 167.

77. *Standards for Adoption Services*, revised edition (New York: Child Welfare League of America, 1973), p. 2.

78. These data are reported by: A. Kadushin, "Children in Adoptive Homes," in *Social Service Research: Reviews of Studies*, ed. Henry S. Maas (Washington, D.C.: National Association of Social Workers, 1978), pp. 39–89.

79. Shyne, *National Study*, pp. 126–32.

80. William Meezan, Sanford Katz, and Eva Manoff Russo, *Adoptions Without Agencies: A Study of Independent Adoptions* (New York: Child Welfare League of America, 1978), p. 1.

81. Subcommittee on Child and Human Development of the Committee of Human Resources, United States Senate, *Opportunities for Adoption Act of*

1977, 95th Congress, 1st session (April 1977), U.S. Government Printing Office, Washington, D.C., p. 110.

82. Joyce A. Ladner, *Mixed Families* (Garden City, N.Y.: Anchor Press/ Doubleday, 1977), p. 57.

83. *Test of Regional Planning in Adoption, Progress and Evaluation Report of the First Program Year, August 15, 1975 –August 14, 1976* (Albany, N.Y.: Welfare Research, Inc.); *Harlem-Dowling Children's Service* (New York: Spence-Chapin Services to Families and Children, Harlem-Dowling Children's Service, n.d.); Elizabeth A. Lawder and others, *A Study of Black Adoption Families: A Comparison of a Traditional and a Quasi-Adoption Program* (New York: Child Welfare League of America, 2nd edition 1972).

84. Vivian Hargrave, Joan Shireman, and Peter Connor, *Where love and need are One* (Chicago: Illinois Department of Children and Family Services, 1975); Harlem-Dowling Children's Service; *That They May Have Homes: A Report of the Black Child Advocacy Adoptions Program* (Washington, D.C.: Black Child Development Institute, 1974).

85. *Child Protection Report*, Vol. II, No. 25 (Washington, D.C.: William E. Howard, Editor and Publisher, December 2, 1976), p. 2.

86. *Opportunities for Adoption Act*, pp. 342–52.

87. Shyne, *National Study*, pp. 130–32.

88. *Opportunities for Adoption Act*, pp. 342–52.

89. *The Children of the State: Barriers to the Freeing of Children for Adoption: Final Report* (Albany, N.Y.: The New York State Dept. of Social Services, 1976), pp. 134–36.

90. Madison, "Changing Roles," pp. 32–33.

91. A. Kadushin, "Children in Adoptive Homes," *Social Service Research: Review of Studies*, ed. Henry S. Maas (Washington, D.C.: National Association of Social Workers, 1978), p. 49.

92. Hanna Grossman and others, *An Evaluation of the New York State Adoption Exchange* (Albany, N.Y.: Welfare Research, Inc., 1976).

93. Roberta Hunt, *Obstacles to Interstate Adoption* (New York: Child Welfare League of America, 1972), p. 30.

94. *Legal Issues in Foster Care*, p. 45.

95. B. M. Bodenheimer, "The Uniform Child Custody Jurisdiction Act," in *The Youngest Minority*, pp. 45–71.

96. *Trends in Child Protection Laws*, pp. 14–16.

97. Ibid.

98. The remaining children were freed because of their parents' death (4 percent), abandonment (5 percent) and "other" reasons (5 percent). Shyne, *National Study*, p. 127.

99. Theodore J. Stein, Eileen D. Gambrill, and Kermit T. Wiltse, *Children in Foster Homes: Achieving Continuity of Care* (New York: Holt, Rinehart & Winston, 1978), Ch. 4; Arthur Emlen and others, *Overcoming Barriers to Planning for Children in Foster Care* (Portland, Ore.: Regional Research Institute for Human Services, Portland State University, 1977), p. 5; Barbara D. Larsen, *"Reach-Out"—A Program for Children in Need of Adoptive Planning* (Los Angeles, Cal.: Los Angeles County Dept. of Adoptions, July 1978).

100. B. Q. Madison and M. Schapiro, "Black Adoption-Issues and Policies: Review of the Literature," *Social Service Review*, Vol. 47 (1973), p. 533.

101. Ladner, *Mixed Families*, Ch. 7.

102. L. Chestang, "Dilemmas of Biracial Adoption," *Social Work*, Vol. 17, No. 3 (May 1972), p. 103.

103. Ladner, *Mixed Families*, p. 103.

104. Ibid., pp. 122–25.

105. Madison, "Black Adoption," p. 553.

106. Kadushin, "Children in Adoptive Homes," p. 43.

107. Ladner, *Mixed Families*, p. 249; Lucille Grow and Deborah Shapiro, *Black Children-White Parents* (New York: Child Welfare League of America, 1974), p. 239.

108. Joan F. Shireman and Penny R. Johnson, *Adoption: Three Alternatives* (Chicago: Chicago Child Care Society, n.d.).

109. E. V. Mech, "Adoption: A Policy Perspective," in *Child Development and Social Policy: Volume 3*, eds. Bettye M. Caldwell and Henry N. Ricuitti (Chicago: University of Chicago Press, 1973), p. 494.

110. Benson Jaffee and David Fanshel, *How They Fared in Adoption: A Follow-Up Study* (New York: Columbia University Press, 1970); Lawder, *A Study of Black Adoptive Families*, pp. 73–74; W. Feigelman and A. R. Silverman, "Single Parent Adoptions," *Social Casework*, Vol. 58, No. 7 (1977), pp. 418–25; also see note 159.

111. H. B. Taylor, "Guardianship or Permanent Placement of Children," *California Law Review*, Vol. 54 (1966), pp. 741–47.

112. *Standards for Foster Family Service* (New York: Child Welfare League of America, 1975), p. 77.

4

Issues in Child Welfare Services

The preservation of family life is the objective society seeks to attain through the provision of child welfare services. The premium that is set on family life determines the value we place on children being raised in the continuous care of one set of adults. In child welfare this value is expressed in the concept of *permanency planning* which, in addition to highlighting a concern for continuity in the care of children, directs attention to the fact that for many youngsters this goal is not attained fortuitously. Rather, it is the end result of a systematic process of gathering and using information, making informed decisions, formulating case plans, and providing problem-solving services. Impediments and supports to attaining the goals of permanency planning are reviewed in this chapter.

IMPEDIMENTS TO PERMANENCY PLANNING

The preceding chapter explored the structural components of protective services, foster home care, and adoption services. These elements provide a framework for the existence of services. For example, without provisions in statutory law that allow for protective service intervention regardless of whether parents want it, it would be difficult to fully realize the goal of safeguarding children, since it is assumed that an abusive parent will not accept this assistance voluntarily. Likewise, substitute care for children in need of homes would not be possible without a framework for recruiting and providing assistance to adults who are willing to provide this service.

To understand certain of the impediments to finding permanent homes for children we must briefly look at the kind of structure that surrounds the process of service delivery. The elements of process, like the elements of structure, create a framework—in this case, one that gives direction to the day-to-day activities through which service objectives are achieved. For instance, in order to safeguard the well-being of children in their own home, workers must make a series of decisions. They must identify problems that create danger for a child, decide how best to go about solving these problems, and decide when the problems have been resolved so that services can be withdrawn. One element of process that makes it possible to engage in these tasks is a decision-making framework that identifies alternatives and gives direction to the process of selecting from among them. Three elements of process common to protective services, foster care, and adoption are (1) decision making, (2) case planning, and (3) service delivery. The following illustrates the relationships between these elements and goal attainment.

Decision Making

Foster care services are offered to provide temporary homes for children until they can be reunited with their families. If family reunification is not possible, adoption, guardianship, and planned long-term care are alternatives which may provide children with permanent homes. Foster care workers, parents, and children must collaboratively decide which of these options to pursue. Generally, restoration to parents is the alternative of choice when children first enter placement.

Case Planning

Once a decision is made, it is embodied in a case plan, the components of which specify how the objective is to be realized. For example, a case plan for a child in substitute care would stipulate how difficulties that necessitated placement will be resolved. It would include a schedule for parent-child visits, and it would note the time frame for accomplishing service objectives.

Service Delivery

A case plan is activated when the first steps necessary to deliver problem-solving services are taken. Workers monitor parental progress in problem-solving programs and the quality of parent-child interaction during visits. Children are reunited with their parents when evidence shows that problems have been resolved. If problems are not solved, or if parents do not participate in problem-solving programs, alternatives that will provide continuity-in-care are considered.

If workers are to engage in decision making, case planning and service delivery, they must have training, access to problem-solving resources, and support for goal-oriented activities from the agencies for which they work.

TRAINING. As the term is used here, training refers to in-service programs provided for agency staff. They may be offered for a variety of reasons—familiarizing new workers with agency policy and state law, equipping staff with specific decision making and case planning skills, and bringing them up-to-date on innovative methods in the field. Training is important for many reasons. Regardless of academic background or work experience, staff must learn how to work within the rules and regulations of a given agency and within the laws of a given state. When new legislation, such as child abuse reporting laws, is enacted, it is important to inform staff how this will affect their daily practice. It is critical because a significant number of child welfare workers in public agencies do not have an education in either social work in general, or child welfare in particular. In 1977 only 25 percent of the children receiving child welfare services nationally were assigned to workers with social work degrees, generally at the bachelor's level.[1]

An ongoing criticism of public agencies has concerned their failure to provide staff with in-service training.[2] This may be changing, in part because of the availability of training monies under Title XX, and also because of recent developments in the field that provide new substance for training seminars and workshops. At the end of 1976 federal grants-in-aid for training increased over 1975 expenditures in thirty states.[3] However, the impact of these increases did not show up in the data gathered by Shyne and Schroder in their 1977 survey of public agencies. They report an absence of skills training for child welfare staff and they consider this to be one of the most serious gaps in the child welfare delivery system.

RESOURCES. These are the tools child welfare workers use to attain service goals. Foster homes and adoptive homes are examples of resources. Here, the concern is with resources workers can bring to bear to assist families to resolve their problems. Whether a protective service worker can fulfill a case plan to maintain a child in his or her own home may depend upon the availability of day-care services to provide respite for a single parent. Whether a child in foster care can be reunited with biological parents may depend upon the availability of treatment programs to reduce a parent's dependency on drugs or alcohol. While certain problem-solving services may be offered by a child welfare worker, generally they lack the training and time necessary for such activities. The availability of resources varies across communities; generally, however, they are in short supply.

The number of staff in an agency is very important. A shortage of staff means that each worker will carry a large number of cases, thereby reducing the time available to provide services. While this problem affects workers in all service areas, it has been recently highlighted in protective services due to increases in reports of maltreatment following passage of reporting laws. If reports increase while the number of staff remains constant, clearly, investigations will be less than thorough. Legal staff to assist workers in exercising options such as adoption and legal guardianship are also necessary, but unfortunately limited, resources.

AGENCY SUPPORTS.   In-service training and problem-solving resources are staff supports insofar as they enable workers to service clients and realize service objectives. Agency policy manuals, if operationalized, are another form of support. An operational policy contains directives that provide workers with instructions and authority to guide them in attaining service objectives. Such directives would spell out, for example, the steps that protective service workers are to take when a report of neglect or abuse is received. It would delineate the conditions that constitute neglect and abuse, thereby providing guidelines for deciding when intervention is appropriate and when it is not. As was the case with in-service training, operational policy is necessary because of variations in agency rules and regulations as well as those found in state laws. It is essential for staff members with no formal social work education or practical social work experience. Until recent years, few agencies provided staff with operational manuals, although there is reason to believe that this is changing.[4]

Other support systems can also be identified, such as clerical assistance to help staff complete forms that are required by local, state, and federal governments, and to help staff maintain case records. Organizing volunteers and case aides to assist workers in delivering services that do not require professional training can provide additional support. Some of the more routine aspects of helping clients, such as transporting parents to visit their children, or children to medical appointments, can be accomplished by trained aides, freeing workers to engage in case-planning and service delivery tasks requiring greater skill.

If training, resources, and agency supports are this important, why are they in short supply? Many difficulties can be traced to federal and state policy. Two policy issues concern us. The first has to do with its development; the second with incentives. Policy is often developed and its provisions enacted into law without due consideration to the time needed to gear up for its implementation, or to the availability of resources to meet its tenets. This is well illustrated by the child abuse and neglect reporting laws. You will recall that professionals, and in many states lay people, are required to report suspected abuse and neglect, and that there are penalties for failure to report. These laws were implemented by the states despite the fact that few if any had developed guidelines identifying the conditions that must be reported. Nagi informs us that almost one-half of all public health, school, hospital, medical, and social service personnel whom he surveyed report that their agencies do not have procedural guidelines for reporting cases.[5] If on one hand there are penalties for not reporting, while on the other there is a lack of clarity as to what must be reported, it is no wonder that the incidence of reports increased dramatically after passage of these laws. Since the volume of reports was not anticipated, it is not surprising that there were deficiencies in staff to handle them, as well as in resources to assist clients.

The issue of incentives in federal policy is as follows. Federal funding for programs to prevent placement of children or for services to reunify families after children enter care is limited, while funds to maintain children in placement are unlimited.[6] For example, for every child who enters foster care under court order, the federal government reimburses the state for "seventy-five percent of the salaries of service workers, supervisors and support staff and fifty percent of the salaries of eligibility workers, administrative costs, overhead and all other costs."[7] This is a clear disincentive to reunite children and parents or to move children towards adoptions, since these funds are lost each time a child moves out of placement. Likewise, there are no federal supports for adoption subsidies despite their value to the adoption of hard-to-place children.[8]

Since states rely on federal funding to support child welfare programs, decisions made by state legislators and public welfare agency administrators are affected by the availability of federal dollars. It follows from this that state practices will reflect the incentive structure in federal policy.

Insofar as there are fiscal incentives to place children in foster care and to maintain them in foster homes, and insofar as legislators and agency administrators are occupied with budgetary issues, it is not reasonable to expect adequate training, adequate resources, or adequate support systems for workers, since these are mechanisms to prevent placement and to provide permanent homes for children who must be placed.

Some Effects on Attaining the Goals of Permanency Planning

There is more than one way to evaluate the effects of service delivery. One approach would be to see whether service objectives are realized. Thus, the effectiveness of protective services could be measured by the number of children who are maintained in their own homes after receiving this service. Effects can also be evaluated by asking clients whether they found a service helpful. Yet it is possible that clients may render positive evaluations even though service objectives are not achieved. For example, Heck and Gruber, reporting the results of a demonstration project that sought to provide services to children in the community in order to prevent institutional care, found that parents whose children *were* institutionalized evaluated change in the child's behavior more positively than did the parents of children maintained in the community. This was explained with reference to the parents' desire to have their children placed in institutions because of the aversive nature of the child's behavior.[9] Our concern is with the first type of evaluation, which has focused primarily on foster care and the use of adoption to attain permanency.

It has been noted that training, access to problem-solving resources, and agency support systems are necessary for workers to engage in decision making, case planning and service delivery activities, and that these are in short supply. Therefore, the following should not come as a surprise. Evidence suggests that case plans are not formulated for between 31 and 70 percent of all children in out-of-home placement.[10] And services to natural parents are the exception, not the rule.[11] It follows, then, that foster home care is not the short-term arrangement it is meant to be. Estimates are that 25 percent of the children entering care in any one year, plus 50 percent of those already in care, will remain there for long periods of time—many until they reach adulthood.[12] The percentage of children restored to their parents ranges from 10 percent to 17 percent when the status of children is viewed at a single point in time. The percentage reported is higher, ranging from 38 to 56 percent, when the status of children is monitored over a period of years. The percentage of foster children who are adopted ranges from 1 percent, when measured at a single point in time, to 21 percent, when viewed over time.[13] There are no statistics regarding the numbers of children for whom guardianship arrangements are made, nor for those for whom planned long-term care is arranged.

Let us review two aspects of foster care said to be harmful to children. These are the initial separation from natural parents (most particularly from mothers) and serial foster home placements.

Bowlby used the term *maternal deprivation* to refer to the separation of infants from their mothers.[14] Based on deductions from psychoanalytic theory, he hypothesized that partial deprivation "brings in its train, anxiety, excessive need for love, powerful feelings of revenge, and, arising from these last guilt and depression."[15] Empirical evidence does not support the suggestion that deprivation necessarily follows from separation.[16] According to Yarrow, the conclusions that have been drawn about the effects of deprivation were based on observations of immediate and short-term reactions of children, not on long-range or ultimate effects.[17] The results of a follow-up study conducted by Bowlby and others inform us that "damage" to the children was not as extensive as had been anticipated.[18] Likewise, Fanshel and Shinn, in a five-year longitudinal study of children in placement, inform us that there was "little evidence of massive emotional trauma experienced by the children at entering foster care or three years after their entry into care."[19] To the extent that children experienced difficulties, they were associated with the child's age at placement. children who entered care after the age of five—those who might be expected to have strong emotional attachments to their parents—experienced greater difficulties in adjusting to placement than did younger children.[20] The limits of the maternal deprivation hypothesis highlight the limits of our ability to make long-range predictions.

Evidence shows that children rarely experience continuity in foster homes. Almost 50 percent of all youngsters are placed in more than one home, and over 20 percent experience three or more moves.[21] Serial foster home placements are said to be harmful to a child's development.[22]

Wald reports a study conducted by Kent, in which the case records of over 500 neglected and abused children living in foster homes were studied. Kent concluded that the child's health, behavior, academic achievements, and peer relations *improved* following placement. However, the improvement declined when children experienced multiple placements.[23] Palmer's study of 200 children in foster care informs us that children who experienced "disruptions" in their placement were less likely to develop their "intellectual potential" than children in stable foster homes. And the incidence of social problems was higher for children who experienced instability than for those in more stable placements.[24] From a follow-up study of children in foster care in Oregon, we learn that the child's *sense of permanency*, not the fact of it, was the best predictor of a youngster's well-being. It made little difference whether the child was returned to natural parents, adopted, or placed in a legally planned foster home.[25] Problems may result from the ambiguity that surrounds unplanned long-term care, rather than from anything inimical in this type of placement.

Even when a child in placement displays problems after entering a foster home, caution must be exercised in explaining these with reference to separation. Difficulties may have existed before the placement occurred and may have been instrumental to the placement decision. It is also important to consider whether a child was prepared for the move into a foster home. Was the child introduced to the foster parents prior to entering their home? Does the child blame himself or herself for the move? Problems that emerge at later stages of a child's placement career may not be the result of substitute parenting services. Parental visits with children decrease as the child's tenure in placement increases.[26] Thus, a child may feel deserted by parents with whom he or she has strong emotional ties. We must also ask ourselves what are the effects on children of knowing that their parents have been labeled inadequate?

While evidence regarding the effects of out-of-home care are equivocal, the issue of finding permanent homes for children should not, as Wiltse suggests, rest on our ability to "prove that long-term foster care is clearly psychologically damaging."[27] The issue of permanent homes should be cast in the framework of rights—those of the child to be raised by its own parents, or in lieu of this, to be raised in another permanent setting; and the right of natural parents to raise their own children with minimum state interference.

SUPPORT FOR PERMANENCY PLANNING

Legislative Activity

The concept of permanency planning reflects a philosophical departure from the traditional view that the rights of natural parents and their children are always synonomous. While this position is still paramount it is slowly giving way to a recognition that children have rights that may be independent of those of their parents. Redressing the imbalance of rights is essential to realizing the objectives of permanency planning. For example, it is difficult to reconcile actions to terminate parental ties—a necessary course of action to achieve continuity for some children—with a position that parents' rights are inalienable. Social custom and law require us to recognize natural parents' rights in the first instance by giving them every opportunity to retain custody, care, and control of their children. However, the full intent of permanency is realizable only when we recognize that there is a point in time when, having given parents the opportunity to exercise their rights, attention must shift to the child's right to a permanent home. This change in thinking is reflected in the Model Placement Statute, legislation which seeks to "protect the needs of children for continuous care," and which proposes that the concept of *psychological parenthood* be adopted as a legal guideline in custody cases in order to promote the objective of permanency.[28]

Psychological parenthood refers to the fact that the bonds existing between parents and children are borne and nurtured in the context of ongoing, caring relationships and that these bonds may develop between a child and a primary caretaker exclusive of blood ties.[29] This position has been advanced by foster parents who have challenged traditional practices that subordinate their interest in a child to the interests of biological parents. It also challenges the position of child-caring agencies which suggest that foster parents have no "standing" with regard to the children in their care. While court decisions vary, some have supported foster parents in their claim that they be given consideration when decisions affecting the welfare of children in their care are made.[30]

The thrust to permanency planning is reflected in other pieces of federal legislation, as well as in legislative activity at the state level. The Foster Care Adoptions and Reform Act, which seeks to "establish the fundamental right of children to a suitable permanent home," illustrates federal activity in this area.[31] Preventing out-of-home placement by providing services such as day care, homemakers, and crisis counseling is stressed. When foster care is necessary, the act calls for written, individual case plans that include a detailed description and timetable for reuniting families. When reunification is not possible, the act recommends that a determination be made whether the child "should be freed for legal adoption through termination of parental rights." And it calls for federal assistance to the states in order to develop laws to permit termination so that adoptive placement can be expedited.

Alaska's Children's Code, adopted in 1977, is illustrative of state-level activity. The code seeks to limit intervention by restricting it to situations where "actual or imminent harm to the child is shown." Before a youngster can be placed in foster care, information must be presented to the court describing why the child cannot be protected or adequately rehabilitated at home. All efforts that have been made to work with parents and the child in the home must be described, and the parents' attitude toward placement must be reported. Case plans for all children must be submitted at mandatory review periods, at which time the court determines whether continued placement is appropriate. Plans must specify the behavioral changes that are to be demonstrated by parents and children in order that reunification occur. Unless a preponderance of evidence shows that the conditions under which the child's case was adjudicated still exist, the law requires that a child be returned to parents at the review hearing.[32]

Juvenile Court Activity

Realizing the intent of permanency requires that the status of children be monitored to assure that plans are made and implemented in accordance with the child's sense of time. Monitoring mechanisms are found in court, agency, and citizen review boards, one or another of which exists in thirty-three states.[33] At review hearings, workers submit case plans which include recommendations (for example, that protective service intervention be continued, or that a child be returned to the care of biological parents) to a judge or review panel.

The Concern for Children in Placement Project (CIP), initiated in 1974 under the auspices of the National Council of Juvenile and Family Court Judges, illustrates review procedures. This project uses citizen volunteers who are sworn to confidentiality to review the records of children in out-of-home care. Review forms, which contain information considered vital for permanency planning, are prepared for judges. Information describing the reasons why a child is in care, the length of time the child has been in placement, the frequency with which natural parents have contact with the child, the child's legal status, and current treatment plans are reported. As of late 1979, CIP projects had been implemented in thirty courts across the United States. While not fully evaluated, available evidence suggests that this review format can increase the number of children for whom permanent plans are made.[34]

The importance of review is evidenced by federal legislation recommending that all states establish procedures for impartial review of case plans.[35] It is also supported by the efforts of the National Council of Juvenile and Family Court Judges, who are endeavoring to explicate exact review procedures for members of the bench to follow in order to increase the chances that children will move into permanent homes.[36]

Innovations in the Field of Practice

Professionals in social work have endeavored to find new approaches to working with families in order to increase the numbers of children for whom permanent plans are made. The Alameda Project was a two-year experimental program that sought to increase permanence for children by involving natural parents in decision making and case planning. Three child welfare workers with master's degrees in social work received training in decision making, case planning, and behavioral methods that could be used to help resolve family problems viewed as impediments to reunification. Written contracts between workers and clients provided a framework for case planning. Plans identified parental objectives for future living arrangements of their children, specified goals for resolving family difficulties, and delineated case worker and client tasks in achieving objectives and goals. At the end of two years, 114 children in experimental units (79 percent) in contrast to fifty-nine children in control (40 percent) were either out or headed out of foster home placement. Long-term plans were made for the remaining thirty-one children in experimental units (21 percent) and for eighty-nine children in control (60 percent).[37]

The Freeing Children for Permanent Placement Project (generally known as the Oregon Project) used a different approach to attain permanency goals. The project involved 509 children from 15 Oregon counties. All the children were considered unlikely to be reunited with their parents, and all were viewed as adoptable. Eleven caseworkers were trained to pursue permanency either through restoration to biological parents or through aggressive action to terminate parental rights. Full-time legal assistance was provided to assist casework staff in pursuing the latter objective. As in the Alameda Project, workers used written contracts between themselves and clients as frameworks for case planning. Goals were articulated, and time limits for attaining them were spelled out. Despite the fact that children were considered unlikely to return to their parents, 27 percent were, in fact, restored. Adoption plans were formulated for 52 percent, and 8 percent were placed with relatives, while "other" plans were made for the remaining 10 percent.[38] The procedures used in both the Alameda and Oregon projects have been implemented elsewhere in the country. Initial reports are optimistic. They suggest that these methods can be applied to other demonstration projects, to different populations and to nonexperimental public agency settings.[39]

New Models for Practice

The tasks involved in permanency planning, including decision making, case planning, and providing services to resolve family difficulties, are beyond the skills of any one person. Even if this were not so, the large caseloads of child welfare workers, when viewed in the context of other worker responsibilities (such as administrative tasks) make it clear that time constraints preclude assigning all these tasks to one worker. Also, most child welfare staff do not have the extensive training that is a prerequisite for developing and implementing treatment programs. A majority of workers in public settings do not have social work degrees, and in-service training is not always available.

For these reasons, professionals in child welfare have made considerable efforts to rethink the role of the worker, mindful of these realities of practice and the demands of permanency planning. These endeavors have resulted in new models for providing services to children and their families. In one approach, services are delivered by a *team* of professionals, generally including persons whose diagnostic and treatment skills play a role in serving families said to be neglectful or abusive. Social workers, psychologists, psychiatrists, medical, legal, school, and law enforcement personnel, as well as volunteers, may be involved.[40] The child welfare worker may offer certain problem-solving services and may fulfill the role of case coordinator. A coordinator arranges for necessary services, gathers information describing client progress in case plans, disseminates information to members of the team, and calls team conferences.[41]

The second model identifies the child welfare worker as a *case manager*. A case manager bears responsibility for all permanency planning tasks with the possible exception of providing problem-solving services. It is expected that these services (such as marital counseling or addressing problems in parent-child interaction) will be offered in the community by persons who have expertise in solving specific problems. In this model the worker as case manager always functions in the role of case coordinator, in contrast to a team approach, where the worker may assume these responsibilities or they may be assigned to another.[42]

In practice, the processes of providing services may bear many similarities, whether one employs a team or case management approach. The models are conceptually different, however. In the case management approach, the locus of case control resides in the child welfare worker, thus defining a clear line of responsibility that is not defined in team approaches.

The tenets of permanency planning embody well-established social work principles. As a statement of purpose, the intent of permanency is not new. What is new, however, is the specificity with which procedures are delineated, and the support and commitment found in legislative activity, case review procedures, and professional research and development efforts.

SUMMARY

The concept of permanency planning expresses the value American society places on children being raised in the continuing care of one set of adults.

Attaining permanency goals requires workers to engage in a systematic process of decision making, case planning, and providing problem-solving services.

If workers are to engage in these processes, agencies must provide skills training, access to problem-solving resources, and support for goal-oriented activities. Evidence suggests that all three are in short supply.

Difficulties can be traced to federal and state policy which creates problems of two sorts: Policy is often enacted and implemented without allowing sufficient "start-up" time for training and for community education, and without due consideration of the fact that necessary resources are not available; incentives in federal policy, reflected in the decision-making behavior of state legislators and agency administrators, are geared more to maintaining children in care than they are to moving them out of placement.

Given deficits in training, resources, and support systems, it is not surprising that case plans are not always formulated and that problem-solving services are not always provided for children and their families.

Significant numbers of children grow to maturity in unplanned, long-term foster care, experiencing a number of changes in placement.

Evidence suggests that out-of-home placement, per se, is not harmful to children, although multiple foster placements may be.

The issue of permanency should not hinge on proving that placement is detrimental to a child, but rather on a child's right to be raised in a permanent home.

The thrust to permanency is supported by the following:

A philosophical position that recognizes children's rights as distinct from those of natural parents in some instances.

Court decisions which have recognized the right of foster parents to participate in decision making when the future of children for whom they have provided ongoing care is affected.

Federal and state legislation which seeks to establish children's right to a permanent home. Maintaining children in their own homes is stressed. Written case plans describing how continuity-in-care will be attained are required for children who must enter placement.

Increased use of court review procedures to monitor a child's progress toward permanency.

Results of demonstration projects, which indicate that the numbers of children for whom permanent homes are found can be significantly increased when systematic case management procedures are used.

New models for practice, reflecting professional efforts to rethink the role of the child welfare worker in light of the fact that the tasks involved in permanency planning are beyond the skills of any one person, and also, the realities of practice in public settings.

NOTES

1. Ann W. Shyne and Anita G. Schroeder, *National Study of Social Services to Children and Their Families* (Washington, D.C.: U.S. Dept. of Health, Education and Welfare, DHEW publication No. (OHDS) 78-30150, 1978), p. 77.

2. Jane Knitzer, Mary Lee Allen and Brenda McGowan, *Children Without Homes: An Examination of Public Responsibility to Children in Out-of-Home Care* (Washington, D.C.: The Children's Defense Fund, 1978), p. 7; Report of the National Commission on Children in Need of Parents, *Who Knows? Who Cares? Forgotten Children in Foster Care* (New York: Child Welfare League of America, 1979), p. 15; Shyne, *National Study*, p. 148.

3. Toby H. Campbell and Marc Benedick, Jr., *A Public Assistance Data Book* (Washington, D.C.: The Urban Institute, October 1977), pp. 150–51.

4. See, for example; *The Case Management Model: Concept and Process Definition: Volume 1* (Athens, Georgia: Regional Institute of Social Welfare Research, Inc., 1977); *Court Referral Project: Final Report* (Bismark, N. Dak.: Division of Community Services, Social Service Board of North Dakota, 1978); *Report of the Task Force on Alternatives for Families At Risk* (n.p.: Utah State Division of Family Services, 1975).

5. Saad Z. Nagi, *Child Maltreatment in the United States: A Challenge to Social Institutions* (New York: Columbia University Press, 1977), p. 19.

6. Knitzer, *Children Without Homes*, p. 123.

7. Jessica S. Pers, *Government as Parent: Administering Foster Care in California* (Berkeley, Cal.: Institute of Governmental Studies, University of California, 1976), p. 83

8. Committee on Finance, United States Senate, *The Social Security Act and Related Laws*, 94th Congress, 1st session (February 1975), U.S. Government Printing Office, Washington, D.C., p. 181. Federal legislation through which the states would be reimbursed for subsidies is pending. See: Committee on Finance, United States Senate, *Adoption Assistance and Child Welfare Act of 1979*, 96th Congress, 1st session (1979), U.S. Government Printing Office, Washington, D.C.

9. Edward T. Heck and Alan R. Gruber, *Treatment Alternatives Project* (Boston, Mass.: Boston Children's Service Association, 1976), pp. 218–19.

10. Edmund A. Sherman, Renee Neuman and Ann W. Shyne, *Children Adrift in Foster Care: A Study of Alternative Approaches* (New York: Child

Welfare League of America, 2nd printing, 1974), pp. 49–50; Shyne, *National Study*, p. 58.

11. *Where Are the Children?* (n.p.: Nebraska Department of Public Welfare, 1976), p. 79; Alan R. Gruber, *Children in Foster Care, Destitute, Neglected . . . Betrayed* (New York: Human Sciences Press, 1978), pp. 183–85; Theodore J. Stein, Eileen D. Gambrill and Kermit T. Wiltse, *Children in Foster Homes: Achieving Continuity of Care* (New York: Holt, Rinehart & Winston, 1978), pp. 63–64; Knitzer, *Children Without Homes*, p. 5.

12. Victor Pike and others, *Permanent Planning for Children in Foster Care: A Handbook for Social Workers* (Portland, Ore.: Regional Research Institute for Human Services, 1977), p. 1.

13. A review of studies on this subject can be found in: Stein, *Children in Foster Homes*, pp. 24–27.

14. John Bowlby, *Child Care and the Growth of Love*, 2nd edition (Baltimore: Penguin Books, 1968), p. 14.

15. According to Bowlby, foster home care results in partial deprivation since the child is raised by a foster mother, who may be a relative stranger to the child. Complete deprivation results when children are placed in institutions where there is no one person responsible for ongoing child care. Ibid.

16. For a review of studies on this subject, see: E. V. Mech, "Adoption: A Policy Perspective" in Bettye M. Caldwell and Henry N. Ricuitti, eds. *Child Development and Social Policy: Volume III* (Chicago: University of Chicago Press, 1973), p. 471.

17. L. J. Yarrow, "Maternal Deprivation: Toward an Empirical and Conceptual Re-Evaluation," *Psychological Bulletin*, Vol. 58 (1961), pp. 459–90.

18. J. Bowlby and others, "The Effects of Mother-Child Separation: A Follow-Up Study," *British Jour. of Medical Psychology*, Vol. 29, Pts. 3 and 4 (September 1956) pp. 211–47.

19. David Fanshel and Eugene B. Shinn, *Children in Foster Care: A Longitudinal Investigation* (New York: Columbia University Press, 1978), p. 412.

20. Ibid., p. 391.

21. Shyne, *National Study*, p. 118.

22. Gruber, *Children in Foster Homes*, p. 95; Janet Lahti and others, *A Follow-Up Study of the Oregon Project: A Summary* (Portland, Ore.: Regional Research Institute for Human Services, Portland State University, September 1978), p. 27.

23. M. S. Wald, "State Intervention on Behalf of Neglected Children: Standards for Removal of Children from their Homes, Monitoring the Status of Children in Foster Care and Termination of Parental Rights, *Stanford Law Review*, Vol. 28, No. 4 (April 1976), p. 647, fn 114.

24. Sally E. Palmer, *Children in Long-Term Care—Their Experiences and Progress* (n.p.: Welfare Grants Directorate of the National Department of Health and Welfare, 2nd edition, 1976), pp. 123–24.

25. *Case Record*, Vol. 3, No. 1 (Portland, OR: Permanent Planning Project, Regional Research Institute, Portland State University, February 1979), p. 1.

26. Fanshel, *Children in Foster Care*, pp. 88–89.

27. K. T. Wiltse, "Foster Care in the Seventies: A Decade of Change," *Case Record*, Vol. 2, No. 4 (November 1978), p. 2.

28. Donald Brieland and John Lemmon, *Social Work and the Law* (St. Paul, Minn.: West Publishing Co., 1977), p. 456.

29. Joseph Goldstein, Anna Freud and Albert J. Solnit, *Beyond the Best Interests of the Child* (New York: Free Press, 1973), p. 19.

30. *Children's Rights Report*, Vol. 1, No. 4 (New York: Juvenile Rights Project of the American Civil Liberties Union Foundation, December 1976– January 1977); *Legal Issues in Foster Care* (Raleigh, N.C.: National Association of Attorneys General, Committee on the Office of Attorney General, 1976), Ch. 13.

31. United States House of Representatives, *Foster Care and Adoption Reform Act of 1977*, 95th Congress, 1st session, U.S. Government Printing Office, Washington, D.C., p. 3.

32. C. Kleinkauf and B. McGuire, "Alaska's Children's Code," *Child Welfare*, Vol. LVII, No. 8 (September/October 1978), pp. 485–96.

33. W. E. Claburn, S. Magura and W. Resnick, "Periodic Review of Foster Care: A Brief National Assessment," *Child Welfare*, Vol. LV, No. 6 (June 1976), pp. 395–406; Local or statewide computerized data banks provide another framework for monitoring. Information deemed pertinent to permanency planning, such as the child's legal status, current case plan, length of time in care and the frequency with which parents visit with their children, is stored, thus allowing child welfare personnel to track a youngster's movement in the system, thus preventing "drift" and increasing the child's chances for being placed in a permanent home. See, Stein, *Children in Foster Homes*, pp. 17–19 for a discussion of issues related to this type of monitoring system.

34. For a more detailed discussion of this project, see: J. P. Steketee, "The CIP Story," *Juvenile Justice*, Vol. 28, No. 2 (May 1977), pp. 3–14; data on the effectiveness of this system comes from the State of Rhode Island which reports a 50 percent increase in the number of termination petitions filed and a 100 percent increase in the number of petitions to adopt. Len Trout, *Annual Report of the Project Evaluator* (Reno, Nev: Research and Educational Planning Center, College of Education, University of Nevada, unpublished report, 1976):

35. *Foster Care and Adoption Reform Act—1977*, p. 13.

36. Roberta Gottesman, *Bench Book—Draft* (Rena, Nev.: National Council of Juvenile and Family Court Judges, University of Nevada, unpublished).

37. Stein, *Children in Foster Homes*, p. 64.

38. Arthur Emlen and others, *Overcoming Barriers to Planning for Children in Foster Care* (Portland, Ore.: Regional Research Institute for Human Services, Portland State University, 1977), p. 5.

39. Data on the results of implementations of the Oregon Project are reported in *Case Record* (November 1978), p. 3. The procedures developed and tested in the Alameda Project were implemented in three group homes in New Jersey. Permanent plans were made for 52 percent of the 101 adolescents involved. Grace Sisto, *Dissertation Draft—United* (Bogota, N.J.: Children's Aid and Adoption Society, n.d.); These procedures were scheduled to be implemented in the New Jersey public welfare system in two southern counties in early 1980. Likewise, they are being implemented in Greensboro and High Point, NC and throughout the state of Arkansas.

40. B. Q. Madison, "Changing Directions in Child Welfare Services," in Francine Sobey, ed. *Changing Roles in Social Work Practice* (Philadelphia: Temple University Press, 1977), p. 44; *The Community Team: An Approach to*

Case Management and Prevention: Child Abuse and Neglect—the Problem and Its Management: Volume III (Washington, D.C.: U.S. Department of Health, Education and Welfare, DHEW publication No. (OHD) 75-30075, 1975) pp. 2–3.

41. C. A. Grosz and M. R. Lenherr, "The Coordinator's Role in Evaluation," in *The Child Protection Team Handbook,* ed. Barton D. Schmitt (New York: Garland STPM Press, 1978), pp. 153–69; M. H. Lenherr and C. A. Grosz, "The Coordinator's Role in Treatment," ibid., pp. 289–302.

42. *Protective Services for Abused and Neglected Children and Their Families: A Guide* (New York: Community Research Applications, Inc., n.d.), Ch. 2; *Case Management: Concept and Process: Volume 1; The Case Management Model: Implementation Requirements: Volume II* (Athens, Ga.: Regional Institute of Social Welfare Research, Inc., 1977).

Part II

PROVIDING SERVICES TO CHILDREN AND FAMILIES

INTRODUCTION

Preservation of family life is one of the strongest of American values. It is expressed in social policy, reflected in court decisions, and supported by a series of programs providing support to families-at-risk. In part one we looked at some components of the multitiered structure that has evolved to formulate policy, fund programs, enact and enforce legislation, and provide services to families. This macrocosmic view will now yield to a close scrutiny of social work practice in providing child welfare services in the areas of protective services, foster care, and adoption.

Chapter five addresses a subject that is central to effective practice in all areas of social work: information. The review begins with a description of information sources, including a framework for evaluating information derived from each source. The topic of recording information is reviewed, contents of case records described, and the uses of information discussed. The chapters that follow are organized around functions that child welfare workers perform in providing assistance to their clients. These functions—illustrated with case examples from practice—are assessment, investigation, case planning and service delivery, and case termination and follow-up. A final chapter reviews future directions in this area of social work practice.

5

Information

Decision making at every level of case management is predicated upon information supplied by clients and collateral resources, as well as that found in case records, central registries, and court reports. It is important, therefore, to learn about the types of information that are available from each source, as well as their quality. Figure 5.1 identifies information sources, the context in which information is gathered, and the method of collection. Information sources are evaluated in four ways: (1) ease of using the data gathering method, (2) accuracy of the information obtained, (3) flexibility of the method (is it limited to gathering specific types of data or can it yield information on a wide range of events?), and (4) whether detailed information can be secured.[1]

Five ways of eliciting information from *clients* are identified. These are self-reports, checklist responses, personality inventories, projective tests, and information gained by self-monitoring.

Self-Reports During Interviews

Interviewing is the most consistently and frequently employed social work technique for eliciting information from clients.[2] Interviews may

119

TABLE 5.1

Advantages and Disadvantages of Different Sources of Information

Source of Information	Information Gathering Context	Method of Gathering Information	Ease of Use	Accuracy	Flexibility	Data Detail
Client:						
Self report during interview	Office/natural environment	verbal exchange	H	L–H	H	L–M
Checklists	Office/natural environment	paper & pencil	H	L–H	M	L
Personality inventories	Office	paper & pencil	H	L	L	L
Projective tests	Office	paper & pencil	M	L	L	L
Self-monitoring	Natural environment	observation/recording	M	M	H	M
Professionals:						
Observation by trained staff	Office/natural environment	interviews simulations	H	M	M	H
Observation by trained staff	Office/natural environment	nonparticipant observation	L–M	M	L	H
Collateral Resources	Office	any of the above	H	L–H	L–H	L–H
Case records	Office	read/abstract data	L–H	L–H	L–H	L–H
Court reports	Office	read/abstract data	L–H	L–H	L–H	L–H
Central registries	Office	read/abstract data or telephone	H	L–H	L–H	L–H

Adapted in part from: Eileen D. Gambrill and Theodore J. Stein, *Supervision in Child Welfare: A Training Manual* (Berkeley: University of California Extension Press, 1978), p. 103.

L–Low   M–Medium   H–High

be done face-to-face in the worker's office or the client's home, or they may be conducted over the telephone. This method of acquiring information rates high in ease of use since all the process requires is that the worker "talk to the client." Interviews also rate high in flexibility. Using this format, information can be gathered that is not available from other sources (such as a description of past events, future expectations, private thoughts, feelings, and behaviors).

The accuracy of information is a function of its correspondence to observed events. If two people who viewed the same incident gave independent parallel descriptions, the information would be considered accurate. The skilled interviewer tries to obtain accurate information by asking carefully formulated questions and by posing follow-up questions if answers are vague. For example, if a client reports that her teenage son "never does anything when he is asked to," the worker might ask: "Can you describe the first thing that your son does after you've asked him to do something?" Skillful questioning is important, but it is not a guarantee of accurate information. This is best understood by recognizing that accuracy may be affected if clients exaggerate the severity of problems, by the fact that they are being asked to recall past events, the memory of which may have been distorted by time, as well as by the extent of positive change following a treatment program. The clients' perception of how they are expected to behave during interviews can reduce accuracy, as can "embarrassment" caused either by a lack of information or by fear of the consequences of actions. Children's accounts of events are no more accurate than those of adults. For these reasons, the information gained through client self-reports is rated low to high in accuracy. Most of us do not scrutinize our own behavior in detail, which accounts for the low to medium rating on this dimension. The information clients supply will range from very general, in which the behavioral referrants of a problem cannot be identified, to the specific, where details are offered. It is not likely that clients will be able to provide all the information necessary for case planning. Workers usually seek confirming information from members of the client's family, by direct observation of parents and children, and by soliciting reports from community resources who have knowledge of the family.

In addition to fact gathering, "the interview serves as a vehicle for establishing a helpful client-worker relationship."[3] The worker lets the client know that he or she is interested in family difficulties and in helping the client resolve them. While focusing the dialogue on areas in which information must be gathered, the worker also informs the client that he or she will be receptive to hearing other issues. The statement "I would like to get all of the information we need on your reasons for seeking assistance, and then we can discuss other issues that are troubling you," can assure a client of worker interest. Concern is also communicated when a worker describes the services offered by the agency, explains the process by which help will be offered if the case is accepted, or assists clients with referrals to other resources when agency services are not deemed appropriate. Reassuring a client that his or her problems are not uncommon, and adopting a non-judgmental stance when a client describes behavior that might be abhorrent to the worker, are important factors in establishing a relationship.

Checklists

A checklist contains a series of items designed to elicit information in selected areas. A client may be asked to rate a child on each checklist item by indicating whether the child completes household chores or returns home at an agreed upon time, "all of the time, some of the time, rarely, or never." A checklist can be especially useful when a client is not able to articulate reasons for saying that a child is not cooperative.

Checklists are easy to use, requiring only that the respondent check an item. Since they can be developed to gain information on various behaviors occurring in diverse situations, they are flexible. However, flexibility may be reduced by the fact that attention is focused on a set range of items, which might omit data. Some of the issues covered regarding the accuracy of information gained in interviews apply here. Responses can be affected by a client's perception of events and concern with presenting a positive image. Behavior may be modified as a function of monitoring, thus yielding information that is not totally accurate. Checklists rate low on detail. Client's responses can serve as a basis for gathering detailed information, which is not covered by checklist items, during interviews and observation periods.

One problem with checklists is that they may focus on negative aspects of behavior and feelings. Questions may stress weaknesses and problems, omitting items that would identify strengths. If positive items are included, the worker learns about client strengths and can use these "assets"[4] in developing problem-solving programs. The client is given the opportunity to see that the situation is not as bleak as initially reported. Despite their limitations, checklists are useful for gaining information because they direct attention to areas in which further assessment data are needed. They may be particularly useful as tools which clients can use to monitor their own behavior.

Personality Inventories

Workers often seek information to confirm hypotheses about client difficulties or to gain information which they cannot gather themselves that they need to reach decisions. When this occurs referrals can be made to professionals who are skilled in administering personality inventories or projective tests. Personality inventories, such as the Minnesota Multiphasic Personality Inventory (MMPI) or the California Psychological Inventory (CPI) are based on the assumption that individuals exhibit certain traits or constant ways of dealing with situations. The presence or absence of specific traits, or the degree to which one possesses a certain trait, is inferred from paper and pencil responses to a series of inventory items. For example, a series of questions might ask whether you defer to suggestions made by others (where to eat, what movie to attend, and so forth) and the frequency with which you defer or assert your own feelings. An inference that you are "submissive" could be drawn if your responses indicate that deference is a common way of dealing with such situations.

Insofar as the instructions for use are clear, personality inventories are easily administered. There are questions regarding their accuracy, however. If the information is to be useful, the behaviors reported must be indicative of how people behave in nontest situations. Classifying a person as submissive based on answers to a paper and pencil test would mean little if in a real-life situation the person acted in an assertive manner. In fact, correlations between responses to a paper and pencil test and non-test behavior are generally weak.[5] This is because such tests cannot take into account the affect on behavior of environmental variables that are present when the behavior is displayed, or of one's "state of mind" at any given time. For example, you may be assertive in the presence of some people and deferential in the presence of others. Or you may be assertive only when you have a strong investment in how you spend your evening, and this may vary as a function of "mood."

Flexibility is low, since these instruments are designed to acquire information on a predetermined range of issues in a set manner. Detail is poor, since the data obtained describes global responses to general situations, rather than providing specific information descriptive of response variation in different situations. One critic states, "Reports based on personality inventories should be used with skepticism in terms of possible helpfulness in decision making."[6]

Projective Tests

Tests such as the Rorscharch and Thermatic Apperception are indirect measures of assessment. The underlying assumption, derived from psychodynamic theories, is the "personality is revealed by highly indirect behavioral signs," such as reactions to inkblots or the descriptions provided by a client to pictures such as those presented in Thermatic Apperception Tests.[7] Indications from over 2,000 articles appearing on these tests indicate that their validity is so poor as to render them of little or no value for individual treatment decisions. While moderately easy to administer, the subjectivity involved in interpreting test results renders them low in accuracy. Since the objective is to infer unconscious process, they do not provide detailed information and their flexibility is limited by their narrow focus. Extreme skepticism is suggested when reports about clients are based on data obtained in this way.

Self-Monitoring

Self-recording and self-observation are synonymous terms that refer to a process of observing and recording one's own behavior. Checklists are one form of self-monitoring; tape recording and maintaining journals, diaries, and logs are others. Data gathered in this way can be invaluable insofar as they yield detailed information that clients cannot recall during interviews and also because information descriptive of private thoughts, feelings, and behaviors can be monitored in a variety of situations, providing data that may not be gathered in other ways.

Self-recording rates high in flexibility because of the range of behaviors that can be monitored and the variety of situations in which monitoring can occur. Information detail receives a medium rating. Unless the observer has thorough training and practice, it is not reasonable to expect extensive detail.

Self-recording is facilitated if predeveloped forms with clear instructions are given to clients. Instructions should specify the overall duration of recording (for example, 10 days or 2 weeks), when it is to take place (every hour, or after every meal), the behavior, thought or feeling to be recorded, and who is responsible for recording.

Self-monitoring may create positive or negative changes in the behaviors observed. A client confronted with self-recorded information showing the frequency with which he engages in an undesirable behavior may modify this behavior; but it is also possible that problematic behaviors may increase, or desirable behaviors decrease. The effects of self-monitoring usually dissipate over time.[8] The information gathered by self-recording will no longer be accurate if behaviors are modified as a result of this procedure. While positive changes may be maintained after monitoring, it is also possible that they will be lost. If clients want to present their "best face" to a worker, information will not be accurate. Accuracy can be enhanced if positive, rather than negative, behaviors are monitored (if the behaviors being observed are aversive to the client, monitoring may not occur or occur only sporadically); if specific instructions are provided; and if the client is given the chance to practice recording during interviews. If recording is intrusive and interferes with other activities, accuracy may be diminished. It can be increased, or problems in recording identified, if two people monitor the same behavior and their information is checked for reliability.

Worker Observations

Observations may occur in the office or in the client's environment. They can be made while clients reenact certain situations (stimulations), or they may consist of naturalistic observations during home visits.

Stimulations are a way of creating situations wherein clients are asked to display certain behaviors. A sample of what clients describe as problematic verbal communication, for example, may be elicited if they are asked to discuss a topic of concern to them, for a set period of time. Information can be gained on who dominates the conversation, whether each gives the other the opportunity to talk, how responsive the listener is to the speaker and so forth. Clients can be asked to role play with others: A worker may play the part of a job interviewer; the client, the role of job applicant. Workers also make observations during interviews. Nonverbal behavior may give indications as to client comfort or discomfort in interview situations. These may be relevant to the client seeking employment or applying for an AFDC grant. It is important to bear in mind that behaviors observed in simulations or interviews are displayed under artificial conditions and may not be representative of what occurs in real life. Therefore, confirmation through client self-monitoring or worker observation in the client's environment may be necessary to gain additional data. For example, the content of conversations that a client tapes at home can be compared with samples of dialogue gained in simulations.

Observation in the client's natural environment is an invaluable source of information. Structured observation can be carried out during home visits. Concern is often expressed that what is observed will be artificial. While this may occur in the earliest stages of observation, evidence suggests that participants get used to the presence of an observer and begin to interact in normal ways.

Observations during simulations and office interviews rate high in ease of use. They are convenient, and they generally restrict the range of behaviors (relative to naturalistic observations). Also competing stimuli, which may distract the observer, can be reduced or eliminated. Naturalistic observation is not as easy due to the time involved in going to a client's home, the greater diversity of behaviors, and distracting stimuli.

Accuracy requires training. Decisions must be made as to what behavior is to be observed out of the multitude displayed. Having to observe more than one person at a time can be difficult. Accuracy is also relative to the worker's skill in simply describing, rather than drawing inferences from, observations. Checklists for recording observations are a valuable aid. They can enhance accuracy and allow for the gathering of detailed information. This is because checklists permit the worker to record the presence or absence of behaviors with minimum attention to the recording process. Flexibility ranges from low (natural environment) to medium (simulations). Simulations are more flexible because clients can be asked to recreate a wide range of situations and to enact a diversity of behaviors. The objective in environmental observation is to observe behavior as it occurs, not to create situations.

The opportunity to observe behavior in real life settings is an advantage of observation in the client's natural environment. Information that is not available through self-report measures can be obtained, and the opportunity to acquire detail is high. (The latter is also true of simulations.) The inconvenience in going to the client's home, the fact that observation is limited to gathering data on overt behaviors, and the possibility that such procedures are intrusive are disadvantages.

Collateral Resources

Information from collateral resources may have valuable assessment or treatment potential. Such data may also be found in case records, court reports, and central registries. If information is made available to a worker, time can be saved that would otherwise be spent gathering data. Information describing a family's past experiences in receiving social services and other types of assistance, their response to these, and outcome information can limit the range of treatment options. Ineffective ones can be excluded and effective ones considered.

The ease of acquiring information from any of these sources varies. Gaining information from collaterals or registries rates high because it generally requires only that the worker contact the resource, explain the need for information, and request a report. Both case records and court reports rate from low to high. The ease or difficulty in using these sources depends upon where information is stored, the requirements for access, and the volume of information contained in either type of record. Privacy and confidentiality requirements may limit access. Further, records are often unorganized and voluminous, making it difficult to find specific items.

Information supplied by collateral resources, as well as that contained in records, may have been gathered by any of the methods reviewed above. To evaluate accuracy, flexibility, and detail, a worker must have information describing the data-gathering method to which the criteria reviewed in the preceeding pages can be applied.

In considering the utility of information supplied by collaterals and contained in case records, the age of the material must be considered in relation to the purpose of its acquisition. For example, problems that necessitated out-of-home placement of a child generally must be resolved before family reunification can occur. If a new worker inherits an "old" caseload, caution must be exercised in accepting the problems identified in records as accurate reflections of a client's current situation. Problems may have been reduced or eliminated over time, and this information may not appear in the reports that are supplied. Thus, information is best viewed as suggestive, directing attention to areas in which additional data must be acquired. The usefulness of information supplied by others may be increased if one has access to the person responsible for initial recording and if this person is able to supply details not presented in records. However, the fallibility of memory and the possibility that information has been distorted by the passage of time suggest caution in accepting ex post facto recollections as reliable.

RECORDING INFORMATION

Recording information is a major task at each stage of the case management process. The case record is the core of an information network. It is often the single repository of data on clients and the focal point for both storing and retrieving information. The record may be the only constant in a client's experience with a public welfare agency. It is what is "left" after workers and collaterals depart and everyone involved in service delivery has long forgotten the particulars of a case.

Information in the case record is critical for providing uninterrupted services for clients. If worker turnover is high, as it is in public welfare settings, and the information in the record is vague, or if facts are missing, a new worker may be unable to provide ongoing services. There may be little choice but to begin service delivery from "scratch," thus punishing clients for their involvement to date and possibly reducing the clients' commitment to further participation. Even when the same worker remains on a case, ambiguous recording and data deficits can prevent clients' reaching their goals. Information needed to support a court request—for example, that parental rights be terminated—may not be available.

If records are to have utility, information must be recorded in a standardized manner and in language that cuts across disciplinary boundaries. The American Bar Association argues that language should be descriptive, not inferential, and that summary conclusions and labels should not be used "unless the underlying factual basis . . . [is] explained in terms that are understandable to a nonprofessional person and their use is necessary."[9] Descriptive writing serves a client's best interests. Labels, while professionally expedient, suggest more than the facts will support. They facilitate the creation and maintenance of stereotypes and, as such, their use is a disservice to the person labeled.

It has been suggested that a useful guideline for recording information is to assume that cases will go before the court.[10] Many cases never do, and it is not being suggested that court action is always desirable. However, the court is instrumental in initiating services in many instances, and some cases go to court even though such involvement seemed unlikely at the outset. Caseworkers are being called to testify in court with greater frequency than in the past, and the information in the case record may be the only resource from which a worker can refresh his memory prior to a court appearance.

Workers should therefore be familiar with court rules for evidence so that information can be documented in a manner that is consistent with these requirements. Three types of evidence are reviewed here: direct evidence, real evidence, and hearsay evidence.[11]

Direct Evidence

This type of information comes from firsthand knowledge. It consists of facts describing what a worker and client heard, saw, said, and did. An example will illustrate the difference between descriptive and inferential recording of information.

You are a worker whose clients, the Donaldsons, have a five-year-old son in foster care. Observing parent-child interaction during weekly visits which are to occur in the home of the natural parents is part of your case plan. On two out of three occasions there is no one at the family home when you arrive. You wait for fifteen minutes, then attempt to locate the parents by asking a neighbor if he has seen them and by looking for them at a local park. Your efforts prove fruitless. In recording this information you can draw the conclusion that the parents "are not receptive to services," or that they "do not want their child returned to their care," since they have neither cancelled nor maintained two of three appointments. Or, you can maintain a log of contacts with parents in which you record the date, place, and time of each appointment and describe what occurred during visits. In this case, you would record that there was no one at home, that you waited for a time and then attempted to locate the parents (if possible record the name and comments of the neighbor), and that you attempted to find them in the park. The suggestion that parents are not receptive to services, as well as the suggestion that they do not want their child returned to them, is an inference drawn from observations. The information recorded in a log presents a descriptive account of events. Neither receptivity nor parental interest are observed events. Both statements go beyond the facts recorded in log entries. They may be correct, but then again, they may not be. Without recorded facts you cannot substantiate your inferences and the information is relatively useless to a person reading the record. It is unlikely that such data would be admitted as evidence in a court of law.

Real Evidence

Documents and photographs constitute real evidence. A copy of school attendance records showing a high rate of absenteeism and certified by school authorities is one type of real evidence that may be presented to the court to support an allegation of educational neglect. X rays and photographs may be important evidence in substantiating allegations of abuse. Written contracts, signed by worker and client, evidence a worker's efforts to provide services and the client's agreement to participate in them. Letters that are sent to clients and returned by the post office bearing the legend "moved, no forwarding address," show efforts to locate parents and may be used in support of an abandonment charge.

Recognizing the importance of documents as evidence cues workers to seek out certain types of information. For example, the identity of a child abuser is often induced circumstantially from real and direct evidence, since the abusing act itself is rarely observed. Knowing this, the worker is directed to seek out real evidence, such as X rays, and to record direct evidence. When this information is coupled with other information, such as the identity of the person responsible for child care when an abusive incident occurred, conclusions can be drawn regarding the identity of the abuser.

Hearsay Evidence

Secondhand information is called hearsay evidence. Its reliability cannot be ascertained through cross-examination of the person who supplied it. Unlike direct evidence, which is based on firsthand knowledge of what one saw, said, heard, and did, hearsay consists of information provided by others. The statement, "Mrs. Guy told me that she saw

Mr. Young beat his child," is an example. Unless Mrs. Guy is willing to appear in court and give direct testimony describing what she observed, and thus be subject to cross-examination by the client's attorney, it is unlikely that a judge would view her statement as supportive of an allegation of abuse.

To the extent that caseworker and collateral reports contain third party information and unsubstantiated inferences, they are not likely to be admissible as evidence under hearsay rules. In situations where the person who supplied information cannot appear in court, and both sides are agreeable, written, signed statements known as "depositions" can be taken and entered into evidence. The statutes of some states provide for agency records to be classified as "official records," making them admissible in court.

Knowledge of what constitutes hearsay evidence can alert a worker to gather supportive information (such as depositions) to be presented at court. The worker can separate hearsay from real and direct evidence, thus judging the strength of the case for court presentation. This knowledge is also crucial when a worker is called upon to testify in court. Social workers may increase their credibility with the court by providing well-founded facts and effective testimony.

CONFIDENTIALITY

The number of persons having access to data, and the extensive uses to which it is put, directs our attention to the subject of confidentiality. The concept of confidentiality is "based on the individual's right to privacy, expressed or implied."[12] The National Association of Social Worker's Code of Ethics admonishes workers to respect the privacy of the people they serve and to use information that is gained in professional relationships in a responsible manner. In part, respecting confidentiality means that the information in a client's record will not be disclosed without the client's consent and only under certain circumstances for the purpose of helping the client.

The growth of data banks, such as central registries, increases concern about maintaining confidentiality because "computerization ... facilitates access to personal data within a singe organization and across boundaries that separate organization entities."[13] Forty-six states have laws requiring that child abuse and neglect be kept confidential.[14] While not undermining the importance of such legislation, the documented abuse of juvenile justice records—despite the long-standing principle that such records be kept private—suggests the need for stringent safeguards.[15] Recommendations in this area include granting clients the right to inspect their records, creating panels to which a client may appeal to have inaccuracies corrected, and giving access to legal services to assist them in such efforts. It is suggested that clients be informed of records kept on them and of each time information is released, and that records be expunged when allegations of suspected abuse or neglect are not confirmed.[16]

Since information must be released to persons within the system, administrative safeguards are also suggested, including a requirement that the identity of each person requesting information be confirmed and that agreements be drafted to preclude the dissemination of information to a second party without prior authorization from the agency initially providing the data. It is also recommended that committees of citizens and public officials be established to monitor information management and assure that clients' rights are protected.

The individual worker can further a client's right to privacy by reporting information in a descriptive manner. This informs the client and the attorney of the basis of any allegations, allowing the facts to be challenged. In the face of any challenge, the worker is protected from charges of arbitrary decision making and unprofessional conduct.

THE CONTENTS OF CASE RECORDS

The objective in building and maintaining case files is to record information descriptive of all transactions that occur between the client and agency representatives throughout the process of service delivery. Information in files can be categorized as (1) agency records, (2) court records, and (3) collateral records. Each of these areas can be subcategorized to reflect specific types of data. The exact items of information contained in case records are determined by agency policy, so the following must be viewed as illustrative.

Agency Records

Included here are statistical reports and specific case information in which transactions between client and agency staff are described. Our concern is with case information, which includes social histories, case planning information, service delivery information, and case notes.

A SOCIAL HISTORY.   This is a report describing a recipient family on a number of dimensions, including demographic characteristics (age of family members, race, and education), personal histories (such as a parent's childhood experiences in interacting with his or her own parents) and a family's service history, including prior experiences with social services or other community agencies.

Social histories also contain current information and in this sense the term "history" is somewhat misleading. Present information would indicate the service requested (such as adoption or protective services), the reason or reasons why a request is being made, or why a case is being referred, and by whom. Current information may also include descriptive accounts of the circumstances surrounding an incident of abuse and parental attitudes toward providing ongoing child care and working with social services. Finally, worker impressions of a family (such as whether they "appear" cooperative) and recommendations as to the appropriateness of agency services are recorded.

CASE PLANNING INFORMATION. This kind of information describes: the objectives of services (for instance, for a parent to decide to keep a child or relinquish a child for adoption); the goals that must be reached to attain objectives (for example, to familiarize a parent with the legal ramifications of adoption); and the process by which a worker will facilitate goal attainment, including identification of service providers. For example, an appointment may be arranged for a client to see an agency attorney who will undertake the task of providing necessary legal information. Time limits for reaching objectives are included in case plans.

Planning information comes from clients, workers, collateral sources, and the courts. Clients select case objectives and provide information describing past experiences with services, which the worker records in the social history (and which directs worker attention to possible approaches to problem solving). Workers use their expertise to suggest alternative approaches for resolving difficulties, to formulate the steps in a case plan, to marshal community problem-solving resources, to allocate responsibility among all parties to a case plan, and to gather data that can be used to evaluate progress toward case objectives. Collaterals describe work that they have done with clients and the extent to which they are willing to cooperate with current case plans. The court frequently requests certain reports (such as psychiatric evaluations) and may require parental participation in treatment programs. Court requirements must be incorporated into case plans.

With increasing frequency *contracts*—verbal or written agreements "clarifying arrangements between two or more parties such as a worker and client, or two clients"—are being used as frameworks for case planning.[17] The components of a contract include the case-planning information just reviewed as well as the names of persons who will sign the agreement. Consequences for not carrying out contractual responsibilities are included. Consequences make explicit the alternatives that will be pursued to provide children with permanent homes. For instance, a worker will recommend to the court that a child be returned from foster care to the home of her parents, or that termination of parental rights with subsequent adoption will be pursued if parents do not remain involved in case-planning activities.

Contracts can provide a useful and a necessary framework for case planning. The process of helping clients realize their objectives is complex because of the number of problems that frequently must be resolved before an objective can be attained and because many people participate in the problem-solving process. It is essential, therefore, that workers have a framework for organizing case-planning activities and for describing all of the tasks in which they, their clients, and collateral resources must engage to solve problems and move cases toward their objectives. Contracts provide such a framework. From the client's perspective, a contract can serve as protection from arbitrary demands for change, particularly in the event of worker turnover. The client possesses a document showing the exact conditions that were set for attaining his or her objectives and containing the worker's agreement to support these objectives when stated conditions are met. Further protection is offered if the contract expressly states that any requirements for change will be linked to the child's safety, thereby reducing the chances that change can be demanded in areas unrelated to the well-being of children. Stein, Gambrill and Wiltse report that the "probability of children being restored when their parents sign a contract is significantly greater than when they refuse." Seventy percent of the children in the Alameda Project whose parents signed written agreements were restored, whereas 84 percent whose parents would not sign a contract were categorized as long-term cases. The authors note that "the predictability of either outcome, given information as to whether a contract was signed, was 57 percent."

Contracts have been used as a framework for short-term case planning (for example, to describe conditions for a one-week trial visit between parents and their child who is in substitute care); for long-range planning (relative to overall case objectives) to facilitate decision making by spelling out the range of alternatives for a given child and by describing the process that will be used to help a client reach a decision; and to coordinate the service delivery activities of all service providers.[19]

SERVICE DELIVERY IINFORMATION. Decision making—whether to restore a child, dismiss protective services, or to move a case toward adoption—proceeds on the basis of this kind of information. It describes client progress toward the objectives and goals identified in a case plan. Services offered to resolve family difficulties are described and parental participation in service programs and the outcome of such efforts are reported. This information tells workers when programs are not being effective in resolving family problems so that plans can be altered and clients helped to realize goals and objectives.

Necessary information is compiled in different ways. Workers maintain logs in which they record the date of each appointment with clients, the time and place of the meeting, its purpose, whether the appointment was kept and if so whether its purpose was accomplished. Logs containing similar information are maintained to record visits between parents and their children in foster home care. Clients monitor their own progress by recording on forms provided by workers. Collateral resources compile data on client progress in problem-solving programs. Case-planning and service delivery information is summarized on a regular basis and reported in narrative form. This provides an overview of case progress in all areas in general, rather than specific, terms.

CASE NOTES. Information recorded immediately following interviews with clients and collaterals is recorded in case notes. They are generally informal summaries of what transpired during contacts. They can serve two purposes. First, case notes "bridge-the-gap" between interview and formal recording times. Unless interviews are taped, notes must be taken soon after meetings or workers run the risk of forgetting and therefore losing valuable information. Also, as the lag between observation and recording time increases, so does the likelihood that what occurred in an interview will be distorted, as interim impressions become concretized.[20] Information should be transcribed into permanent records as soon as possible after an interview. A method for recording case notes should allow for ease of recording while simultaneously preserving information detail.

A second use of case notes is to record hypothetical information. There are situations in which observations are made that seem important, but whose relevance is not immediately clear. For example, one might hypothesize, based on a client's verbal reports, that the client's parents are applying pressure for her to relinquish for adoption a child that she wishes to keep. Recording this suggestion in a case note can serve as a clue to the worker that he or she should try to interview the client's parents to learn of their position on this issue.

Once the utility of hypothetical information is established it should become a part of the permanent record. Thus, notes should be as descriptive as possible. Case notes should be discarded if the information does not prove to be relevant.

Court Reports and Records

Workers prepare reports and compile documentation for the juvenile court. They also make specific requests of the court which, in turn, supplies reports to child welfare staff. Exhibits such as X rays, photographs, and documentation in the form of depositions, are submitted for jurisdictional hearing to help a judge determine if a child has been maltreated as defined in state law. Social histories are often used at the dispositional phase to assist the court in determining where a child will live. Formal papers, such as birth, death, and marriage certificates, are submitted for adoption hearings.

To comply with the court's need for information on cases over which they have jurisdiction, workers summarize case-planning and service delivery information and submit summaries for review hearings. Using the evidence describing client progress toward case objectives, recommendations are formulated (for instance, that a case be continued in its current status or that a court dependency be dismissed) that the court is free to accept or reject.

Requests of the court consist of *petitions*—formal requests filed at the initial hearing at which the court was asked to make a "particular finding" (for instance, that allegations of maltreatment are true and that the court should therefore assume jurisdiction over a child).[21] When a foster care worker wants to return a youngster to its family for a trial visit, an ex parte order may be filed, which asks the court for permission to make such a return. A worker may ask the court to issue a subpeona, which is a "summons to appear before a particular court at a particular time," in order to assure the presence of a witness whose testimony is needed at a hearing.[22] Court reports in which judicial decisions are summarized and treatment orders noted are presented to workers following court hearings.

Collateral Resources

Community professionals involved in service delivery contribute to the case record in various ways, many of which have already been discussed. These include psychiatric evaluations, psychological tests, and other diagnostic and medical reports. Information is also provided describing services offered to clients and the results of these endeavors.

USING INFORMATION

Child welfare workers gather information from a variety of sources. This information is used for decision making and case planning. Data that workers collect throughout the process of service delivery serve as a basis for establishing accountability in practice. In the following pages the uses of information are reviewed with reference to decision making and accountability. Additionally, decision-making constraints that affect both worker and client and the respective roles of each party in the decision-making process are discussed.

The objective of *decision making* is to select the most appropriate course of action from a range of alternatives. The options for a child in foster care are: restoration to natural parents; adoption; guardianship; or planned, long-term placement. The decision maker's task is to select which of these is most appropriate for any given youngster. Decision making involves three steps: developing criteria; using criteria as guides for gathering evidence during assessment; and evaluating the information that is gathered by applying criteria to evidence in order to reach a decision.[23] This process will be illustrated with an example that should be familiar.

You have to choose an elective course this semester. Your first task is to gather information about course offerings, so you get a university catalog. Unless the range of electives is extremely limited, you will need guidelines to approach this task because there is a considerable amount of information in a university catalog. In short, you must have some method of sorting the relevant from the irrelevant. Your work will be simplified if you have criteria to guide you. A brief digression will illustrate the importance of criteria to decision making in child welfare.

Criteria are developed from standards, which are an expression of values derived from statutory law, policy, or practice. The desire to raise children under conditions presumed to be optimal to their growth and development is a social value that is expressed in the "best interest standard." If we could specify all or most of the conditions that further this end, these specifications would serve as criteria to guide us in assessing whether the conditions under which a child is living further or impede progress toward this goal. We can, of course, specify certain minimum conditions. For example, immunizing children against disease, providing a balanced diet, and requiring a minimum amount of schooling are viewed as serving a child's best interests. In any given case, we can determine whether this interest is furthered by checking medical and school records for information regarding immunizations and classroom attendance, and by testing a parent's knowledge of nutrition and meal planning. We encounter difficulties when trying to specify conditions at the other end of the continuum—those under which a child will feel loved, wanted, and secure. If the conditions cannot be identified, criteria cannot be specified. Without criteria, decisions are not likely to be made nor case plans formulated. If they are, the criteria used are apt to be highly subjective. The difficulties that result were succinctly expressed by protective service workers, public health nurses, and other professionals who work with abused and neglected children. Sixty-nine percent strongly agreed or tended to agree with the statement, "It is difficult to know what is and what is not child maltreatment." It is therefore not surprising that 79 percent responded in a similar manner to the statement "It is difficult to know when parents should have their children returned."[24] This adds a further dimension to our understanding of why case plans are not made and permanency not achieved for so many children in out-of-home placement. (See part one, chapter four.) The absence of decision-making criteria also contributes to the poor quality of case records, specifically in regard to the excess and extraneous information that investigators have found they contain. Without criteria, it is tempting to document everything in sight in the hope that some of what is recorded will prove relevant. In short, it is possible, in the absence of criteria and given the subjectivity that follows, to argue that everything is pertinent to a decision.

What would happen to you if your standards for selecting courses were as broad as those implied by the best interest standard? Say, for instance, that you want to take courses to help you to "become a better person," but you have no idea of how to attain this goal, or you have a wealth of ideas. In either case, you will be in trouble. In the first instance, you will not know what to look for; in the second, you will look for so much that the semester will be half over before you are able to sort and evaluate the information that you have collected. What you need is a standard that can be operationalized—one that can be translated into observable criteria to guide you in selecting information.

Let us say that your standard for choosing an elective is that it increases your knowledge of different ethnic and cultural groups that you might work with after graduation. This standard reduces the number of options by focusing attention on those with ethnic content. However, you are still faced with the task of developing criteria so that you can collect information about available courses. What criteria might you use? Assuming that you have never had a course in this area, the following considerations might guide your choice. You want to learn about one particular ethnic group because members of that group are the largest numerical minority in the community in which you expect to practice. You want to take a course that will provide you with information about the history of this minority in America, and familiarize you with contemporary issues. You think it best to study under a professor who is a member of the minority group on which the course focuses, and you prefer to study under someone who has done community work, rather than one whose experience is wholly academic. Finally, your experience is that you learn best in situations that involve both academic and practical experience. Thus, you have a preference for any course that includes work in the community, as opposed to one that is solely classroom based. You are ready to apply these six criteria to the range of courses listed in the catalog to which they might be applicable.

To save time in recording information and to make sure that pertinent data are not omitted, you develop a checklist. In addition to having space for identifying information such as the course title, department, professor's name and class time, the checklist contains the six criteria noted above. Thus, one item might say "Ethnic groups covered: _____ Black, _____ Mexican-American, _____ Native American, _____ Asian," and so forth. A second item might be "Course covers historical content: _____yes _____no _____don't know." When the checklist is completed, you duplicate it on three-by-five cards and for each identified course you read the catalog descriptions and complete one card. Some of the requisite information may not be available in the catalog. A check in the column headed "don't know" will show you that you will have to seek this information elsewhere. The process of completing these cards should reduce your options. If you are lucky, all of the requisite information will be in the catalog and only one course will meet your requirements. Your decision will be made. What do you do when two or more courses fit the bill, or when none meet all of the criteria, but several meet some?

In anticipation of this outcome, you have assigned values to each criterion. Values, in this case numerical ones, express a hierarchy of personal preferences. In professional terms these values are referred to as "weights." Criteria can be weighted in several ways. Ideally, they reflect our knowledge of the relative contribution of each variable in a decision matrix to the overall decision. The following example illustrates a checklist developed at the University of Colorado Medical Center as an aid in assessing the safety of a child's home for protective service work.[25] This checklist contains ten items on which the worker is expected to gain information. These items are:

1. Parent repeatedly beaten or deprived as a child.   _____
2. Parent with low self-esteem or socially isolated.   _____

3. Child is unwanted or at risk for poor bonding. _____

4. Parent has criminal or mental illness record. _____

5. Parent suspected of abuse in past. _____

6. Multiple crisis or stresses. _____

7. Rigid expectations of child's behavior. _____

8. Violent temper outbursts. _____

9. Harsh punishment of child. _____

10. Child difficult or provocative. _____

The process of collecting information will not concern us here. Gathering assessment data is the subject of the next chapter. We are concerned with how these are weighted to facilitate decision making. The authors assign lowest weights to the first three items. They suggest that these factors are relevant because they have been found in abuse cases. However, since they are "common in society," their presence alone is not necessarily indicative of a high-risk family situation. Intervention is not warranted based solely on their presence. Greater weight is assigned to the next four items. Numbers four and five are said to be indicative of "pathology" in the parent's lives, number six is viewed as a precipitating factor in abuse and seven, as justification in the parent's eyes for abusing the child. The greatest weights are assigned to the last cluster of items. Numbers eight and nine are rated highest "because they demonstrate that the parent currently is displaying aggressive behavior toward society and the child." Number ten rates high because it is evidence that the "child is capable of precipitating the abuse." The decision to intervene is based on a parent's total score. Weightings were derived subjectively. The greatest values are given to those items which clinical experience and other research data suggest are the best indicators for assessing the safety of a child's home. Subjective judgment is acceptable because, as we saw in the third chapter of part one, we do not know enough about the causes of neglect and abuse to assign values on wholly objective grounds. However, we do need guidelines to direct data gathering and to facilitate decision making. Combining scores from several items reflects caution. It is an acknowledgment of the current limits to our knowledge and a recognition that the decision to intervene has serious implications for families and should only be made when the bulk of evidence suggests that a child is at risk. Reaching a decision on the basis of a combination of factors is characteristic of professional decision making and no doubt reflects the process we use as individuals.

Let us return to our example. You have six criteria to which you assign a value of five points each. Extra points can be given when certain combinations appear. For instance, let us assume that your highest priority is to learn about the history of black people in America and to gain knowledge of contemporary issues affecting them. In addition to the fifteen points that any course covering all three criteria would receive, you assign a bonus of five points to reflect the priority you place on these variables. For any course focusing on this ethnic minority that covers either, but not both, of the second and third criteria, you assign a bonus of five points, again reflecting your priorities. No bonus points are assigned to courses covering other ethnic groups. You could also decide to assign extra points to any course offering both classroom and community experience and to ones where the professor has a combination of academic and community experience.

Next to each criterion item on each card you insert the number of points according to your guidelines. These are totaled and the course with the highest score selected. What do you do if two courses tie for first place? It is possible to approach the task of tie breaking by having on hand "backup" criteria. These would be indicators that are not crucial determinants of a decision. For instance, you may break the tie between courses by reviewing the session hours of the tied electives, selecting that course which meets closest in time to required classes. Tie breaking in professional decision making should be guided by agency policy or practice guidelines. Let us say, for example, that each of two preadoptive homes meets all agency criteria, but that only one child is available for adoption. Policy might state that, all things being equal, preference be given to adoptive applicants below a certain age or to those who have been waiting the longest.

DECISION-MAKING CONSTRAINTS

Certain constraints limit the range of decisions a worker can make. Some cases come to worker attention with decisions already made by others. For instance, a foster care worker may receive a case after the court has assumed jurisdiction. The court may have ordered a course of treatment that, in the worker's opinion, is not the best solution to the problem at hand. However, there may be little choice but to comply with the court directive. The best plan of action may not be possible because of resource deficits. Homemaker services to provide temporary care for a child when a parent is hospitalized may not be available, thwarting the worker's efforts to maintain a child at home.

Decision making is generally shared with supervisors, with collateral resources, and often with other workers in the agency. Some staff view sharing as limiting their autonomy to act on behalf of their clients; others welcome this opportunity.[26] Sharing decision-making responsibilities may increase the willingness of workers to take risks which are unavoidable (since we cannot predict whether a child will be safe in the long run after cases are terminated). The concern that this generates may contribute to the absence of case planning.

The Client's Role in Decision Making

Natural parents and children, if they are old enough, should participate in decision making. Social and professional values demand that biological parents and children be extended this right. Some of the constraints on worker decision making affect parents and children. Judicial decisions, agency policy, and resource availability set boundaries defining the range of alternatives. Social values regarding the responsibilities of parenthood can impose constraints. They may, for example, make it difficult for clients to choose to relinquish their child for adoption. And values can force a decision—for instance, the parent who wishes to relinquish a child may instead take the youngster home from foster care. A child's role in decision making may be limited if the child feels pressure to agree with adults and conflicting loyalties to both foster and natural parents. A major constraint on natural parents is whether their status is voluntary or involuntary.

Clients are considered *voluntary* when they initiate or agree to participate in services without court intervention. When their involvement is court ordered, they occupy an *involuntary* status. In principle, voluntary clients may withdraw from service at any time. Involuntary clients do not have this option. I say "in principle" because the maintenance of voluntary status may be contingent upon ongoing participation in service. If a client has voluntarily accepted protective services, for example, and then decides to withdraw against the worker's advice, the worker may be forced to petition the court to make the child a dependent. A foster care worker may do the same, even though not compelled by law, if the worker thinks that the client's withdrawal may endanger a child's well-being. Thus, the distinction between voluntary and involuntary status can "blur" when acceptance of the former is based on knowledge that not cooperating may lead to court action. Involuntary clients are still able to participate in decision making. However, their involvement must be viewed in the context of the constraints imposed by knowledge of possible court action. With this in mind, let us look at some factors related to the role of clients in decision making.

Clients must have available to them all of the information necessary to make informed choices. Providing information is the worker's responsibility. The objective of any particular service must be described—for example, that protective services seek to safeguard children in their own homes, while foster care services provide short-term, substitute care. When applicable, the legal ramifications of parental involvement or noninvolvement must be identified (for instance, that court action may be invoked if evidence of abuse is found, that failing to play an active role in case planning can result in court referral, and that nonparticipation in planning for children in foster care may result in action to terminate parental rights). The legal consequences of placing a child for adoption, as well as those of adopting a child, must be clarified. The client has a right to know what it means to participate in services—what he or she must do, when, where, and how, as well as what will be done for the client. Some of this information is not known to the worker in the early stages of assessment and planning. Describing the client's role in service delivery with any degree of specificity is not possible until problems are identified and treatment options become known. Thus, the process of informing clients is an ongoing one.

What can be said about the division of responsibility between worker and client in reaching decisions? It is the client's right to reach the initial decision to participate or not to participate in services. The worker's responsibility is to provide information in the areas outlined above. Given knowledge that coercive intervention is possible or that parental rights can be terminated, it is likely that clients will agree to cooperate. However, clients may elect to "fight" by engaging their own attorney. It is the worker's task to explain the client's right to do so, and to direct the client to legal services if they are requested.

Assuming that a client agrees to participate, the division of responsibility in future decision making allows for the fact that the child welfare worker has the greatest expertise with regard to agency and court procedure as well as with the alternatives that are available for solving problems. The client's expertise derives from knowledge of his or her children and from the ability to hypothesize which of the alternatives is most likely to succeed. The worker's responsibility in helping the clients reach decisions is to describe the process involved in each alternative (what will be expected of the client and what assistance will be given to the client, as well as the expected outcome of participation). Given this information, client and worker can develop a collaborative relationship in selecting the most appropriate approach to problem solving.

ACCOUNTABILITY

The demand for accountability in practice is steadily increasing. It is evident in federal and state legislation requiring that plans be submitted for each child receiving services, and it is clear from the thrust to implement external review procedures so that permanent planning efforts can be monitored. The increased use of written contracts, and the requirements that goals and time limits be established and that information be presented in descriptive language that crosses disciplinary boundaries and can be understood by nonprofessionals further evidence this concern.

Accountability is not an exact term. It takes on different meanings in relation to the question: "Accountable to whom?" Child welfare workers are accountable to the public that funds service programs, to the agencies that administer them, to the profession, to the courts, and to clients. Agencies may judge accountability in different ways. Requirements may be satisfied if workers prepare thorough statistical reports needed to justify a budget, or they may demand a showing that permanency is being achieved for the majority of children receiving services. Similarly, accountability to the public means different things. One constituency may be satisfied if reports show only that services are being utilized, while another may want to see evidence that services are effective in reducing or eliminating the problems that led to their development. This brief discussion will focus on accountability to clients for whose benefit public welfare services are designed. Accountability requires the following:

1. Evidence that services were required reinforces a commitment to family privacy. The grounds for intervention in family life should be specified to the fullest extent possible. Parents have a right to know when their behavior violates the law. Vague standards that allow personal values to bias decision making run counter to this end. This requirement for accountability can be met if the standard for decision making, the criteria used, and the method of applying criteria to evidence to reach decisions are made explicit.

2. Evidence that services were provided is another yardstick for measuring accountability. Court decisions have recognized that clients have a right to treatment as a necessary balance to the loss of freedom resulting from court intervention.[27] Since child welfare services are often initiated on an involuntary basis, evidence that rehabilitative services were provided is of critical importance. If case plans are formulated; if objectives, goals, and the process of realizing these are clearly explicated and the process monitored, this requirement for accountability can be met.

3. Evidence that the problem-solving services selected are the most effective ones available for reducing or eliminating family difficulties is a third criterion for establishing accountability. Workers must be familiar with the clinical and research literature describing the effectiveness of intervention methods and the particular problems for which these methods are reported to be useful. Workers must also be familiar

with the intervention techniques employed by community resources whose services are brought to bear in solving problems. There is a tendency in practice to use whatever services are available without clear comprehension of how these will further goal attainment. The "mystical reliance" workers place on the healing powers of mental health professionals is often misplaced.[28] It is intrusive insofar as clients are forced to disclose private behaviors that may be totally unrelated to the safety of their children, and it can impede, rather than enhance, goal attainment. If the goal to be realized by participating in any service program is not clear, there is no way of evaluating when services should be terminated. The service of choice may not be available, and there are situations in which one service may be substituted for another. Group counseling, for example, may be a viable alternative to individual counseling, even though the evidence may suggest that the latter is more appropriate. When substitutions are used, workers should report the intervention of choice, as well as the one used, and they should document the reasons for selecting a particular service. Not only does this reflect the worker's efforts to provide the most appropriate services, but it also provides information that may be useful for funding decisions when new services are developed.

4. Evidence that services provided are effective in achieving case goals is an important dimension of accountability. Ongoing monitoring is necessary to show that services are effectively reducing family difficulties and, as such, are moving cases toward objectives. When expected results are not attained, the changes made to achieve these must be recorded.

5. Evidence that clients had information that enabled them to reach informed decisions with reference to their participation in service delivery. The discussion of the division of decision-making responsibility between client and worker is pertinent here. Clients must have all of the information that workers are able to provide if they are to participate in an informed manner. If contracts are developed in accordance with the guidelines reviewed in subsequent chapters, an outside evaluator is able to see that clients were given necessary information for informed consent.

6. Information that is recorded must be factual and documented in a language that is understandable to lay persons and is least likely to be detrimental to the client. The relationship between language and accountability is straightforward. Accountability cannot be established unless persons reading the record understand what is in it. To the extent that professionals from different disciplines and lay persons who have read the contents of a report can independently describe its content in their own words, and to the extent that these reports are in agreement, this requirement is satisfied.

SUMMARY

Information supplied by clients and collaterals, as well as that found in case records, court reports, and central registries, is used for decision making at every stage of case management.

Workers gather information from clients during interviews and periods of direct observation, in the office or the client's natural environment.

Clients add to this information by completing checklists and by observing and recording their own behavior.

Collateral resources provide information about clients using any of the methods child welfare workers use, as well as by administering personality inventories and projective tests.

Each method of gathering data can be rated in terms of ease of use, flexibility (judged in relation to the narrowness or breadth of the data gathered), likelihood of producing data that are an accurate reflection of client behaviors, and global or detailed information yield.

The case record is a central repository for data on clients.

If recorded data are to be useful for providing ongoing services and helping clients attain their goals, information should be descriptive, not inferential, so that persons reading the record can independently agree on its contents.

Documenting information in a manner that is consistent with court requirements can further this end.

Direct evidence comes from firsthand knowledge of events, expressed in terms of what a worker saw, heard, said, and did.

Real evidence consists of documents such as school attendance records, birth and marriage certificates, photographs, and X rays.

Hearsay evidence consists of information descriptive of what others heard, saw, said, and did.

Confidentiality refers to a client's right to privacy, which is respected when (1) the client's consent is obtained before information is disseminated, (2) clients have access to their records, (3) when mechanisms are established so that clients can challenge the accuracy of information, (4) access to records is restricted to persons who require information in order to assist clients, and (5) clients are informed of the release of information and the reasons for releasing it.

A case file contains agency records, court reports, and collateral reports.

Information in agency records describing transactions between worker and client are found in social histories, case planning and service delivery information, and in case notes.

Social histories contain descriptive data on recipient families including demographic characteristics, individual personal histories, and the service history of the individual and the family unit. Current problems are recorded, as well as the worker's impressions of the family and recommendations regarding the appropriateness of the case for the services of the agency.

The objectives to be achieved in providing services, the goals that must be realized to attain objectives, and the process by which goals will be pursued (including identification of service providers and the time frame for reaching objectives and goals) are described in case plans.

Written contracts provide a framework for ordering case-planning information. The complexity of the problems child welfare workers confront and the number of people involved in fulfilling the tenets of a case plan direct attention to the importance of having such a framework.

Service delivery information is recorded by workers and collaterals as they monitor client progress toward objectives and goals.

Transactions between worker and client, worker observations, and hypotheses as to possible sources of difficulty are summarized in case notes prepared immediately after an interview.

Factual information is then transcribed into permanent records. Hypothetical information is transcribed when and if its utility for case planning or service delivery is established.

Court records consist of (1) reports that workers file in order to comply with the court's need for information on cases over which it has jurisdiction, (2) formal documents such as petitions, ex parte orders, and subpeonas, and (3) summary information supplied by the court in which decisions are noted and treatment recommendations are made.

The objective in decision making is to select the most appropriate course of action from a range of alternatives.

The process requires that criteria be developed and used to guide data gathering during assessment and that information be evaluated by applying criteria to evidence in order to reach a decision.

Criteria are developed from standards, statutory law, policy, or practice knowledge.

Criterion items may be written in a checklist format which can be used to guide data-gathering activities.

To assist in evaluating information, weights or scores may be assigned to criterion items, signifying the relative importance of each item to the overall decision.

A final decision is generally based on a client's total score, which is arrived at by viewing combinations of criteria, rather than resting on any single item.

Criteria not used in reaching the initial decision can be applied to break ties.

Worker decision-making autonomy is constrained when choices are made before the worker receives the case, when resources are in short supply, and when decision-making responsibility is shared with others.

Clients have the right to participate in decision making.

Their autonomy is constrained by law, policy and resource deficits, and social values that make certain options, such as relinquishing a child for adoption, difficult to select.

A child's role in decision making may be restricted if adults apply pressure, and by conflicting loyalties to foster parents and natural parents.

Clients are voluntary when they initiate services or agree to participate in them. Involuntary status means services are provided under court order.

Maintenance of a voluntary status may be contingent upon ongoing cooperation in service delivery.

Knowledge that court action can be invoked may be an added constraint on a client's decision-making autonomy.

Within these constraints clients can still exercise their right to participate in selecting options.

They have the right to make the initial decision whether to participate in services, the right to be involved in selecting treatment options, and the right to continue to participate.

The worker, as expert, supplies clients with all of the information necessary to reach an informed decision.

Establishing accountability to clients requires evidence (1) that services were required, (2) that they were provided, (3) that those provided were the most effective for reducing or eliminating the problems, (4) that services provided are effective in achieving case goals, (5) that clients had information to help them to decide whether to participate in service delivery, and (6) that evidence be descriptive and recorded in a factual manner so that the information is not likely to be detrimental to clients.

NOTES

1. Part of this section is based on material from Eileen D. Gambrill and Theodore J. Stein, *Supervision in Child Welfare: A Training Manual* (Berkeley, Cal.: University of California Extension Press, 1978), Ch. 3.

2. Alfred Kadushin, *The Social Work Interview* (New York: Columbia University Press, 1972), p. 7.

3. Gambrill, *Supervision*, p. 102.

4. Arthur Schwartz and Israel Goldiamond, *Social Casework: A Behavioral Approach* (New York: Columbia University Press, 1975).

5. Walter Mischel, *Personality and Assessment* (New York: John Wiley and Sons, Inc., 1968), pp. 77, 79.

6. Gambrill, *Supervision*, p. 110.

7. Mischel, *Personality*, p. 110.

8. A. E. Kazdin, "Self-Monitoring and Behavior Change," in *Self-Control: Power to the Person*, ed. M. J. Mahoney and C. E. Thoresen (Monterey, Cal.: Brooks Cole, 1974), pp. 218–46. Cited in Gambrill, *Supervision*, p. 113.

9. Institute of Judicial Administration, American Bar Association, Juvenile Justice Standards Project, *Standards Relating to Juvenile Records and*

Information Systems—Tentative Draft (Cambridge, Mass.: Ballinger Publishing Company, 1977), p. 71.

10. C. Bell and W. J. Mlyniec, "Preparing for a Neglect Proceeding: A Guide for the Social Worker," *Public Welfare*, Vol. 32, No. 4 (1974), pp. 26–37.

11. Part of this section is based on material from Brieland, *Social Work and the Law*, p. 269.

12. M. M. Reynolds, "Threats to Confidentiality," *Social Work*, Vol. 21, No. 2 (March 1976), pp. 108–13.

13. Report of the Secretary's Advisory Committee on Automated Personal Data Systems, *Records, Computers and the Rights of Citizens* (Washington, D.C.: U.S. Department of Health, Education and Welfare, 1973), p. 12.

14. *Trends in Child Protection Laws–1977* (Denver: Education Commission of the States, 1978), pp. 20–21.

15. C. E. Lister, "Privacy, Recordkeeping, and Juvenile Justice," in *Pursuing Justice for the Child*, ed. Margaret K. Rosenheim (Chicago: The University of Chicago Press, 1976), Ch. 10; Institute of Judicial Administration, *Standards*, p. 115.

16. For a discussion of these issues see: Theodore J. Stein, Eileen D. Gambrill and Kermit T. Wiltse, *Children in Foster Homes: Achieving Continuity of Care* (New York: Holt, Rinehart & Winston, 1978), p. 135.

17. Theodore J. Stein and Eileen D. Gambrill, *Decision Making in Foster Care: A Training Manual* (Berkeley, Cal.: University of California Extension Press, 1976), pp. 25–44; Victor Pike and others, *Permanent Planning for Children in Foster Care: A Handbook for Social Workers* (Portland, Ore.: Regional Research Institute for Human Services, Portland State University, 1977), pp. 48–52; *Lower East Side Family Union Newsletter*, Vol. 1, No. 3 (Fall/Winter, 1977–1978), p. 1. Edward T. Heck and Alan R. Gruber, *Treatment Alternatives Project* (Boston, Mass.: Boston Children's Service Association, 1976), p. 208; E. Fein, L. J. Davies and G. Knight, "Placement Stability in Foster Care," *Social Work*, Vol. 24, No. 2 (March 1979), pp. 156–57.

19. See Stein, *Decision Making*, pp. 25–44; Gambrill, *Supervision*, pp. 157–59.

20. J. C. Horn, "The Prejudiced Remembrance of Things Past," *Psychology Today*, Vol. 21, No. 9 (February 1979), p. 23.

21. Brieland, *Social Work and the Law*, p. 140.

22. Ibid., p. 277.

23. Saad Z. Nagi, *Child Maltreatment in the United States: A Challenge to Social Institutions* (New York: Columbia University Press, 1977), p. 107.

24. Ibid., p. 15.

25. C. A. Carroll, "The Social Worker's Evaluation," in *The Child Protection Team Handbook*, ed. Barton D. Schmitt (New York: Garland STPM Press, 1978), p. 93.

26. Theodore J. Stein, Eileen D. Gambrill and Kermit T. Wiltse, "Dividing Case Management in Foster Family Cases," *Child Welfare*, Vol. LVI, No. 5 (May 1977), pp. 321–31.

27. Carol M. Rose, *Some Emerging Issues in Legal Liability of Children's Agencies* (New York: Child Welfare League of America, 1978), Ch. 2.

28. E. D. Gambrill and K. T. Wiltse, "Foster Care: Plans and Actualities," *Public Welfare*, Vol. 32, No. 2 (Spring 1974), p. 14.

6

Assessment— The Beginning Phase

Assessment is the first step in case management. The process requires that workers gather and evaluate information and make decisions as to whether the services offered by their agencies are appropriate in response to a client's request for assistance. Because assessment involves a number of discrete steps and a series of decisions, the process is described in two chapters. Flow charts at the beginning of each chapter depict the steps to be reviewed. This chapter describes the initial phase of assessment, which begins with a request for services and ends when cases are dismissed or when arrangements are made to visit with clients in their homes. The processes reviewed are illustrated with case examples.[1] Chapter seven reviews a second phase of assessment, which begins with an investigation into the circumstances surrounding a request for services or a report of maltreatment, and ends when cases are dismissed or when data needed to formulate case plans have been gathered. The case-planning process is described in chapter eight. The beginning steps in assessment, shown in Figure 6.1, are reviewed next.

INTAKE

Intake is the gateway to services. Cases come to this point in one of three ways. Clients may request services themselves, or agencies in the

FIGURE 6.1 Assessment Flow Chart—First Phase

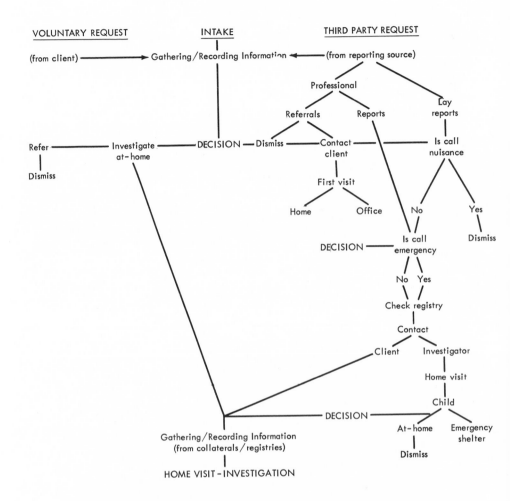

community may refer their clients to the child welfare agency for services. Reports of abuse or neglect are the third way. The worker's first task is to learn why services are being requested or why referrals or reports are being made. The process begins with a question: Why have you come to the foster care, protective service, or adoption unit? In the case of referrals or reports, the worker asks: Why are you referring this case or making this report?

The answer tells the worker something about the client's or caller's knowledge of agency services. The worker then describes services and the conditions under which they are provided so that any misunderstandings can be clarified. An initial screening occurs at this point. Cases may be referred elsewhere if the agency does not offer the requested service, or if eligibility requirements cannot be met. For example, day care may be provided only to families receiving protective services or only if the family is currently receiving AFDC (or is eligible for benefits). If the request indicates that agency services may be appropriate, the process of gathering additional information needed to reach a final decision gets under way.

The process of assessment differs according to the way in which cases come to the attention of an intake worker. Requests for service require direct contact with clients unless a report is evaluated as a nuisance call or when a referral is inappropriate. Voluntary requests generally begin with direct contact, which involves fewer steps to reach a decision than referrals from other agencies. The latter involve additional steps because information must be exchanged with the referring source before direct contact occurs. Reports of suspected abuse or neglect involve even more steps. When the reporter is a lay person, calls may be screened to eliminate "nuisance" reports. Once this is done, a decision is made as to whether the report constitutes an emergency requiring an immediate response. This is done whether the referral is from a professional or nonprofessional. If the call is an emergency, fast action must be taken to protect a child, so workers contact the person or agency charged with responding to emergency calls. Emergency investigations may result in: a child being removed and placed in a temporary shelter; or being left at home (if, in the worker's opinion, the child is not in imminent danger); or in a dismissal of the report if the facts do not warrant further investigation. In responding to reports, the first contact with clients will occur immediately if the family has a telephone. If there is no phone, it will occur when a worker visits the family home. In emergencies this generally occurs within hours of receiving a report; in nonemergencies it takes place within twenty-four to forty-eight hours, depending upon state law. If time permits, a worker will check registry information to see if there are prior reports on a family before visiting. A more thorough search for information occurs before a formal investigation of the family's circumstances takes place. Let us review the beginning steps in assessment with a voluntary request for services.

THE ANDRES FAMILY

Raymond Andres, a 41-year-old white male, came to the foster care intake unit of a metropolitan child welfare agency. In response to the worker's question: "Why have you come to the foster care intake unit?" Andres said: "The situation at home is not good. My wife isn't well, my daughter does all of the housework, and my son is unmanageable. I don't know what will happen if we don't get some help. A neighbor told me that you might be able to place my son in a foster home for a while, until things get straightened out at home." The worker assured the client that he could arrange for some assistance. He explained that out-of-home care is a temporary service that is provided only if a parent has to be hospitalized for a short period of time and no other child care arrangements can be made, or to provide protective shelter for children whose safety is endangered in their home. "We have other resources," he continued, "that can provide assistance while your son remains at home. In order to find out what is best for your family, I need more information." The following dialogue illustrates how the worker proceeded to gather more specific data about the family's problems from the client.

W: You said that your wife isn't well. Can you briefly describe what is wrong with her?

C: Well, about two years ago she had a nervous breakdown. That's what the doctors called it, a nervous breakdown. She was hospitalized for two and one-half months. Since she's been home things haven't been the same.

W: What do you mean when you say that things haven't been the same?

C: She stays in bed almost all day. Used to be she'd cook, and clean, and take care of the kids. Now, my oldest daughter does everything.

W: How old is your daughter?

C: Fifteen.

W: Isn't she in high school?

C: Yes. She does all of the work after school and on weekends.

W: Have you talked with your wife's doctor about when she'll be well enough to resume her household responsibilities?

C: Yes, I did. All he says is that we shouldn't put any pressure on her to do anything.

W: You said that your son is "unmanageable." Can you give me one example of something that he does that makes you say this?

C: He doesn't come home after school. He knows that he should help his sister, but he doesn't do it.

W: Do you know what he does after school?

C: No, but I'm sure that he's up to no good.

W: Specifically, what has he done that makes you sure?

C: I have no proof. I just feel it—pick it up from his attitude.

W: Does he spend his time with other boys?

C: Yuh, sure.

W: Do you know any of these boys?

C: Well, yuh, sure, some of them have been friends since he was little.

W: Do you have reason to think that these boys are likely to get into trouble?

C: No, I guess not.

W: How old is your son?

C: Ten.

W: How is he doing in school?

C: OK, I guess. At least his report cards are all right, and I haven't had any complaints from the school.

W: What time does he usually come home each day?

C: Five o'clock, six o'clock. Whenever he feels like it.

W: What do you say to him when he comes in?

C: I used to scream at him. Once tried talking to him but it didn't do any good. He'd go into his room and lock the door or run outside again. My wife got upset and my daughter would start crying when we fought. So now I don't say anything.

W: Does your son know exactly what chores he is supposed to do each day?

C: Sure, he knows that he is supposed to come home and do whatever his sister says needs doing. Go grocery shopping, help to clean the house. You know what has to be done to keep a house up.

W: Are there days when he does come home directly from school?

C: Sometimes.

W: Does he do his chores on those days?

C: I guess so.

W: For how long has this situation been as you describe it?

C: The last year or so.

W: Have you received any help for this—from a counselor or clergyman for example?

C: No. I just kept thinking that we could work it out.

W: Now that we've talked about your family, I would like to learn something about you . . .

Objectives of the Interview

Let us review the worker's objectives in this conversation. The client referred to each member of his family in general terms ("my wife isn't well, my son is unmanageable"). And he noted that things haven't been the same at home since his wife's illness. The worker's first goal is to get more specific information; so he asked a series of questions, repeating the phrases used by the client and requesting descriptive examples in the client's own words. Different clients use similar terminology to refer to different problems. The worker wanted to learn what this client means when he says that his wife is ill or his son unmanageable. He also wanted to find out whether the father has factual information to support his statement that his son is "up to no good." The question,

"What has he done to make you sure?" plus the worker's attempt to elicit information regarding the youngster's friends and his schoolwork are directed toward clarifying this issue. The worker is interested in learning about the interaction between father and son relative to the problem presented. Hence the question "What do you say to your son when he comes in?" If Raymond Andres had answered by stating that he responded in a physical manner (fights or punishment) the worker would have a clue as to whether there was a risk of physical abuse.

At difficult times all of us are prone to evaluating our situations as bleaker than the facts warrant. If the client is able to identify non-problem situations, the worker can help him to see that the difficulties are not as pervasive as initially thought; thus the inquiry into whether the son ever comes directly home and, if so, whether he does his chores on these occasions.

Whether the problem is of recent origin or of long duration has relevance for further questioning. If Raymond Andres had stated that the difficulty had recently emerged, the worker would have asked a series of questions to identify whether a recent family crisis, such as the loss of employment, specific marital problems, or a death in the family, had precipitated the crisis. Information describing prior assistance is also important. If services had been used, the worker would want to learn about them and their effects from both the client and the service provider. If there had been services, the worker would have asked the father to sign a "consent to release information form" giving him permission to contact the service provider and request information covering the assistance offered and the affect it had on reducing or eliminating family difficulties. When the worker meets with the entire family he will obtain the name of the mother's physician and the names of the schools attended by the youngsters, and he will request permission to contact these sources. Permission to obtain information should always be requested.

At the end of the dialogue the worker asked the father a series of questions (not shown here) from which he learned that Andres is employed in construction work and has been with the same firm for ten years. He does not assist with household chores, nor does he think it is his place to do so.

Profiling Problems

The information acquired during interviews must be organized, preferably in writing. This allows worker and client to view the range of problems that are identified and reduces the margin for misunderstandings that may occur when trusting to memory. Constructing a problem profile is one approach to this task.[2] (Table 6.1) It is begun during the interview and will be completed during a home visit, at which time other family members may contribute examples of the problem or identify difficulties not noted during the office visit. Problems are numbered for purposes of cross-referencing the information gathered at this time with information collected later. The problems that necessitated the request for services are listed in the column headed "label." The client's terminology is the source of this information. The person who identifies the problem is noted next. This is important because problems may be identified by different sources. For example, during a home visit the worker may notice exposed electrical wiring or broken windows with jagged edges. These conditions should be remedied because of the potential danger they pose for children and adults. In the label column, the worker would write "condition of the home," and identify himself in the column headed "who labels," identify the family in the next column under "who has the problem," note the date on which this issue was first observed, list exposed wiring and broken glass as examples, and cite the family home as the situation. If this case had been referred for services or reported to protective services, the reporter would be named in the column "who labels." When more extensive information is needed, this directs the worker to the source most likely to have pertinent data.

The person said to have the problem is identified in the next column, followed by the date on which the problem was reported. The importance of examples was discussed in relation to the different ways in which labels are employed. The information is recorded directly from the father's description. Situations are identified for two reasons. First, the occurrence of a problem is often situationally specific, occurring in certain contexts and not in others, or only in the presence of certain people. This information is necessary to direct attention to those situations requiring additional data. The behavioral examples will serve as cues to focus worker attention during periods of observation. Identifying the situations where a problem occurs is another way in which clients may be helped to see that difficulties are not as pervasive as initially suggested. In the column headed "assets" the worker lists strengths that the client identifies in relation to the problem cited, which places family difficulties in perspective by balancing the problem view with whatever positive information is provided. As we will see, this is useful when the final decision on whether to provide services or to make a referral is made.

In order to profile all the difficulties that relate to the request for services, the worker asks if there are other problems pertinent to the client's request. In this case, the father said "no." At the end of the

TABLE 6.1

Problem Profile

Problem Number	Label	Who Labels	Who Has The Problem	Date	Examples	Situation	Assets
1	Wife ill	Husband	Family	6/5/78	1. nervous breakdown	1. hospitalized	1. now at home
2	Situation at home is "terrible"	Husband	Family	6/5/78	1. wife: in bed all day	1. at home	1. daughter attends school
					daughter: does all chores		
3	Son is "unmanageable"	Husband	Family	6/5/78	1. won't do chores	1. at home	1. comes home and helps sometimes
					2. does not come home after school	2. whereabouts unknown	2. doing well in school
					3. no information as to where he goes		3. no evidence of misbehavior
					4. father suspects son gets in trouble		4. no reason to think friends misbehave
							5. father doesn't use physical punishment

interview the completed profile is shown to the client, who is asked if the information is an accurate reflection of what was said.

The interview serves purposes not revealed in the dialogue. The worker gained demographic information—a part of the social history—from the father. The information recorded cn the profile will later be turned into a narrative, and it too becomes a part of the social history.

In the process of exchanging information workers lay the groundwork for a positive working relationship with clients. Much has been written about the importance of this relationship to case work service delivery.[3] Yet the components of it and the precise part it plays in problem solving remain elusive. At minimum, a positive working relationship rests on showing respect for and interest in the client. Both are evidenced by the information the worker provides regarding agency services and the worker's statement that he or she will arrange for assistance by direct intervention or by referral. Concern is also evidenced when the worker asks questions to clarify the nature of the family's difficulties. It is also reflected in nonverbal behavior, by paying careful attention to the client's statements (evidence of which is seen when the worker poses specific follow-up questions) and by not "judging" clients even though their behavior and attitude may be "different" and at times personally repugnant.[4] Respect is also shown by asking the client's permission before attempting to gain additional information on the family, by explaining why this information is important and how it will be used, and by describing the process to be followed during a home visit.

Impressions of clients are formed during interviews. These may be important later and should be recorded. However, they should not become a part of the case record until the relevance of the information is shown. Memos in which workers describe their impressions are completed as soon as possible after the interview.

A word about information in relation to the time frame for gathering it is in order. While it is possible to list the items that are needed to reach a decision, and while it can be said that this information should be acquired by the end of the second or at the most the third interview, it is not appropriate to say that items "one and two" will be gathered in the first interview, and items "three and four" in the second. The process of gathering data does, however, follow certain logical rules. For example, while the problem profile and the social history may be completed in one or two interviews, all of the information concerning any single problem should be ascertained when the difficulty itself is pinpointed. This is not to suggest that data cannot be added should the client later recall pertinent information. It does suggest, however, that

TABLE 6.2

Client Contact Log

Family Name	Date of Apointment	Type of Contact	Place	Time	Person(s) in Attendance	Purpose	Results
Andres	6/5/78	office visit	welfare office	4 p.m.	Raymond Andres	request: out-of-home care for son	1. completed profile 2. made appointment for home visit
Andres	6/15/78	home visit	334 Smith Street	5 p.m.	Raymond Andres Marie Andres Michael Andres Elaine Andres	1. gather information from all family members re: request for service 2. make initial determination re: appropriateness of services.	

once a problem is identified, the issue is pursued until all of the information accessible to the client is elicited.

The information gathered thus far is not sufficient for reaching a decision regarding the appropriateness of services. The problems described by Raymond Andres do not rule out the possibility of agency intervention. Observing the parent, the child, and the home environment is necessary to acquire the data needed to make a final determination. Two home visits are generally sufficient for this purpose.[5] In terminating the interview the worker made an appointment to visit at the client's home at a time when all family members would be present. He entered this in his contact log along with information regarding the office visit. (Table 6.2) The "results" column in the log will be completed following the home visit. We will return to this case in chapter seven. The next case briefly illustrates one of the ways in which workers handle referrals from community agencies.

THE KYLE FAMILY

Richard Fong, a counselor at Stevens Community Mental Health Center, telephoned the protective service intake unit at a satellite office of Burke County Child Welfare Services. He was seeking assistance for twin girls, aged nine, whose parents participated in a marital therapy group that he conducted. The young girls, according to their parents, were having "serious problems at school." They were truant and failing in several classes. Fong explained that his marital therapy group did not include children and that his agency had no services to offer for this problem.

The worker inquired whether the young girls' school retained a school social worker or other counselor and, if so, if either the parents or Fong had contacted this person. According to Fong, the parents reported having spoken with "someone" at the school. They did not, however, receive any assistance. The worker suggested that Richard Fong contact the school, with the parents' permission, to learn what services were available and what, if anything, the school had done or planned to do to deal with this difficulty. "This situation may not be an appropriate referral for the services of the child welfare agency," she said. This is so because it is possible that the school has resources to deal with problems of truancy and failing grades. The situation would be appropriate for child welfare services if there are no school resources. If some exist, it would be appropriate only after they were brought to bear and then, only if the truancy constituted educational neglect. For this to occur, there would have to be evidence that the parents were in some way responsible for keeping their children at home.

This case illustrates a growing trend of making referrals to child welfare agencies for issues that are not clearly within the legal and social mandate of the agencies. Because of staff shortages and the pressures created by high caseloads, workers must be familiar with agency policy describing the types of difficulties that they are mandated to deal with, with resources in the community whose services were developed to address various family problems, and with the statutory definitions of neglect and abuse in order to reach correct decisions about the appropriateness of services.

THIRD-PARTY REPORTS

The procedure for handling third-party reports of abuse or neglect varies according to whether the reporter is a nonprofessional or professional. There are differences in state laws and in professional thinking as to whether all reports should be investigated. In some states, the person receiving a report has the discretion to "screen" calls, eliminating inappropriate referrals; while in others, there is a statutory requirement that all reports be investigated.[6] Professional thinking differs; one position is that all reports should be investigated, the other, that a screening process should occur. The former position recognizes the possibility that a decision not to intervene may be made when, in fact, the report is valid.[7] One runs the risk that a noninvestigation decision may lead to a child's being injured. Additionally, if abuse is proven later, the agency may be vulnerable to legal sanctions if no one responded to the report. The other side of the liability coin is that unless reports are screened before investigation, law suits may be instigated charging "harassment," of the investigated family. Thus, a decision for face-to-face contact in every case has certain liabilities.[8] We lack the information necessary to evaluate the possibility of risk to a child when a decision not to conduct an investigation is made. If we knew, for instance, that the probability of a child being harmed was greater than the probability that family privacy would be violated, we would have a reasonable basis for making the decision to respond to every call. Without such information, other variables, such as the number of staff and the volume of reports, are important policy considerations. We know that the volume of reports has increased dramatically with the advent of mandatory reporting laws and that investigative staff has not increased proportionately. If the quantity of cases increases and the number of staff remains constant, the quality of investigations will suffer. So there is further risk in responding to every call; namely, that cases where neglect or abuse has really occurred will not receive the attention they merit.

Making sure that the caller understands the purpose of the abuse or neglect reporting line is the worker's first task. Thus, the process begins in a manner similar to that described under voluntary requests. The worker ascertains the reason for the report and describes agency services. An exception to this occurs when a lay reporter wants only to present information and to get off of the phone. When this happens, workers record minimum information without which there can be no response.

The fact of reporting abuse, particularly when the caller is a non-professional, can be disquieting. The reporter may have witnessed an abusive act or seen a child with severe physical injuries. In order to obtain necessary information the worker must often calm the reporter. Statements such as "I understand that making this report is difficult . . . I know how traumatic it is to have seen bruises on a young-ster," coupled with assurances that assistance will be provided, may help to put the caller at ease. The informant may be reluctant to provide information, due perhaps to a concern with becoming involved beyond the fact of making the report. Most state laws give the caller the right to remain anonymous and this must be explained to the caller.[9] While this right is respected, workers point out that the reporter's willingness to be identified and interviewed at a later time may be invaluable for establishing evidence for a case. For example, if the caller's information is based on direct observation, his or her testimony in court can be crucial to sustaining allegations of maltreatment (when real evidence is missing) or for identifying the abuser. Even when the caller is iden-tified, anonymity can be protected by the agency until the case goes to court and thereafter at judicial discretion.[10]

A caller may be prejudiced against the family, and the report may reflect attempts at harassment. The informant's inability to provide a rationale for the report is a clue to this possibility. Statements such as "I (we) think that they are not doing a good job with their kids," or, "Their kids always look unkempt and dirty," alert the worker to the possibility of a nuisance report. Follow-up questions are asked. When an infor-mant says that "Mrs. Thomas isn't taking care of her children," the worker inquires into what the reporter has observed or heard that leads to this conclusion. The caller's speech patterns, whether they sound "incoherent, inconsistent or confused," are further clues that the report may not be valid.[11]

Lay persons should not be asked to gather information nor should they be asked to make judgments or draw conclusions. When the reporter is not a professional, every effort is made to get all of the information needed at the time of the call. Persons may be unwilling to be interviewed or may agree, only to change their minds at a later time. Also, the accuracy of the information provided can decrease with the passage of time. When reports are made by professionals and the situation defined as an emergency, this is accepted without screening. The rationale for this is discussed on page 165.

The worker taking a report seeks information in four categories.[12] Ideally the necessary information is arranged in a checklist to allow for fast recording and to reduce the likelihood of missing important items. Information categories should be organized according to their importance for responding to a call. The first category covers the identification of the family being reported—name, address, and phone number. Then the worker seeks to determine the reason for the report (category number two) by formulating questions to discriminate between firsthand information (what the caller saw or heard) and secondhand information (what they were told) and impressions (what the informant thinks happened). Checklist items would permit the worker to record that the reporter observed an abusive act, the date and time of the observation, and the frequency if more than one observation is being reported. Other items would allow for information descriptive of the child's condition (bruises or burns seen) what the person heard (crying or threats to a child) what they were told by a youngster ("I have been beaten ... I am afraid to go home") or by another ("my next door neighbor told me that he saw ..."). The information provided may serve to alert the worker to the emergency nature of the report. The statement "I have heard this child crying hysterically for two hours and I cannot locate the parents," indicates the need for immediate action. However, if the caller says "I think that there is a problem in the Jones family because I can hear the parents fighting and the child crying," while suggesting that follow-up work may be appropriate, does not, by itself, indicate that emergency action need be taken.

The reporter is described in the third category. Whether the caller is a lay person or professional is noted. If the former, and the caller is willing to be identified, the name, address, and phone number are recorded and willingness to be interviewed in person is indicated. Professionals are identified by discipline and by agency affiliation if they are in public sector employment. Otherwise, a business address and telephone number are requested. Their opinion as to the emergency nature of the situation is ascertained and the worker asks whether they have evidence such as X rays and photographs. Whether the parents know that the report is being made, and, if so, when they were told and how they responded are recorded as the final pieces of information. All checklist categories allow for the worker to document "other" relevant bits of information supplied by the reporter. Here is an illustration of the process for handling emergency cases.

THE BATESON FAMILY

At 9:30 P.M. on the night of January 4, 1979, a telephone call was taken at the emergency switchboard of a reporting center. The anonymous caller said that his neighbor's children had been "screaming their heads off all night." It sounds as though "someone is being murdered," he said. The worker was given an address and the family's last name, Bateson, before the caller hung up. The worker first tried to obtain a telephone number for the family, but none was available. He reported the call to the crisis unit of the local police department, which was charged with responding to "domestic crises," including reports of maltreatment, received after business hours.

Approximately two and one-half hours later, an investigating officer reported back to the switchboard. She said that she had gone to the address given by the caller, found no one at home, but heard muffled cries coming from inside the apartment. She tried the door, which was unlocked, and entered the apartment. Two children, approximately four and five years old, were found in a back bedroom. There were no adults present. The officer's report noted that the children were sitting together on one of two beds in the room. Their crying ceased "momentarily" when she entered the room. There were no outward signs of injury. She was able to calm the children somewhat, but not sufficiently to ask if they knew where their parents were. She left, telling them that she was going to look for their mother and father and that she would be right back if she could not find them.

After knocking on the doors of several nearby apartments, the parents were located. The officer informed them of the report and described what she had found upon entering the flat, and what she had done to try to quiet the youngsters down. The parents said that they often left their children by themselves when visiting with friends in the same building. Furthermore, they added that they saw nothing wrong with this practice and wished that people would "mind their own business." The officer explained the reporting requirements in the state law and told the parents that while she could understand their position, that the children could be hurt when left alone and that they would be held responsible under state law if anything were to happen.

She said that she would file a report of her findings with the county protective service unit, and that the parents would be contacted by a worker from that unit within forty-eight hours.

The switchboard worker completed a memo in which he summarized the content of the original report and noted that an emergency call had been made to the Bateson home and the time of the call. The officer was identified by name and by precinct number. The information provided by the police officer was briefly summarized and the fact that she would file a detailed report was recorded. This memo was attached to the checklist on which information had been recorded when the initial phone report was received, and this material was left for the day worker.

The day worker did two things with this information. First, she telephoned the central registry to find out whether there were prior reports on the family and found that there were none. Then she wrote them a letter in which the information presented by the caller was noted and the actions taken by the police officer described. The section of state law requiring the report and investigation of suspected abuse and neglect was quoted in the letter. She stated that if protective service intervention occurred, it would by law proceed under court order. The letter was sent to the Batesons by registered mail, return receipt requested. A copy of the letter, along with the officer's report and the information compiled by the switchboard worker, were filed in a case record and recorded in the registry office. Thus the worker documented all activities taken, as required by agency policy. This information is important should a report on this family be received at a later time.

Decision-Making Guidelines for Emergency Home Visits

The initial decision to make an emergency home visit to the Bateson family was made using guidelines provided for crisis workers. These are reviewed next, followed by a commentary on why this case was terminated with a letter to natural parents.

Decision making in this case and in all others presented in this text was guided by a standard requiring evidence that a child: had been abused or neglected; was in immediate danger of being maltreated; or was at risk (not necessarily imminently) of being abused or neglected. Criteria for judging whether an emergency response is appropriate are: (1) a professional reporter defines the situation as an emergency; (2) a lay person cannot locate a parent or is not willing to do so (and the child can be heard crying or is observed to be in a dangerous situation and, if the latter, the caller told the child to come indoors or to play elsewhere and the child would not listen); (3) a child came to a neighbor asking for help and is afraid to return home; (4) the caller observed an abusive act within the past twenty-four hours *and* the child is a preschooler, or the child is of school age and school is out of session; (5) the caller describes an emergency situation and hangs up before additional information can be obtained.

The potential for violating family privacy is present whenever an emergency house call is made. While this can be justified to safeguard a child's well-being, we must, in fact, have good reason to believe that this purpose will be served. The rationale for accepting professional definitions without screening is that we assume the actions of professionals will be more considered—less likely to be guided by emotional reactions—than those of nonprofessionals. Professionals have a vested interest in protecting their credibility. Since they generally identify themselves when making reports and since workers later inform them of protective service action, their own best interests are served when they exercise caution in defining a situation. And some professionals— medical personnel for example—are trained to identify abuse and certain conditions that constitute neglect. While these assumptions may be incorrect, the consequences for children are such that it is safer to accept them as accurate until proven otherwise.

As no rationale exists for making similar assumptions when the caller is a lay person, safeguards for the reported family are found in screening criteria. Notice that the second and third items require evidence that the reporter took certain actions (tried to locate the parents, called to the child to come indoors) in *combination* with what the reporter heard (the child crying), observed (the child in a dangerous situation), or was told by a youngster. Whether the caller tried locating a parent or admonishing a child to come indoors are useful ways to discriminate between emergency and nonemergency situations. The actions may not have been considered. If suggested by the worker and acted upon by the reporter, the immediate danger may subside, thus obviating the necessity of an emergency call. The informant may refuse to take action and should not be prodded to do so. This is explicitly recognized in the fourth criterion. Having observed an abusive act, a caller may, understandably, be hesitant to speak to the parents. If abuse was observed and it occurred more than twenty-four hours previously, it should not be deemed an emergency unless the caller explains the delay in reporting by some statement such as "I was afraid to call," or, "I didn't know what to do," or, "I didn't want to burden anyone, but after some thought I decided to telephone."

The potential danger in a situation must be evaluated in relation to a child's age—an important decision-making factor, yet an arbitrary criterion. If a youngster is of school age, it is possible to avoid an emergency home visit by contacting the school and asking if the child attended classes that day. If so, it is reasonable to expect that severe injuries would have come to the attention of a school authority. Even if they did not, the fact that the youngster went to school implies that injuries may not be so severe as to warrant immediate action. Remember, investigation occurs within twenty-four to forty-eight hours in nonemergency situations. It is also important to bear in mind that older children are able to take certain actions on their own behalf. Emergency action may be avoided by telephoning parents, describing the report, and eliciting their explanation of the incident reported. The worker can ask to speak with the child. If a school cannot be contacted, is not in session, or the parents cannot be reached by phone, an immediate home visit is called for. When the reporter describes an emergency situation and hangs up before additional information can be elicited there may be no option but to initiate an immediate home call.

If the switchboard worker had found a phone number for the Bateson family he would have attempted telephone contact prior to initiating emergency action. The parents would have been informed of the report and asked for their explanation. Children cry for many reasons. The neighbor's call might be more indicative of discomfort in hearing a youngster cry than of any family difficulties. How do you know if parents are being truthful? There is no totally satisfactory answer to this question. The worker can, however, seek confirming evidence. If the children's crying is explained by illness, she can inquire if the child has been seen by a physician. If so, she would ask if the parents are willing to tell her who the doctor is and if they would mind if she telephoned to inquire into the diagnosis. If a child is of school age the school can be contacted as suggested above. Registry files should be checked for past reports which, if they exist, indicate the correctness of a home visit. If parents provide a reasonable explanation for the child's crying and there are no prior reports, there is little basis for emergency action.

Reasons for the Bateson Decision

The reasoning behind the Bateson decision was based on the fact that there were no prior reports, the family's explanation was not unreasonable, and there was no evidence that the children had been harmed. The parents' statement that they frequently left their children alone when visiting with neighbors in the building and the officer's expression of understanding for this position are important. Individual child-rearing practices do not always readily conform to changes in the law. If leaving children unattended reflects a pattern of ongoing child care there is nothing to be gained by telling parents that this is "wrong." From their perspective it is not. It may be inappropriate, and if continued it could result in harm to the children and in protective service intervention and court action. This should always be explained. However, if the parents view their behavior as appropriate and if there is no evidence that a child has been harmed, value judgments can create barriers between parents and professionals that don't serve the objective of helping child-caring adults see that their behavior conflicts with the law. The officer, by giving information to the parents at their home, and the child welfare worker, by formulating this information in a letter, were performing important educational functions. The signed, return receipt will be evidence that the worker has provided the parents with information, as required by agency policy.

One possible outcome of an emergency home visit is that a child may be taken into protective custody. In each state certain persons are empowered to remove children from their parent's home in an emergency without parental permission. Therefore, emergency referrals must be made to the person or agency designated to take such action. In locations where this power is vested in law enforcement personnel, a social worker may accompany the police officer to the home. If the police officer who responded to the report in the Bateson case had not found anyone at home or in the building, she would have taken the children and placed them in a temporary shelter.

Guidelines for Initial Contact

Before we review criteria for intervention in nonemergency cases, let us review general guidelines for initial contact with parents following a report of abuse or neglect. It is important to bear in mind that we are discussing services initiated by a third party, not requested by the parents. Families may resist the intrusion, especially if they recognize that their behavior constitutes maltreatment. Resistance can also stem from misunderstanding the purpose and possible consequences of an investigation. Workers represent an authority that parents may fear. Difficulties are exacerbated when parents deny that there are family problems and thus hinder the process of investigation.[13]

The initial approach to parents can enhance or impede their willingness to cooperate. The worker must inform them that a report has been received (without violating the confidentiality of the reporting source) and describe what has been reported, the state law under which an investigation is mandated, and the possible consequences (court action) of not cooperating with the investigation. The worker apprises the clients of their right to counsel and offers to assist them in obtaining legal assistance if they desire this but do not have their own resource. Parents have the right to refuse entry to their home. This should be explained, as well as the fact that if they refuse entry, the worker would have to request a court order for entry. The family is told that the worker wants to assist them. Since so much of this initial information has to do with legal requirements, the chances of evoking a fearful and consequently resistant response are increased. The manner in which information is shared is critical. A nonaccusatory, nonblaming stance on the part of the worker is essential. A nonjudgmental position in forming a casework relationship is important here.

The likelihood of parental cooperation may be increased if workers make appointments for the first interview in nonemergency situations, thus showing respect for the family's privacy. If a home visit is resisted (and the report is not of an emergency nature) the worker can offer to see parents for the first time in a situation that is comfortable for them. The first contact can occur outside of the home, "the worker can offer to see parents in her car, in a local coffee shop, while taking a walk or in their front yard."[14] The worker is of course interested in seeing all family members as soon as possible. However, an initial contact in a situation suggested by the client may lay the groundwork for a cooperative working relationship. The consideration the worker shows by meeting the parents in a situation that is comfortable for them may dilute some of the concern raised by knowing that he or she is a court representative.

Offering immediate, concrete help at the first visit (food stamps, financial or medical assistance) evidences the worker's intention to assist the family. This can counterbalance the law-enforcement aspects of the worker's role and potentially increase the likelihood of parental cooperation. The process of investigation is described and a schedule for gathering information is established. Workers endeavor to arrange visits in accordance with the parent's work schedule. Parents are told that information regarding past experiences with social services and other community resources is needed and why, and they are asked to sign release of information forms. Parents should be allowed to participate in the process at every stage. They should have the opportunity to explain the conditions surrounding the reported incident and to suggest ways to conduct the investigation. It should be assumed that they will cooperate unless evidence suggests otherwise. First contact by telephone may make parents more comfortable and may be necessitated by time constraints imposed on workers. However, in-person contact is preferred.[15] All efforts to contact families are documented in logs such as the one illustrated in the Andres family case.

CRITERIA FOR INVESTIGATING
NONEMERGENCY REPORTS

As in the case of emergency reports, a professional recommendation for an investigation is accepted as a sufficient basis for action. When reports are made by lay persons, the first criterion is whether the condition or situation described suggests maltreatment as defined by state law. Investigation is precluded if, for example, the reporter describes a situation of neglect and the reporting laws in your state cover only abuse.[16] It is useful if workers have a checklist categorizing the types of abuse and neglect covered by law (such as supervisorial neglect, material neglect, and physical abuse) and listing the conditions that suggest the presence of maltreatment. The worker's task is to compare the information provided by the caller with checklist items. Under supervisorial neglect we might find any of the following: child age six or under is unsupervised between his or her return from school and the parents' return from work; child is left unsupervised when parents go out in the evening; child of six is responsible for supervising two younger siblings; parent is home after school hours, but child (age six or under) plays unsupervised in heavily trafficked area.

The worker is concerned with whether the informant is reporting a condition or a situation that affects a child, as opposed to describing marital squabbles, where there is no indication that a child has been implicated. In deciding whether to respond to reports made by nonprofessionals, criteria direct the worker to seek additional information before reaching a decision. Telephone contact with the parent or parents is attempted, the report is explained to them, and they are given the opportunity to present their side of the case. Investigation is called for: (1) if they cannot or will not explain the incident, (2) if their explanation is reasonable but there have been prior reports, or (3) if they cannot be contacted by phone. Since we have so few criteria that enable us to predict the likelihood of abuse or neglect, prior reports assume particular significance. When a report involves a child or children of preschool age it should be investigated unless the parent presents a reasonable explanation of the incident and this is confirmed by other sources. Preschool children often do not come in contact with others outside the immediate family and so they are especially vulnerable. When children are of school age and the situation is "borderline" (evidence for an investigation is not strong) information from the child's school may swing the decision one way or another. For example, if a teacher, nurse, school social worker, or other counselor reports that the child regularly attends school and if, in this person's opinion, there is no reason to think that the child is being neglected or abused, a noninvestigation decision is appropriate. However, without information from an outside source, it is correct to pay at least one visit to the family. Also, when children ask for help, a home visit is called for.

Interim Information

Most states allow a twenty-four to forty-eight hour period of time between receipt of a report and an investigation in nonemergency situations.[17] Workers use this time to gather information preparatory to the first home visit.[18] If the report is made by a collateral resource the worker asks what type of sustaining evidence is available. Workers also conduct a search to see if there is information in registry files or case records from which they can learn something about the family's history in areas related to child care. If documentation is on hand, a worker is able to approach a family with more than the hearsay information that may be all that was provided by a reporter. This is useful when parents deny that there are problems, because the worker can refer to prior reports and other information to support a claim that an investigation is necessary.

Knowing that reports are available, even if there is no time to read them prior to the visit, permits the worker to counter a denial by referring to available documentation and by informing parents of his or her intention to review related material. When an investigation proceeds solely on the basis of hearsay information, workers approach parents with caution, bearing in mind that what parents have to say is not, ipso facto, any less reliable than what a reporter had to say.

In addition to preparing a worker for a first home visit, the existence of information from other sources may be decisive in reaching the decision to conduct a full-scale investigation. If the worker makes a home call because the family does not have a telephone, with no information other than the report, the case may be dismissed if the parents offer a reasonable explanation for the reported incident. The Bateson case illustrated this. A word of caution regarding registry information: If unsubstantiated cases are not expunged, prior reports have little utility for decision making, at times reflecting little more than recorded nuisance calls. Workers must be familiar with policy and practice (which are not necessarily the same) regarding the handling of unproven reports.

At this point, workers seek general information, such as whether reports were substantiated, and if so, whether the corroborating evidence was real, direct, or hearsay. The type of maltreatment, and whether the case was dismissed or investigated should also be learned. More specific information, such as whether intervention took place, the type of service provided, who provided service, and the service provider's evaluation of outcome, will be gathered if a decision for a full-scale investigation is made. The following case illustrates the process of responding to nonemergency reports.

THE CARR FAMILY

The Carr family is headed by Sharon Carr, aged thirty-one, mother of Nita, fourteen; Barry, seven; and three-year-old twin girls, Susan and Maria. As of mid-1976, the children's father, Matthew Carr, had not been seen by Sharon Carr for almost three years, and his whereabouts were unknown. The case was brought to the attention of protective services by a worker in the county foster care department who had worked with the family for one year, during which time the twins had been in foster placement with a maternal aunt. The foster care worker said that Sharon Carr had called him one morning asking that he "come and get the twins and put them back in foster placement . . . [because she was] unable to manage with "all of the children in the home." It had been three months since the twins were returned to their mother's care and the court dependency was still open. The initial petition alleged that Sharon Carr had "abandoned" her children to the care of her sister. The twins were placed in the aunt's home under court order and had remained there for one year. The older children stayed with their mother.

The foster care worker reported having told Sharon Carr that he could not immediately comply with her request, but he would try to get a protective service worker to her home as soon as possible. He asked whether she thought she could manage for a day or two, to which she responded affirmatively. He told the intake worker that Sharon Carr was prone to exaggerate and that, in his opinion, she would be all right if the worker telephoned and set up an appointment for the next day. The worker agreed to do this and said that she would drop by the foster care unit to review the case record prior to the home visit. She reached the new client by telephone and made an appointment for late the next day. Court documents in the case record were reviewed next, including the initial petition for dependency, the worker's report to the court for the jurisdictional and dispositional hearings, a summary of court action provided for the worker by the court officer, and a description of the worker's report for the review hearing. The tasks involved in the investigation are described in the next chapter.

The *petition* requests a particular finding from the court at the jurisdictional phase of the juvenile court hearing. On it, the name, date of birth, residence address, and city and state of residence of each child named in the petition are shown. The same information appears for each parent, the child's legal guardian, or the nearest known relative. The section of the state code under which dependency is requested appears in the body of the petition, and the applicable part of the code is quoted directly from the statutes. The facts that serve to establish grounds for dependency are reported as follows:

> Said minor(s) has been abandoned by h_____ (their) parent(s), guardian or custodian in that:
> On July 10, 1966, Mrs. Sharon Carr, mother of Susan Carr and Marie Carr, minor children, left these children in the care of their maternal aunt, Mrs. Andrea Thomas. On July 13, 1976, Mrs. Andrea Thomas reported to the County Welfare Department that her sister Mrs. Sharon Carr had not returned for the children, nor had she telephoned her sister informing her of her whereabouts.

The request being made by the petitioner is shown next, for example, "that the said minor be adjudicated a ward of the court." The petitioner (child welfare worker designated as the court representative) signs the petition on oath stating that "I have read the foregoing petition and that the matters alleged therein are true and correct to the best of my information and belief."

Notice that the petition names only the two youngest children. Prior to filing, the mother voiced the opinion that she could continue to provide care for the older youngsters. The aunt agreed to care for the twins, thus the decision to file the dependency only for them.

The casework report to the court is divided into two parts: The first, the *jurisdictional* report, establishes the facts of the case in greater detail than on the petition. This is used by the judge to determine whether the evidence is sufficient to assume jurisdiction over the children. The second part of the report, headed social study, is less factual. The information here is abstracted from the social history and is illustrative of what is contained in such documents. This is used at the *dispositional* phase of the hearing to assist the judge in determining where the children should be placed.

The jurisdictional report contains nine items of information.[19] In the first three, the parents and children are named, their ages are reported, the marital status of the adults is noted and their current address, if known, is indicated. Items four and five satisfy legal requirements. The fourth section notes that the parent was served notice of the hearing and given a copy of the petition. Item five reports that the parent was informed of her right to counsel and her response to this (that she waived this right, or that she will be represented by counsel).

The reason for the hearing is spelled out in section six. The information here must be factual. Thus, the worker uses direct quotations when possible and phrases information in terms of "I saw . . . I heard . . . I was told." For example, this section of the report included the statement, "Mrs. Thomas [Sharon Carr's sister] said, "My sister left her kids with me on Wednesday night [July 10, 1976] and has not come back for them." She continued by stating that this was her "sister's customary practice [and that she would] keep them for today, only. Either my sister or somebody from the welfare had better come and get them."

Because witnesses are not always called in juvenile court hearings, section seven includes information telling the judge what a witness will report if called upon to testify. If this had been a report of medical abuse, the facts of which were substantiated by medical evidence or opinion, the information contained here might state that "if subpoenaed, Dr. Jones will testify that he has examined the child [who is named], who is suffering from multiple bone fractures which, in his opinion, could not have been caused by accidental means." What the parent is expected to say with regard to the allegations is reported in item number eight. Sharon Carr did not dispute her sister's testimony. However, she did explain her failure to return for her children by stating that she had been "stranded 48 miles from her home when a friend's car broke down and that she did not have access to a telephone from which to call her sister." Parents do contest allegations. When this occurs, the report informs the judge of this by noting, for example, that "Mrs. X. can be expected to deny the allegations," which would be followed by a summary statement of what the parent will say in his or her own behalf. Item nine contains a pro forma request that the court find the allegations cited in the petition to be true.

The social study shown in its entirety in Figure 6.2 contains information on the family in several areas. If a parent had an arrest record or was hospitalized under psychiatric orders, the date(s), place(s) of incarceration, and reason(s) for incarceration would be reported. Previous history (section three) refers specifically to background information related to the petition. Hence, if the youngsters had been in foster care in the past, the date(s), reason(s) for placement, location of the placement facility, and a brief summary of service provided and changes in the family would be reported. Section four contains information regarding family history and a brief description of their physical environment. The parent's explanation of the conditions leading up to the incident and other relevant comments are summarized. Item five informs the court of Sharon Carr's sister's position with regard to providing care for the children. If they were to be placed in an as yet unidentified facility, a section would be included in which the worker

FIGURE 6.2   Report to the Brooks County Juvenile Court
Social Study

Section Number	Concerning	
1	Arrest Record for Parent	None
2	Psychiatric Hospitalization for Parent	None
3	Previous History	None pertinent to this petition
4	Family History and Environment	Sharon Carr, mother of the minors, was born in Richmond, Virginia, March 23, 1945. She was the youngest of three children born to Anna and Stephen Warren. One sister, Andrea Thomas, lives in Brooks County An older brother, Phillip Warren, is reported to live in Fort Lauderdale, Florida. Sharon Carr moved to Brooks County in April or May of 1970, with her husband and daughter Nita, then 8 years of age, and infant son Barry, then 1 year of age.

They moved from Richmond, Virginia, where the parents met, and were married on May 23, 1961. Both Nita and Barry were born in Richmond. The expectation that Matthew Carr would obtain employment in the aerospace industry was cited as the reason for the move. However, Sharon Carr reports that her husband lacked the educational and skill requirements for such employment. Instead, he worked as a television and refrigeration repairman until the time of their divorce and his "disappearance" in 1973. Sharon Carr's father is deceased. Her mother is said to

(continued)

FIGURE 6.2 *(continued)*

Section Number	Concerning	
		reside in Fort Lauderdale with her older brother.
		The couple married following what Sharon Carr describes as a "whirlwind courtship," that began prior to her sixteenth birthday, at which point she had known her fiance for "two to three months." Her parents reportedly disapproved of the marriage, but gave in when their daughter applied pressure. Sharon Carr was awarded custody of all minor children at the time of her divorce in 1973. Mr. Carr was ordered by the court to pay the sum of $125 per month for child support. However, according to Sharon Carr, payments were never made. Welfare records indicate an unsuccessful search for the father in early January 1974 following his wife's application for AFDC benefits. A grant was awarded and has been the only known source of income since that time. Sharon Carr has no marketable work skills. She has never held a job, but did acquire her high school diploma by passing a GED test. She reports that she would like to enter a training program to acquire work skills.
		The mother says that she "dates" but does not have a steady boyfriend, and is not "particularly interested in getting married again."
		She informed this worker that she cannot "cope" with all four of her children. The twins in

(continued)

FIGURE 6.2   (*continued*)

Section Number	Concerning	
		particular are "difficult to manage," especially since her eldest daughter "will not help." She describes herself as "frequently depressed," and says that she does not engage in any activities outside of the home save for an "occasional date." Without some respite from ongoing child care she reports that she will "go crazy [or] leave her children once again." The Carr family resides in a five-room, three-bedroom apartment, located on the second floor of a six-unit apartment building. The building is located in a residential area in the northwest section of the city. The three girls share one bedroom, the boy the second, and the mother occupies the third. The family's residence is within walking distance of the school attended by the older children and is in close proximity to a playground and neighborhood shopping area. The apartment appears to be adequate for the family's needs.
5	*Statement of Andrea Thomas: Sister to Sharon Carr*	Andrea Thomas, who has no children of her own, and whose husband is deceased, states that she will provide care for the twins if she is able to get financial assistance and if her sister "understands that under no circumstances will she babysit over night for the two older children." Furthermore, she reports that she is willing to provide care for a limited period of time only, in order to "help my sister get back on her feet."

(*continued*)

FIGURE 6.2 (continued)

Section Number	Concerning	
6	Additional Statement from Sharon Carr	Sharon Carr states that, "I would like my sister to take care of the twins," and she agrees not to ask her sister to assume child-care responsibilities for the older children. She agrees to cooperate with the welfare department in a program designed to resolve her difficulties such that she can resume full time care of the twins, hopefully, in one year or less.
7	Brooks County Welfare Department Report	Jonathan Walden, an AFDC service worker, reports having had supervisorial contact only with the Carr family. He informed me that Sharon Carr never discussed the difficulties referred to above. His records show that she is currently receiving AFDC and Food Stamp benefits which, when combined, amount to $411 per month. The family is eligible for Medicaid. Sharon Carr has been a continuous recipient of benefits since 1974. The grant will be reduced, accordingly, if the two younger children are removed from her care. Grace Briggs, County Foster Care supervisor, reports that Andrea Thomas's home is suitable for licensing and that she is eligible for board and care payments at the current relative-placement rate.
8	Evaluation and Recommendations	There seems to be little doubt that the allegations shown in the petition and jurisdictional report are correct. The mother

(continued)

FIGURE 6.2 (continued)

Section Number	Concerning
	readily admits that her behavior was inappropriate, however, she thinks that her situation justified her actions. Furthermore, her suggestion that she will do this again should, I think, be taken seriously. Since this family has no prior service record, and since there are no reports in central registry files, it is premature to evaluate her potential for change. Since the sister is willing to provide care and since this would reduce the pressure on Sharon Carr while assistance is provided, it is respectfully recommended that Susan and Marie Carr be made dependents of the juvenile court and that they be placed in the care of their maternal aunt, Andrea Thomas of 456 Ridgeway Drive, City. It is further recommended that there be no court action with regard to the older children who will continue to reside with their mother. A complete assessment of the mother's situation with subsequent services to resolve identified problems is recommended so that the younger children can be returned to the mother's care at the earliest possible time.

would describe the plan to be followed in order to locate a suitable placement. If the children had been in emergency care prior to the hearing, a report from some person with knowledge of their behavior during this time and information as to whether the parent visited with the children would be included. Information describing the results of any examinations of the children (medical or psychological) is also reported. The parents' wishes, if any, with regard to the placement plans are noted in section six.

The financial status of the parent(s) is shown next. If Sharon Carr had resources other than AFDC this section would have been headed "Parental Resources" and the source of income described. The report concludes with the worker's evaluation and recommendations for disposition of the case.

A *summary of court action* is generally submitted to the child welfare worker by a court officer shortly after the hearing. In this document, the judge's decision is reported, the date at which the court will review the case is noted, and judicial recommendations related to assessment, planning, and treatment are reported. The worker must follow up on these or risk being held in contempt of court. The summary submitted in the Carr case contained the following information:

> The court made a finding of dependency under California Civil Code 300, section (a). Both Susan and Marie Carr, minor children, were placed in the care of their maternal aunt, Mrs. Andrea Thomas. The court did not take action in regard to the older children who will continue to reside in the home of their mother. The date for case review is January 28, 1977, six months from this time. The court recommends a speedy and thorough assessment of the family situation and admonishes Mrs. Carr not to leave her children overnight in anyone's care without first obtaining permission from Richard Avedo, Foster Care worker for the Brooks County Department of Social Services, or an authorized representative of that agency. Mrs. Carr is further admonished to cooperate in every way with the assessment process and with the plans subsequently developed. The worker is ordered to return to this court at the review hearing with the results of the assessment and with recommendations for treatment and information regarding any treatment currently underway and client progress therein.

The caseworker's *report for the review hearing* was the last court document in the case record. Regular review hearings can be instrumental in preventing children from drifting into long-term foster care. Whether they serve this function depends upon the specificity of information required by a judge, and, if required, whether the provision of information is monitored and how carefully it is reviewed. If data are not available, the judge should request it. The content of a report should be goal-oriented and process specific. The reviewer should be informed of the case objective (for example, to return a child from foster care to the home of natural parents), the goal or goals that must be attained to reach the objective (reducing or eliminating alcohol consumption, for instance), the process to be followed to attain goals, the progress to date (how far along the path to goal attainment the client has moved), what remains to be done, and the time frame for accomplishing the remaining tasks. Thus, the reviewer is informed of the approximate date at which goals should be realized and overall case objectives attained. Reports should also include a log of contacts between worker and parent and between parent and child. The judge also has information regarding the frequency with which services are provided and whether the parent has maintained contact with the worker and with the child or children.

When a case that was active (as in the Carr family) is transferred to a new worker, this information can be very valuable. If fully documented, the new worker has a clear description of case-planning and service delivery activities.

Although court expectations of material to be presented for review were noted in the summary of court action, all of the information requested was not provided. There was no evidence in the record to suggest that the judge ordered the worker to produce the missing information. The report to the court contained three brief paragraphs. The first stated that Sharon Carr was in counseling (the counseling resource was named) and noted that, according to her counselor, she was "making progress in group therapy." The goals of the group were not reported, progress was not defined, and assessment information (indicating why group counseling was chosen) was not provided. In the second paragraph, it was reported that "the children are doing well in the foster placement [and that] no problems have been reported to this worker during the past six months." It continued with the information that "Mrs. Carr visits with her children at her sister's home approximately once each week." The final paragraph contained the worker's recommendation that "placement be continued until the next review hearing on July 8, 1977."

This material is of marginal use to the new worker since it does not contain specific information descriptive of the processes that occurred between worker and client or between the client and counseling resource. The case record contained a progress note from the counseling center. However, it did not yield additional information. The worker's narrative account, which should contain specific information descriptive of worker-client contacts, was vague. For example, with reference to contacts, it was noted that "the worker has seen the client several times in the past six months." There was no information about the purpose of contacts, nor any way of knowing whether the client had been consistent in maintaining contact, since a detailed log listing all appointments and whether they were kept was not available.

SUMMARY

The objective of assessment is to reach a decision whether the services offered by the child welfare agency are appropriate in response to requests for assistance.

Assessment begins at intake, the gateway to child welfare services. Cases come to intake when clients voluntarily request assistance, when they are referred by community agencies, or when a professional or lay person files a report of abuse or neglect.

Since requests for service require direct contact with clients, the tasks involved in assessment differ according to the way in which cases reach intake.

Voluntary requests begin with direct contact, which involves fewer tasks than either referrals (where information is exchanged with the referring source prior to contacting the client) or reports, in which a screening process to eliminate "nuisance" calls may occur, and which require that the intake worker decide whether the report is an emergency requiring an immediate investigation.

Voluntary requests and professional referrals may result in referrals to other agencies, or dismissal of the case (when the request is inappropriate for the services of the child welfare agency), or in a decision to conduct an investigation in the client's home (during which time additional information is compiled prior to reaching a decision to open, refer, or dismiss the case).

Emergency reports are investigated immediately. A child may be removed to a temporary shelter or left in the parent's home with plans for further investigation. Cases may be dismissed when the facts do not warrant further home study. Nonemergency reports are investigated in the client's home within twenty-four to forty-eight hours of the report. The case may be dismissed, referred to another community agency, or opened to the child welfare agency.

Requests for service, whether made directly by the client or indirectly by referral, warrant a home visit if: the service requested is offered by the agency, the client is eligible for the service requested, and if the difficulty described falls within the agency's mandate.

Workers prepare for home visits by gathering and recording information from clients when the request is voluntary, or from the source referring or reporting the case. Additionally, workers check central registries for prior reports and case records for information descriptive of past services, if any.

All reports by professional persons, emergency or not, are investigated.

Whether a report by a lay person requires an emergency response is determined by considering combinations of factors such as actions taken by the reporter (efforts made to locate the parents), along with what the reporter saw (an abusive act), heard (a child crying), or was told by the child or another person.

Nonemergency reports made by lay persons in states that do not mandate investigation of all reports are followed up if, for example, the conditions or situation suggest maltreatment as defined by state law; if the parents cannot be contacted by phone or, if contacted, they do not offer a reasonable explanation for the incident reported; or if the child is a preschooler and not visible to others.

Workers may attempt to verify the information in a lay person's report prior to a home visit by telephoning the parents, describing the report, and asking for their explanation; or by checking with a child's school or day-care center to learn if the child attended school or if injuries were observed by school personnel.

Because protective services are generally initiated by a third party, posing a violation of family privacy, and because workers represent a legal authority which parents may fear, workers endeavor, in nonemergency situations, to increase the likelihood of parental cooperation by making appointments for initial interviews, by seeing parents in situations that are comfortable for them, and by offering immediate, concrete assistance with financial or medical help.

NOTES

1. All identifying information has been removed to safeguard client confidentiality.

2. E. D. Gambrill, E. J. Thomas, and R. D. Carter, "Procedures for Socio-Behavioral Practice in Open Settings," *Social Work*, Vol. 16 (1971), pp. 51–62; For a detailed discussion of problem profiles, including examples of their use, see: Theodore J. Stein and Eileen D. Gambrill, *Decision Making in Foster Care: A Training Manual* (Berkeley: University of California Extension Press, 1976).

3. Carol B. Germain (ed.), *Social Work Practice* (New York: Columbia University Press, 1979); Beulah Roberts Compton and Burt Galaway (eds.), *Social Work Processes* (Homewood, Ill.: The Dorsey Press, 1975), Ch. 4; Alfred Kadushin, *The Social Work Interview* (New York: Columbia University Press, 1972), Ch.2; Helen Harris Perlman, *Social Casework: A Problem-Solving Process* (Chicago: The University of Chicago Press, 1957), Ch. 6.

4. There is no simple prescription for learning to contain one's "shock or surprise," at information revealed in interviews. This skill may be partially learned in classroom simulations where students observe models and enact what they observed and in field placements where exposure to experienced practitioners is possible. In large measure, skills are acquired over time with the accumulation of practice experience.

5. *Protective Services for Abused and Neglected Children and Their Families: A Guide* (New York: Community Research Applications, Inc., n.d.), p. 53.

6. Barton D. Schmitt and Leimalama Lee Roy, "Team Decisions on Case

Management," (ed.) Barton D. Schmitt, *The Child Protection Team Handbook: A Multi-Disciplinary Approach to Managing Child Abuse and Neglect* (New York: Garland STPM Press, 1978), p. 188; *Utah State Division of Family Services: Task Force on Alternatives for Families-at-Risk* (n.p.: Utah State Division of Family Services, October 1975), p. 9.

7. *Protective Services for Abused and Neglected Children*, pp. 49–50.

8. Ibid.

9. *Court Referral Project: Final Report* (Bismark, N. Dak.: Division of Community Services, Social Service Board of North Dakota, 1978), p. 55.

10. Ibid.

11. Schmitt, "Team Decisions," p. 188.

12. Agency policy or practice may dictate that additional information be gathered.

13. *Protective Services for Abused and Neglected Children*, p. 54.

14. Ibid., p. 52.

15. Ibid., p. 50.

16. Protective services may still be offered if requested directly by the client.

17. *Protective Services for Abused and Neglected Children*, p. 50; *Utah State Division of Family Services*, p. 9.

18. *Protective Services for Abused and Neglected Children*, p. 50.

19. This may vary from state to state.

7

Assessment—The Investigation

Figure 7.1 depicts steps to be taken at the investigative stage of assessment. The process begins when workers visit in the family home and ends with either a nonintervention decision, or when data necessary to develop a case plan have been accumulated.

Gathering, recording, and evaluating information are at the heart of this process. Since workers look for indicators that abuse or neglect has occurred, or for evidence suggesting that a child is at-risk of either, a decision must be made whether the expertise of others is needed at this time. If a worker's task is to investigate a report of medical neglect, he or she will decide prior to the first home visit whether to ask a public health nurse to go along. The decision to involve collateral resources may be reached only after the first visit, at which time data that are gathered may suggest medical neglect or physical abuse. Thus, gathering assessment information may involve a division of responsibility between child welfare staff and others. When the expertise of others is needed to establish the basic facts of a case (for instance, whether there is evidence to sustain an allegation of physical abuse or medical neglect), workers gather secondary data which contribute to the diagnosis and to assessment of the safety of the home, so that decisions can be made to provide services in that setting or in substitute care, if neces-

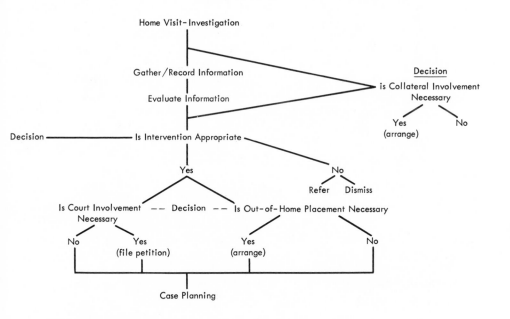

FIGURE 7.1   Assessment Flow Chart Second Phase

sary. When the concern is material or custodial neglect, or when it is hypothesized that problems in parent-child interaction are contributing to family difficulties, evidence is compiled and evaluated by child welfare staff skilled in direct observation, who are trained to isolate indicators of these conditions. So the question: "Who gathers assessment data?" requires knowledge not only of the type of maltreatment being investigated, but also an accurate assessment of one's own strengths and weaknesses in data collection. Some workers may require assistance in compiling and managing information that others have been trained to gather.

Evidence may be available when a report is made. Medical personnel may have confirmed that a child's injuries could not have been sustained accidentally. When this occurs, the worker proceeds to gather the supportive evidence needed to evaluate the safety of the child's home. Factors involved in the decision whether or not to intervene are reviewed later in this chapter.

When agency services are not appropriate, whether the case should be referred or dismissed must be decided. Availability of community resources and family interest in using services are prime considerations. Given an affirmative intervention decision, two questions must be addressed: "Is it necessary to invoke court action?" and, "Can services be offered while the child remains at home, or is out-of-home placement necessary?"

The answer to the first question comes from state law, agency practice, or parental response to intervention. In some jurisdictions, workers must petition the court any time protective service intervention proceeds on a report of maltreatment. If not required by statute, court action may be dictated by agency policy. If court action is not required by statute or policy, it is necessary only when parents are not cooperative. Children should not be removed from their homes unless they are in imminent danger. This critical decision is discussed at length later in this chapter.

PREPARING FOR THE HOME VISIT

Workers prepare for home visits by developing an outline itemizing information they want to exchange with, and elicit from, clients. The structure of the outline depends on information provided when a report or a referral is made, or when a client requests voluntary services. The range of items in an interview outline will vary depending on the reason for the referral or voluntary request, or the type of maltreatment being reported, as well as by the specificity of information supplied. Hence, when investigating a report of supervisorial neglect, the worker would ask questions about the client's perception of the need for supervision (At what age and under what circumstances do you think that a child can stay home alone in the evening or stay home alone between the end of school and a parent's return from work?), the methods of supervision used (Does the client hire a babysitter or give the child a phone number where the parent can be reached?), and whether the client has access to child-care services.

In preparing an outline for a home visit with the Andres family, the worker, John Wilson, identified two topical areas in which he wanted to elicit information. First, he wanted to learn whether the members of the family shared the father, Raymond Andres's, perception of the specifics of the problem. (Did the daughter think that she did all of the chores? What would the son say when asked "What chores do you do around the house?") Since the difficulties described by Raymond Andres revolved around daily activities such as the daughter doing all the housework, and the son neither helping nor returning home from school, each member of the family would be asked to describe a "typical day" and to report how he or she felt about the daily routine.

Questions focusing on changes in family life comprised the second topical area. The worker wanted to learn what the Andres family would like to see altered in their daily lives (Would the daughter like assistance with specific tasks? Would she like one hour each day after school to study?), what each thought they would have to do to bring about change, and what the daily routine would be when changes were made. Answers to these questions would inform the worker as to the specific need of change, whether there appeared to be a consensus about the necessary changes, and whether each person had given thought to his or her role in effecting change. The last question was directed to find out whether their expectations focused on an ideal (which might be defined in terms of the mother, Marie Andres, being completely well) or whether they had considered the possibility that she would not make a full recovery.

The responses of family members would provide cues to the most appropriate type of assistance. For example, if the young boy acknowledged the need for change and agreed to help his sister with household chores, assistance could focus on negotiating an equitable division of household responsibilities. It is possible that the problem has less to do with the boy's willingness to help per se, than with the exact things that he is asked to do. If, however, the son does not think that change is required, but his parents agree that it is, resolution might hinge on identifying reinforcers (such as his allowance or special privileges) which could be given or withheld contingent upon his complying with a program to distribute household responsibility.

An interview outline is directive, and the topics listed serve as cues to direct the worker's data-gathering efforts. An outline is not meant to be all-inclusive. The responses of family members and the questions they may ask can redirect conversation into new, previously unidentified areas. While workers are receptive to enlarging the scope of discussion, they must also retain a focus that assures the collection of information necessary to decide whether services will be offered. An outline increases the chances of retaining such a focus.

Highlights of the Home Visit
With the Andres Family

The verbal reports of family members confirmed Raymond Andres's description of his family's approach to household management. The expectation that Marie Andres would regain her health and that life would "return to normal" was revealed in the responses of both mother and children, none of whom stressed the need for change. For example, the daughter said that she would like "relief" from housework, but immediately stated that this would be forthcoming when her mother recovered. For Marie Andres a return to normal meant that she would resume her role of full-time homemaker; for the daughter it meant having time to spend with friends and time to devote to schoolwork; for the son it meant a diminution of fights with his father and continued freedom to spend his time as he chose. Raymond Andres omitted any reference to his wife regaining her health or resuming her role in the home, suggesting to the worker that he either knew or suspected that Marie Andres would not recover. His suggestions for change were the same that he had offered during the office interview.

This meeting concluded with the worker stating that he would take the tape recording back to his office, review it with his supervisor, and formulate recommendations for the family. He requested permission to contact Marie Andres's psychiatrist (to inquire into the prognosis for her recovery) and the children's school to learn how they were doing in class. A meeting was arranged for the same time the following week at the worker's office.

Immediately following an interview workers record impressions of the family and note questions they want answered. If interviews are recorded, questions and commentary can be made directly on the tape; if not, they must be written down. In addition to asking Marie Andres's psychiatrist for a prognosis, John Wilson also wanted to learn whether there was any chance that her medication was so strong that it was affecting her speech and contributing to her lethargy.[1]

It was the worker's impression that, save for Raymond Andres, the family saw Marie Andres's recovery as the solution to their difficulties. The father's omission of any reference to his wife's recovery suggested that he might have information that he had not shared.[2] If, as the worker hypothesized, Marie Andres was not expected to regain her health in the foreseeable future, resolution of family problems would have to begin by sharing this information with the children and by addressing its implications with regard to household management. We will return to this case following a review of the home visit with the Carrs.

First Home Visit With the Carr Family

The worker's objectives for this meeting were: first, to learn why the mother, Sharon Carr, wanted the twins again placed in foster care; and second, to establish a framework for gathering assessment data beginning with the development of a problem profile. The social history would be updated with information from the interview.

Ann Tripp, the worker, began the session by describing the objective of protective services and by explaining that revised agency policy precluded out-of-home placement until after services were provided in the family home.

Three problems were listed on the profile. These were (1) mother is overwhelmed with housework (does all household chores, receives no help from the children), (2) mother is depressed (feels "dull," says that her situation will never change and that she does not engage in any activities outside of the home), and (3) Nita, the eldest child, is in trouble at school—defined as failing in class. Sharon Carr also reported that little had changed in the year that the twins were in placement, save for her relief from day-to-day child-care responsibilities. She had been in a therapy group, but did not find it helpful. Ann Tripp asked permission to contact Sharon Carr's therapist to ask for an evaluation of the client's progress in group therapy, and the counselor at Nita's school in order to clarify the nature of the girl's problems.

Explaining the need for additional information about the family's difficulties, Sharon Carr was asked to maintain a log of her daily activities and Ann Tripp arranged to observe family interaction.

The log (Table 7.1) was shown to Sharon Carr, and the instructions for recording were reviewed. Clients are asked to record information at set intervals (every hour, for example), to indicate their activities at the time of recording, and to provide the information called for in the remaining columns (where they were when recording, who was present, what they wanted to do, and what they actually did). They are asked to record their thoughts about the preceding information and to evaluate their activities in the column headed "comments." The example at the top of the form is provided as an illustration for the client.

If "exploratory" logs are maintained according to instructions they allow for the acquisition of detailed data that may not be accessible to clients through memory.[3] Behavioral examples, which help to define the problems verbalized in general terms, are made available, and conditions that facilitate and maintain problems may be highlighted by information in the remaining columns. For instance, feelings of depression may emerge only in certain situations, only in the presence of certain persons, or only in relation to certain cognitions. Such discriminatory information allows for the identification of nonproblem situations, adding perspective to what may otherwise appear to be an overwhelmingly negative picture. Knowledge of what Mrs. Carr "wants" can direct worker attention to personally satisfying activities in which the client can engage to reduce feelings of depression. Barriers to engaging in activities may be identified from the information recorded under comments. For example, Sharon Carr may note an interest in going to the movies, but indicate an unwillingness to go by herself and report that she does not know anyone to ask to accompany

TABLE 7.1

Activity Log

Date	Time	Activity	Setting	Who Was There	What Did You Want	What Did You Do	Comments
Example: 8/1/77	6 p.m.	Sitting down, just finished dinner dishes	at-home: living room	son David	1. to have a drink 2. not to think about anything	1. helped son with homework	1. wish I'd had the drink 2. hate thought of spending whole evening alone 3. wish someone were here besides kids

Source: The format for this log is from: Arthur Schwartz and Israel Goldiamond, *Social Casework, A Behavioral Approach* (New York: Columbia University Press, 1975), pp. 164–65.

Instructions:

1. This log is to be kept for the next ten days. Information should be recorded as in the above example. Recordings should be made each hour or as close as possible to the hour, beginning in the first hour after getting up in the morning.

2. Keep this copy of the log at home. Use the 4 × 6 cards given to you to record the same information when you are away from home. Transcribe that information onto this form as soon as possible after returning home.

3. This form, and any 4 × 6 cards with information that has not been transcribed, are to be available for each meeting with your worker.

4. If you have difficulties with recording, telephone your worker as soon as possible after the difficulty arises. Your worker can be called at her office (number) from 8:30 A.M. to 5 P.M., Monday through Friday.

her. Identifying ways in which she can meet others who share her interests could then be included in a plan to reduce her depression.

Ann Tripp said that she wanted to observe family interaction during dinner time. Using a prepared form (Table 7.2) she explained that she would record information describing the chore behaviors of each family member by placing a check mark under the name of the person engaging in a task next to that particular chore. Thus, if Nita "set the table," a check mark would be placed under her name in the row listing this chore. If Barry helped, this would be noted under his name. Also recorded would be whether assistance was requested (rather than volunteered); if so, which person asked for help; who was asked to help; whether the person complied with the request; if so, whether compliance was immediate or offered only after the request was repeated. The information in the last column would indicate the manner in which a request was made. Was it "polite" ("Would you please set the table?") or was it made in a disapproving manner ("Why don't you ever help me set the table?"). Ann Tripp chose to observe during dinner time because it is a period when family members naturally get together, allowing for observation under ordinary, everyday circumstances. Also, preparing, serving, and cleaning up after meals involves a number of varied tasks. This increases the chances of observing cooperative behaviors.

The importance of obtaining information through direct observation was discussed with reference to the ease with which clients overlook cooperative behaviors given a problem focus. Thus, any efforts by the children to help might go unnoticed. Problems with compliance could result from incomplete instructions, in which the message doesn't convey the expectations of the parent, or from the method of delivering the message, such as statements that indicate disapproval or are delivered in a sarcastic manner. Observational data would yield detailed information descriptive of how the Carrs manage tasks related to meal preparation, and might shed some light on conditions that impede compliance by the children.

With Sharon Carr's permission, the worker arranged for a foster grandmother to provide respite child care one afternoon per week for three hours.[5] The client agreed to allow the volunteer to record information regarding the visits, such as the types of activities in which she had the children engage, their response to these activities, and information about any conversations between herself and Sharon Carr. The fact that volunteers are sworn to confidentiality provides a safeguard for the client. The foster grandparent's recordings would complement information gained in other ways (she would have the chance to observe the children at play as well as possibly observing their interaction with their mother) and contribute to the final case plan.

TABLE 7.2

Chore Behavior Observation Form

TASKS	PERSON DOING TASK*					WAS ASSISTANCE REQUESTED		OF WHOM					BY WHOM					NUMBER OF TIMES REQUEST MADE PRE-COMPLIANCE	RESULT		REQUEST VERBALIZED**						
	Mo	N	B	S	Ma	yes	no	Mo	N	B	S	Ma	Mo	N	B	S	Ma		Comply	Non-Comply	P	Y	D	S	W	IN	CN
Prepares food																											
Sets table																											
Serves food																											
Clears table																											
Washes dishes																											
-etc.-																											

*Family members: Mo=mother
                     N=Nita
                     B=Barry
                     S=Susan
                     Ma=Marie

**Verbal Behavior Categories:[4]

P=positive   W=whining
Y=yelling   IN=incomplete instructions
D=disapproval   CN=command negative
S=sarcasm

At the conclusion of the interview, Ann Tripp explained the use of contracts, and said that she would like to draft an agreement and bring it to their next meeting for joint review.[6] Sharon Carr was cautioned not to leave the children in anyone's care overnight without first consulting the worker. The court order was still in effect and the judicial admonition regarding child care was binding.

HIGHLIGHTS OF THE INTERVIEW. The worker's intention to help her client is evidenced in several ways. Completing the problem profile—delineating family difficulties from the client's point of view—is one example. Arranging to gather assessment data is another. Since this information is necessary for the development of problem-solving programs, its collection may be considered an initial step in resolving client difficulties. Additionally, Tripp offered immediate assistance by offering to contact Nita's school and by arranging for the services of the foster grandparent.

Involving the client in the process of gathering assessment data lays the groundwork for a cooperative working relationship and implicitly informs the client that an active role must be taken in problem solving. When the worker requested permission to contact collateral resources and for the foster grandparent to record information, she was showing respect for her client's privacy.

MULTIPLE SOURCES OF ASSESSMENT DATA. The reliability of any single source of information is often weak and subject to bias for reasons reviewed in chapter five. Gathering data from different sources and using different data collection methods can be used as an effort to increase information accuracy and detail. Using different sources produces a more thorough picture of family strengths and weaknesses than is possible when there is only one source of information. In this way Tripp may identify cooperative family behaviors through direct observation that are not observed by the foster grandparent or recorded in Sharon Carr's log.

INFORMATION FROM
COLLATERAL RESOURCES

Exchanging information with other professionals is central to child welfare work. Contacts with collaterals are recorded in logs, and the information provided is put in writing and becomes a part of the case record. The resource person is generally asked to submit a written report, which also becomes a part of the record.

Requests for information are made by mail, by telephone, or in person. The method used depends upon the nature of the information to be exchanged, how quickly it is needed, and the time constraints on all parties. In the Andres case, for example, an in-person interview with the psychiatrist might be called for if the doctor wanted to listen to the tape recording of the interview before responding to the worker's question regarding the effects of medication on Marie Andres's speech. If not, a telephone conference might suffice. Use of the telephone is expedient, and for this reason it is probably the most common method workers use to exchange information with others.

Service providers may have worked with families in areas that are unrelated to the concerns of child welfare personnel. Out of respect for client confidentiality, requests for information must be confined to specific items related to assessment or case-planning needs. This is why, in contacting Marie Andres's psychiatrist, Wilson would restrict his questions to the issues of the mother's recovery and the effects of her medication.

Workers can avoid duplicating certain tasks if specific information is available from collaterals. For example, a resource person may have conducted an assessment of parent-child interaction and have observational data describing the frequency of positive and negative verbal exchanges between clients and the topics of conversation most likely to elicit either type of response. Access to this data may eliminate the need to replicate assessment in this area. Ineffective treatment regimes may be eliminated if process and outcome information has been compiled, reducing the range of treatment options. Or, process data can be scrutinized to see if, with certain modifications, an unsuccessful approach to treatment might be made efficacious.

Workers inquire into whether the resource person is currently offering services to the client and, if so, how long this will continue. If both child welfare worker and collateral are concerned with the same areas of family life, the advantages of a cooperative working arrangement to expedite problem resolution and avoid an overlap in service delivery are considered. Workers also ask if collaterals know of others who have worked or are currently working with the family in related areas. It is possible, for instance, that a resource person may have diagnostic information from a child guidance clinic that was not noted in the case record nor reported by the client. Let us review the manner in which workers record information obtained form collaterals.

The memo shown in figure 7.2 summarizes the information that John Wilson obtained from Marie Andres's psychiatrist. The questions asked by the worker or items of information sought are listed in the body of the memo, with the doctor's response recorded under each item. Direct quotations are used when possible. From the conversation it was learned that Marie Andres's depression was so severe as to "ap-

FIGURE 7.2   Memo: Collateral Contact—Andres Family

Memo No. _____   Date: _____   Time of Recording: _____
Time of Interview: _____   Person(s) Contacted: _____
Method of Contact: in-person _____   phone _____   mail _____

PURPOSE OF CONTACT:

1. Gain diagnostic and prognostic information from Marie Andres's psychiatrist.
   Results: She is suffering from depression so "severe as to approximate melancholia." She is "not responsive to therapy." Dr. Yarrow reports that the chances for a "full recovery, while not impossible, are not good."
2. Is there a relationship between Marie Andres's lethargy and speech patterns (see tape of [date]) and her medication?
   Results: Dr. Yarrow reported that the former is a "symptom of Marie Andres's depression," the latter exists "independent of medication."

COMMENTS:

1. Written report requested from Dr. Yarrow. Copy of signed consent-to-release-information form sent to her on (date).
2. Dr. Yarrow states that Raymond Andres is cognizant of his wife's condition. Whether the children are is not clear.
3. *Recommendations:* Discuss this conversation with Raymond Andres alone. The children should be informed of their mother's condition and the psychiatrist's prognosis as a start toward problem resolution. Agree to review this with all family members if the father agrees.
   (a) Contact Family Service Agency. Determine whether they can assist the family resolve difficulties with household management. If so, discuss this alternative with family.
   (b) Hypothesis: referral and dismissal are likely.

---

proximate melancholia," that lethargy was a symptom of her condition, and that changes in her speech patterns had developed independent of medication. She was said not to be responsive to therapy and would not, in the psychiatrist's opinion, fully recover. Raymond Andres had been told this; moreover, he was cautioned not to expect his wife to resume responsibility for household management, nor to apply pressure for her to do so. The psychiatrist did not know whether the children had been told this information.

In the section headed "comments," the worker noted that he asked the doctor to submit a written report and that he would send him a copy of the signed, consent-to-release-information form. The memo concludes with the worker's recommendation that this conversation be reviewed with Raymond Andres, that the psychiatrist's report be shared with the children, and that Wilson participate in a discussion with them if the father agrees. In item 3a, the worker advises contact with a family service agency to learn if they can provide assistance with problems of household management.[7] The reasons why the worker has indicated referral and dismissal as likely outcomes are reviewed later in this chapter. Next, let us review the events that took place at the second meeting with the Carr family.

Second Home Visit With the Carr Family

The worker's objective for the second meeting with the Carr family was to review her draft of the contract and to make any necessary modifications.[8] *The assessment contract* formulated by Ann Tripp and signed by Sharon Carr and her two eldest children is shown in figure 7.3.

The worker and each member of the family are identified in the first paragraph. That the children are residing in their mother's home is noted, as is the fact that the court dependency on the twins is open. The objective of the agreement—to maintain the children in their own home—is reported next, followed by the statement that the worker's assistance in helping the family realize this objective was contingent upon their compliance with an assessment program.

Realizing objectives generally involves attaining a series of goals, each of which describes the changes that are anticipated for clients as a result of participation in problem-solving programs. However, before problem solving-goals can be written, a period of assessment must occur during which family difficulties are identified with a degree of specificity regarding such goals. Thus, initial contracts always contain an assessment goal. Once this information is collected and analyzed, the contract will be amended to include problem-solving goals and a description of how these are to be attained. This is indicated under the heading "consequences." A problem-solving goal to provide Sharon Carr with assistance for household tasks might state as an intention, "to increase the frequency with which each of the children completes household chores." The exact chores assigned to each child and the frequency and time of completion would be delineated as a series of steps. Progress through these steps signals movement toward goal attainment. Attainment of each goal, in turn, signals progress toward realizing the final case objective.

Steps spelled out in this contract describe each client's agreement to engage in the assessment process—for example, Sharon Carr's agreement to maintain a log of daily activities as well as her agreement

FIGURE 7.3   Assessment Contract—Carr Family

NAMES: This contract is entered into between Ann Tripp, Child Welfare Worker for the New City Public Welfare Department, and Sharon Carr, mother of Nita, Barry, Susan, and Marie Carr, minor children currently residing in the home of their mother. Susan and Marie Carr are presently dependents of the New City Juvenile Court.

OBJECTIVE: In keeping with Sharon Carr's wish to maintain her children in her home and the wish of the children to remain in their mother's care, Ann Tripp agrees to assist the Carrs in working towards this objective contingent upon family compliance with a program of assessment.

GOAL: To conduct an assessment of the Carr home, which both Ann Tripp and members of the Carr family agree is necessary in order to identify the specific behaviors, thoughts, and feelings that define family difficulties as well as to identify the conditions that facilitate and maintain family problems.

STEPS: 1. Sharon Carr agrees to maintain a log of her daily activities using the recording forms provided by Ann Tripp and according to the instructions noted on these forms.

(a) Ann Tripp agrees to review Sharon Carr's recordings at five (5) day intervals throughout the contract period, to assist Sharon Carr in resolving any problems that she encounters in recording, to analyze the completed log and to share the results of this analysis with Sharon Carr.

2. Sharon Carr agrees to permit Ann Tripp to visit her home three (3) times within the next ten (10) days to observe family interaction prior to, during, and immediately following the evening meal.

(a) Ann Tripp agrees to share the results of her observations with members of the Carr family at the end of each home visit. Ann Tripp agrees to notify Sharon Carr twenty-four hours in advance of each visit. The Carrs agree to be at home for each scheduled appointment.

3. Sharon Carr agrees to have the foster grandparent, Ethel Chase, record her observations, following guidelines provided by Ann Tripp, during visits with members of the family.

(a) Ann Tripp agrees to share the results of these observations with members of the Carr

(continued)

FIGURE 7.3   (continued)

family. The Carrs agree to be at home for each appointment with the foster grandparent.

4. Ann Tripp agrees to work with Nita Carr toward resolution of her school difficulties. Ann Tripp and Nita agree to meet for three (3), one-hour sessions within fourteen (14) days of the date of this contract. The purpose of these meetings is to identify the particulars of Nita's school problems in order that the most appropriate approach to resolving these can be identified.

CONSEQUENCES: Ann Tripp agrees to assist the Carrs in resolving difficulties identified through any of the above-noted assessment procedures. Ann Tripp will either develop problem-solving programs or enlist the assistance of other community professionals toward this end. This contract will be amended to include a description of problem-solving programs once these are developed. Ann Tripp further agrees to recommend that the dependency on Susan and Marie Carr be dismissed following resolution of any problems which, if not resolved, might reasonably be expected to endanger the safety of the Carr children. Nita Carr is aware that failure to cooperate in identification and resolution of school problems will be reported to school authorities and that such failure is likely to result in her expulsion from Midway High School.

Failure to comply with this program of assessment will result in Ann Tripp's reporting this to the juvenile court and in a formal request that the court order Sharon Carr's involvement with protective services.

TIME LIMITS: This contract will be in effect for a period of fourteen (14) working days, from _____ 1977 to _____ 1977.

SIGNED:

_____   _____
Ann Tripp, Child Welfare   Sharon Carr, mother
Worker

                                  _____
                                  Nita Carr, daughter

                                  _____
                                  Barry Carr, son

to permit worker observation during the evening meal. Note that worker tasks (such as reviewing Sharon Carr's log) are delineated relative to each assessment item, as is Tripp's intention to share all assessment data with her clients.

Clients have a right to be informed of the consequences of participating or not participating in the processes spelled out in contracts. The consequences listed here indicate Tripp's agreement to assist the family in solving identified problems and her willingness to recommend that the court dependency be dismissed following problem resolution. The contract clearly states that Tripp is interested only in problems which, left unresolved, might reasonably be expected to endanger the children. By linking change requirements to the youngsters' safety, clients are protected against arbitrary demands for change that may be unrelated to the objectives of protective services or foster care.

Sanctions for noncompliance are reported; for example, that Nita's failure to cooperate with Ann Tripp in resolving school difficulties will be reported to school authorities and that, should this occur, Nita will be at risk of expulsion. The contract notes that assessment was to be completed within fourteen working days.

AMENDING CONTRACTS. The objectives and goals of contracts are subject to change. The dates established for home visits may be altered due to illness which precludes adhering to the schedule, necessitating an extension of overall time limits for completing the contract. New goals may be written if difficulties emerge as visits between a parent and child in foster care increase in frequency and duration, or after a youngster is placed in a preadoptive home. When timetables are altered, contracts do not have to be rewritten. They may be amended by adding a footnote, or an attachment if the amendment is lengthy. A footnote added to the original document states which of the goals has changed. It is initialed by all parties and the amended goal is tagged with an asterisk or some other notation. For example, an amendment to extend contract time limits might be worded as follows: "This contract is amended to extend the time limits for an additional seven (7) days, from _____, 1977, to _____, 1977. The conditions for assessment set forth in the paragraphs headed 'goals' and 'steps' apply during this extended time period."[9]

DECISION MAKING

Assessment data are evaluated and a decision made whether to intervene, refer, or dismiss a case. Differences in state law, agency policy, and practice preclude delineating guidelines for intervention that would be universally acceptable. Some jurisdictions, for example, permit voluntary placement in foster care contingent upon a request for this service; others allow this only under court order and require evidence that a child is neglected or abused as defined by state law. Thus, Michael Andres's request that his son be placed in foster care would be sufficient to prompt intervention in some regions and not in others.

The assumption that a child is at risk of maltreatment, and that by offering services we can reduce risk, is implicit in most intervention decisions in child welfare. However, this position is always a hypothetical one. We do not know that any single occurrence of maltreatment, regardless of its severity, will lead to a recurrence. Nor do we know that risk is eliminated given specific interventions. Decisions to intervene and to dismiss cases after intervention rest on hypotheses which are based on current knowledge. We assume, for example, that short-term predictions can be made given knowledge of current behavior. If abuse has occurred because parents use physical methods to discipline their children, our best guess would be that unless the parents learn noncorporal methods of punishment, they will resort to the familiar and thus place the child at risk of further abuse.

However, the antecedents of maltreatment are not always easily discerned. What we want but do not have are methods of calculating the likelihood of abuse or neglect occurring on the basis of the parents' social history, their current attitudes towards themselves and their children, their general patterns of child care, and so forth. Using clinical evidence and survey data, it is not difficult to identify a constellation of factors that are, in some way, associated with acts of maltreatment; the vexing question is how these factors should be combined and weighted so that valid predictions of future risk can be made. Researchers are endeavoring to develop instruments to assess the risk of abuse and neglect.[10] The value of current scales is largely heuristic; none as yet have predictive utility. Therefore, errors will occur: intervention will take place when it is not necessary, and it will not take place when it should.

While we cannot specify the exact conditions that increase risk, it is possible to identify factors which suggest that risk is reduced. Absent any of these factors, it is reasonable to argue for an affirmative intervention decision. These criteria and the reasons that their presence suggests reduced risk are reviewed next.

Two minimum criteria for a nonintervention decision are (1) parents must express an interest in providing ongoing care for their children, and (2) the children, if old enough to verbalize a position, must want to remain at home. Without a reciprocal interest in remaining together, we must assume that risk is increased and that an intervention decision is warranted. Secondly, for reasons reviewed elsewhere, confirmed prior reports of abuse or neglect direct attention to the importance of providing services.

Any incidence of abuse must be *reasonably explained* before a nonintervention decision can be considered. The evidence must rule out the possibility that an injury was inflicted with the intention to harm the child or that it resulted from a loss of control.

INTENTION TO HARM.   Intention to harm is inferred by considering the nature of an injury in relation to the child's age. When medical examination uncovers third-degree burns on the buttocks of an infant, cigarette burns on the child's body, or broken bones that could not have been caused by a fall, conclusions regarding intention are drawn; the youngster's age rules out the possibility that an injury was self-inflicted or sustained during play. Knowledge of who was responsible for child care allows for assumptions about the identity of the perpetrator.

LOSS OF CONTROL.   Loss of control is inferred from marks or bruises on the child's body that suggest a beating with an object and indicate a parent's loss of control during punishment. The child's injury need not be severe to indicate either intentionality or loss of control. If these are imputed, risk is high and intervention appropriate even though the child was lucky enough to escape serious harm.

As stated previously, neglect differs from abuse in that it generally involves acts of omission, rather than acts of commission. With the possible exception of abandonment with no provision for child care, intentionality is rarely an issue in single instances of neglect.[11] Unless the situation or conditions are severe, intervention based upon a single episode is unlikely.[12] Inferences about intention may be drawn when parents are unwilling to accept services that are offered to help them modify behaviors that have resulted in neglect, or to correct conditions in the home that they are able to financially. Loss of control is not an issue in neglect.

FAMILY CRISIS.   A family crisis may precede an incident of maltreatment. Crises are frequently precipitated by an identifiable event, such as loss of employment, desertion by a mate, or a death in the family. These are made known through information provided by clients who describe themselves as depressed; evidenced by a falling off of activities (such as household management and social behaviors); and reflected in a chaotic life style. Resumption of activities whose absence partly define the crisis suggests that it has passed.

VISIBILITY.   The risk for children with visibility—who attend school or day-care programs on a regular basis—is less than for those who are rarely seen by persons outside the nuclear family. When parents are socially isolated, with no contacts outside the nuclear family for extended periods of time, risk may increase because visibility is decreased.

The older the child, the more plausible are *alternative explanations* as to the cause of any injury. For example, a physician may report that a youngster's internal injuries were caused by a beating. We might suspect the parent, but if the youngster reports having been "beaten up after school by a gang of kids" and the parents support this, it may be impossible to prove otherwise. Imputing intentionality or loss of control without a confession from parents or confirmation from the child or others who observed the incident may be impossible. Carelessness, rather than malice or loss of control, may cause an injury. An infant whose parent has forgotten to raise the side of a crib may fall and suffer a concussion. A toddler can overturn a pot of boiling water and sustain third-degree burns. When injuries are explained, or when harm may have resulted from carelessness, the decision to intervene is not easily reached on the basis of single criterion. Being able to view criteria in combination therefore becomes critical.

We can say that risk is reduced if (1) parents offer a reasonable explanation for an incident and the child, if old enough, concurs with the explanation, and there is no evidence of intention to harm or loss of control; (2) if maltreatment was preceded by a single crisis and there is evidence that it has passed; (3) the parent, who is financially able, is willing to correct conditions that resulted in a single incident of neglect by seeking medical assistance, correcting dangerous conditions in the home, or arranging for supervision of a child; (4) there are no prior confirmed reports; (5) the parent wants the child at home and the child wants to remain at home; or (6) the child is of school age or is enrolled in a day-care or nursery program and attends regularly.

Any increase in risk indicates the importance of intervention, but leaves unanswered the question, "intervention by whom?" Is action by child welfare staff always necessary, or can we refer cases to others in the community, and so dismiss the case to the public agency, even though there is evidence of maltreatment? The Child Welfare League of America suggests that:

> Protective services may not be necessary in situations where a child has been found neglected or abused if the parents are able to provide care, when they recognize what is expected, and can accept the worker's assistance in obtaining help from an appropriate agency or resource.[13]

Assuming that day care, homemaker services, and counseling programs are available, and assuming further that parents are willing to participate without a court order, that they are eligible for services, and that there are no waiting lists, it is reasonable to make referrals unless the situation requires services by more than one resource. When multiple referrals are indicated, cases should be opened to the child welfare agency because it is essential that one person assume responsibility for coordinating service delivery.

Information gathered during assessment is organized and the items most pertinent to decision making are summarized. These include (1) information describing the family in relation to the risk-reducing factors listed previously (such as the information that parents and children offer to explain an incident of maltreatment, or the parents' attitude toward providing ongoing care); (2) a list of the methods used to gather this information, allowing for an evaluation of the quality of assessment data (for example, the suggestion that a crisis has passed may be based on the client's verbal reports to that effect, verbal reports by others indicating that the client has resumed activities which ceased during the crisis, and by direct observation from which the worker has recorded increases in positive exchanges between parent and child); (3) other types of evidence—X rays, photographs, and depositions from witnesses, for instance—available to support a charge of maltreatment and listed by the data-gathering source (such as a child welfare worker or physician); (4) the reason a service was requested or a case was referred or reported; (5) the applicable statute, if court action is to be taken; (6) pertinent information summarized from prior reports (such as the type of incident reported and the actions that were taken); (7) information describing prior services provided for related problems and the outcome of client involvement in service programs; (8) options for resolving family difficulties, followed by the worker's hypothesis as to the most appropriate course of action; and (9) the worker's recommendations for case disposition that follow from the preceding information. Workers consult with their supervisors or with team members before a final determination is made.

Supervisory Consultation

Supervisors occupy pivotal positions in child welfare agencies. They familiarize new staff with agency policy and provide training in case management. More experienced personnel are kept up-to-date with changes in agency policy and law and with innovative approaches to practice. Supervisors provide guidance for workers by offering consultation on any aspect of case management, and they monitor case progress throughout service delivery. Persons occupying this position generally have more direct access to agency administrators than do workers. For this reason, they are in a position to interpret administrative concerns to staff and vice versa.[14] More experienced workers act with relative autonomy, submitting pertinent case materials in summary form and consulting with their supervisors when necessary.

The Carr and Andres Decisions Contrasted

An affirmative intervention decision in the Carr case was made on the following basis. First, Sharon Carr's having "abandoned the children to the care of her sister," was similar to a prior confirmed report and the court dependency was still open. Her past behavior may be seen as a response to a personal crisis, defined with reference to her depression and feelings of being overwhelmed with household responsibilities. Eighteen months after the initial placement the situation had not changed, although services were offered; and Sharon Carr did not want the twins at home, as evidenced by her request to renew their placement. In addition, Nita was at risk of being expelled from school, and the school did not have resources for counseling the young woman. While there is no evidence of current maltreatment, the worker hypothesized that unless services were provided to effectively reduce or eliminate the problems, there might be additional supervisorial neglect. Since there were multiple problems, a referral was not appropriate.

The Andres case lacked certain essential elements for an intervention decision. There was no evidence of maltreatment, nor any objective basis for a risk hypothesis, and there were no prior reports. Additionally, resources in the community could provide assistance for solving family problems.[15]

Assessment information for the Carr family is presented in the next chapter, where its use for case planning is illustrated.

THE DECISION TO PLACE CHILDREN IN OUT-OF-HOME CARE

Child welfare workers are often confronted with the decision whether to place children in out-of-home care. This choice is a difficult one, with serious implications for all family members. There is a growing consensus that children should not be removed unless they are clearly in danger in their own homes.[16] Several arguments can be advanced in support of a conservative stand toward placement. First, parents who receive AFDC grants lose some if not all of their benefits following removal of their children. They must then find new housing, unless they are able to replace lost income through employment. Prior to having their children returned, they will have to relocate once again to housing that is sufficient to accommodate all family members. The latter may prove difficult unless state law allows for resumption of AFDC payments at least thirty days prior to a restoration. If this is not possible, and the agency does not have an emergency loan fund, the client must either have employment or must be able to borrow money to relocate. Also, parents can be made to feel inadequate when children are removed, and children to feel that they are to blame for family breakup. So in addition to the problems that necessitated placement, others may be created by the fact of placement. Further, both assessment and treatment occur under artificial conditions once a child enters care. For example, observation of parent-child interaction during one weekly hour-long visit (which often occurs in a worker's office or the foster home) is not the optimal framework for learning about the conditions that facilitated and maintained family problems when the child was at home. And there is no reason to expect changes that occur during placement to generalize to the home situation. Also, problems that necessitated foster care can decrease simply because stress is reduced, only to reemerge once the child is returned. Finally, biological families may accommodate themselves to a new life style, the maintenance of which is contingent upon not resuming responsibility for their children, and parents and their children may become emotionally estranged.

Out-of-home placement in temporary foster care is called for when (1) there is no adult willing to care for a child, or the child is unwilling to stay at home; (2) there is medical evidence that physical abuse or nutritional neglect is so severe as to be life threatening; (3) even if an injury is not severe, there was intent to kill the child, evidenced by poisoning or assault with a deadly weapon, or when a child was repeatedly beaten with a heavy object; (4) there is evidence of abuse or neglect which, without intervention, may threaten the child's life and the parents refuse help; (5) medical evidence of repeated abuse[17] exists; (6) severe abuse or neglect recurs after services were offered; (7) severe emotional abuse is evidenced by extreme behavioral disturbance or withdrawal by the child and parental rejection; (8) evidence suggests that the parent is incompetent and there are no resources (family, friend, or community services) to help in the home while assessment is underway; or (9) if a child has been raped by a related adult, or a nonrelated adult known to the parent and the parent did not attempt to protect the child.[18]

When there is evidence of sexual abuse, some states remove the child, others the parent.[19] Recognizing that, frequently, incest is ongoing, that the uninvolved as well as the involved parent is often aware of it and that both, in fact, may have helped contain it in the family unit for some time before the matter became public, coupled with the equivocal evidence regarding its effects on the child, some professionals have taken the position that the family unit should not be broken up if treatment services are available and the family is willing to accept services.[20]

Incest is often repugnant to professionals and the decision to remove a parent often proceeds on moral grounds. If the act is acknowledged by parents who want assistance and help is available; if the child wants to remain at home; and if the casework objective is to strengthen and restore family life, it can be argued that placement is not appropriate. If any of these criteria are absent, action to safeguard the child by removal becomes more creditable.

THE DECISION TO REFER CASES TO COURT

Given an affirmative intervention decision, another decision must be made as to whether to petition the court to have a child made a dependent. In some states, once a finding of maltreatment has been made, statutory law requires that it be reported to the court. And agency policy may necessitate a court order before a child can be placed in a foster home. Other conditions allow for voluntary provision of services if parents are agreeable and if, in the worker's judgment, this is appropriate.

It has been argued that court involvement can be therapeutic; that the authority of the court may be instrumental in increasing the chances of family compliance with case planning and service delivery. The court's ability to objectively monitor progress toward case goals and reduce the chance that children will drift into unplanned, long-term care is yet another argument in favor of court action.[21] Countering these positions is the suggestion that court involvement is not necessary when parents are cooperative. It is argued that the courts can impede development of a working relationship because they increase the law enforcement dimension of the worker's role. Clients may perceive service delivery as threatening rather than helpful.

There is no question as to the correctness of court action when parents are uncooperative, or if, after accepting a voluntary role, they withdraw against the worker's advice. And there is evidence to support the value of court review in achieving permanent plans. It is possible, however, that this value might be realized with agency or citizen review panels. Data comparing the effectiveness of different review procedures are not available.

Court action is costly in actual dollars and in workers' time, and it is not difficult to argue, in the absence of evidence to the contrary, that it should not be used as long as parents do cooperate. Workers should, however, bear in mind the possibility of court action in documenting cases, despite initial convictions that it is not needed. It is extremely difficult, if not impossible, to reconstruct evidence in a manner acceptable to the court months after it has been gathered and recorded.

If court action is to be taken, parents should be told that a petition is being filed, the basis for it, what their rights are, and the consequences of court action. Workers should assist them in obtaining counsel if they so desire, and when there is a contest between parents and children, separate counsel for each should be appointed.

SUMMARY

The investigative process begins when workers visit families in their homes. It ends with either a nonintervention decision or when data necessary to formulate a case plan have been gathered.

Assessment information is collected by child welfare workers who are skilled in direct observation and are trained to isolate indicators of maltreatment, and by other professionals, such as medical personnel, whose expertise is needed to diagnose medical neglect and physical or sexual abuse.

Given an affirmative intervention decision, workers must decide whether to invoke court action and whether a child can remain safely at home or must be placed in substitute care.

Workers prepare for home visits by developing an outline in which items of information they want to exchange with and elicit from clients are noted. The development of an outline is informed by the data provided by clients, by referring sources, or by persons filing reports of maltreatment.

In order to preserve accurately the information exchanged during interviews, a worker makes notes as soon as possible following the interview.

Multiple sources for assessment data are used in order to reduce the bias inherent in any single method of gathering information and to increase accuracy and detail.

Accordingly, clients may be asked to maintain logs of their daily activities, and workers to engage in direct observation of parent-child interaction, and to arrange for information to be compiled by others important to the client.

Workers exchange information with collateral resources who may have assessment, treatment, or medical data.

Clients' objectives in working with any service may be formulated into written contracts which inform all concerned parties of the goals that must be attained to realize objectives, the steps to be taken by worker and client to realize goals, the consequences for the client of participating or not participating in problem-solving programs, and the time limits for accomplishing objectives and goals.

Initial contracts with clients contain a goal allowing for the collection of assessment data and describing the steps necessary to compile such data.

Implicit in the decision to intervene in family life is the assumption that interventions will reduce risk for the children involved.

It is reasonable to suggest that risk has been reduced without intervention when, for example, parents want to provide ongoing care for children who want to remain at home, when evidence suggests that a single crisis has passed, when parents and children offer reasonable explanations for an incident of maltreatment, and when there are no prior, confirmed reports.

If parents are willing to provide care and will voluntarily accept the services of a community agency, referrals may be made despite evidence of maltreatment.

When family difficulties require the services of more than one community agency, it may be advisable to open the case to the child welfare agency in order for the worker to coordinate services.

Workers generally consult with their supervisors and members of a team before reaching a final intervention decision.

Children should not be removed from their own homes unless evidence indicates that they are in danger if left in their parent's care.

Parental unwillingness to provide ongoing care, medical evidence of repeated abuse, and evidence of severe emotional disturbance accompanied by parental rejection of a child support a high-risk hypothesis and indicate the appropriateness of a child's removal into temporary care.

Opinions differ as to the wisdom of court referrals for all cases.

Those favoring court involvement argue that the authority of the court may increase the likelihood of parental cooperation with workers and that the court can serve as an objective monitor of case progress toward goals.

Opponents of mandatory court action suggest that court involvement may impede the development of a positive relationship between worker and client and that court action is costly in time and dollars.

Unless mandated by state law, it is reasonable to question whether cases should be referred to court when parents are willing to accept services.

NOTES

1. Throughout the interview, Marie Andres responded to the worker's questions with hesitancy. In some instances there was an interval of one minute between completing one statement and beginning another. Many of her sentences were incomplete, wandering from one thought to another, and her speech was slurred.

2. The worker could have asked this directly, but chose not to confront Raymond Andres with this question in front of the children.

3. For a discussion of different types of logs and their value as assessment tools, see: Arthur Schwartz and Israel Goldiamond, *Social Casework: A Behavioral Approach* (New York: Columbia University Press, 1975), pp. 104–12.

4. For examples of the types of verbal statements defining these categories, see: Theodore J. Stein and Eileen D. Gambrill, *Decision Making in Foster Care: A Training Manual* (Berkeley: University of California Extension Press, 1976), p. 99.

5. Foster grandparent programs are generally staffed by senior citizen volunteers. By offering child-care services they provide respite for single parents.

6. Clients must be socialized to the use of written contracts since, in all likelihood, their use will be new to them. The use of written agreements, particularly their advantages to the client, are spelled out in chapter five, p. 133.

7. From contact with a social worker at the youngster's school, John Wilson learned that the daughter's school work was "not up to par." Her grades had dropped over the past year, while her brother had maintained his academic standing. There was no indication of attendance or behavior problems for either youngster.

8. Prior to this meeting, Ann Tripp contacted the community mental health center where Sharon Carr had attended group therapy, as well as the counselor at Nita's school. The person who had led the mother's group was no longer with the center. A supervisor checked Sharon Carr's record for information regarding the mother's progress in treatment. Nothing was available other than what had been reported at the initial review hearing. There was a meeting at Nita's school, attended by Ann Tripp, Sharon Carr, and Nita. It was learned that the young woman had missed an average of two days of school per week for a three-month period, that she was "failing in three subjects" and was at risk of expulsion. Nita had not responded to two memos in which the counselor had requested a meeting to discuss these difficulties. The school had no counseling services save for career related ones, thus there were no school based resources for assisting Nita. The school principal agreed to defer his expulsion edict given Ann Tripp's agreement to work with the young woman toward resolution of school problems.

9. For additional discussion and examples of contract amendments, see: Stein, *Decision Making*, pp. 41–44.

10. R. E. Helfer, "Basic Issues Concerning Prediction," in Ray E. Helfer and C. Henry Kempe, (eds.) *Child Abuse and Neglect: The Family and the Community* (Cambridge, Mass.: Ballinger Publishing Co., 1976), pp. 363–75; C. A. Carroll, "The Social Worker's Evaluation," in Barton D. Schmitt (ed.) *The Child Protection Team Handbook* (New York: Garland STPM Press, 1976), pp. 105–8; Norman A. Polansky and Christine DeSaix, *Roots of Futility* (San Francisco: Jossey-Bass, Inc., Publishers, 1972); N. A. Polansky, M. A. Chalmers, E. Buttenwiesser, and D. Williams, "Assessing Adequacy of Child Caring: An Urban Scale," *Child Welfare*, Vol. LVII, No. 7 (July/August 1978), pp. 439–49.

11. When a parent abandons a child to the care of another adult (the Carr case illustrates this) it is not correct to infer an intention to harm since provisions for child care were made.

12. Evidence of severe neglect might be the child's physical condition which cannot be corrected absent hospitalization (extreme nutritional neglect,

for example) or conditions of the home, such as exposed electrical wiring, which pose an imminent fire hazard (shelter neglect).

13. Child Welfare League of America, *Standards for Child Protective Service* (New York: Child Welfare League of America, Inc., 1973: Revised), p. 26.

14. Eileen D. Gambrill and Theodore J. Stein, *Supervision in Child Welfare: A Training Manual* (Berkeley: University of California Extension Press, 1978), p. 1.

15. Raymond Andres had not told his children that their mother was unlikely to recover. However, the children said that they had "guessed that their mother would stay as she was for a time." The family chose to hire part-time help to assist with heavy household chores and to share responsibility for daily tasks such as shopping and meal preparation. The worker gave them the telephone number of a family service agency and recommended that they contact the agency should assistance with this difficulty be required at a later time.

16. Institute of Judicial Administration, American Bar Association, Joint Commission on Juvenile Justice Standards, *Standards Relating to Abuse and Neglect* (tentative draft, 1977); C. Kleinkauf and B. McGuire, "Alaska's Children Code," *Child Welfare*, Vol. LVII, No. 8 (September/October 1978), pp. 485–96; K. T. Wiltse, "Current Issues and New Directions in Foster Care," in *Child Welfare Strategy in the Coming Years* (U.S. Dept. of Health, Education and Welfare, Children's Bureau, DHEW publication No. (OHDS) 78-30158), pp. 51–89; R. H. Mnookin, "Foster Care—In Whose Best Interest?" *Harvard Educational Review*, Reprint Series No. 9(1974), p. 185; R. Bourne and E. H. Newberger, "Ambiguity and Conflict in the Proposed Standards for Child Abuse and Neglect," in Richard Bourne and Eli H. Newberger (eds.) *Critical Perspectives on Child Abuse* (Lexington, Mass.: Lexington Books, D. C. Heath & Co., 1979), p. 112.

17. This reference is to prior untreated injuries (generally identified through X ray) where the location or type of injury hints at past abuse.

18. It has been suggested that children be removed if a parent is considered dangerous (defined, for example, with reference to police reports and prior incarcerations, drug addiction, or severe alcoholism); see: B. D. Schmitt and L. L. Loy, "Team Decisions on Case Management," in Schmitt, *Protection Team Handbook*, pp. 191, 193–94). The difficulties in trying to predict whether someone is "dangerous" were highlighted in 1974 when the California State Supreme Court ruled that a "therapist must warn [a] *potential* victim of a client's threat." (Tarasoff v. Regents of the University of California 529 P. 2d 553 Cal. S. Ct. 1974). Psychiatric response to this (despite years of using preventative detention by asserting dangerousness to lock people up) was to claim that psychiatry was far too inexact a science to make such predictions, *Law and Behavior Quarterly*, Vol. 1, No. 4 (Champaign, Ill.: Research Press Co., Fall 1976), pp. 1–2.

19. The concept of sexual abuse is not clearly defined. Except for incest (sexual intercourse with other members of the family which should not be confused with rape since the latter always involves force) and acts of oral copulation, the boundaries are not clear. See Michael Wald, "State Intervention on Behalf of 'Neglected' Children: A Search for Realistic Standards," *Stanford Law Review*, Vol. 27 (April 1975), p. 1024, fn 203.

20. Ibid, pp. 1024–27; Blair Justice and Rita Justice, *The Broken Taboo: Sex in the Family* (New York: Human Sciences Press, 1979), Ch. 15; C. E.

Gentry, "Incestuous Abuse of Children: The Need for an Objective View," *Child Welfare*, Vol. LVII, No. 6 (June 1978), pp. 355–64.

21. *Protective Services for Abused and Neglected Children and Their Families: A Guide* (New York: Community Research Applications, Inc., n.d.), pp. 61–62; *Standards for Child Protective Services*, Ch. 4.

8

Case Planning

When the investigation has been completed and the intervention deci-sion is affirmative, case plans are formulated. A case plan begins with a statement of the client's objectives in working with the child welfare agency. Based on an analysis of assessment data, problem-solving goals are established, the most appropriate procedures for solving problems are identified, and decisions are made as to whether services will be offered by the child welfare worker, by others in the community, or by both. The methods that client, worker, and collateral will use to resolve problems are described, time limits for attaining goals and overall ob-jectives are established, and the consequences of client involvement or noninvolvement in the case-planning process are described. (figure 8.1). Written contracts provide a framework within which case-planning information is explicated.

Case plans are implemented when service delivery begins. The activities of service providers are coordinated and client progress toward goals is monitored. The reverse arrow in figure 8.1 highlights the fact that service delivery efforts may be repeated, providing clients every opportunity to realize their objectives before alternatives that will provide permanent homes for children are pursued.

Decision making, gathering and recording information, and court

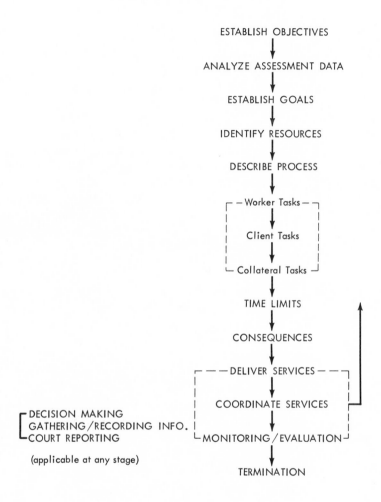

FIGURE 8.1 Case Planning Flow Chart

reporting appear at one side of this diagram in recognition of the fact that the former items occur throughout case planning while court reporting may occur at any time (or more than once) in the life of a case plan.

Termination is the point at which active service delivery comes to an end. It occurs when evaluation of data shows that goals and objectives have been realized. Termination and case follow-up are the subjects of chapter nine. The steps in case planning will now be described in detail.

STEPS IN CASE PLANNING

Objectives

The conditions that all parties to a case plan would like to see when service delivery is complete are called objectives. Objectives are finite, identifiable in relation to the range of outcomes for any area of service. For instance, when a child first enters foster home care, many options are open. The youngster may ultimately be reunited with biological parents, placed in an adoptive home, have a legal guardian appointed, or have a planned, long-term foster care placement arranged or plans for the youngster's emancipation may be formulated. The range of objectives may narrow as the situation of the child and the natural and foster parents changes. Options for a child who has been in out-of-home placement for several years may be limited if he or she cannot be restored to the natural parents and if the foster parents cannot assume the role of adoptive parents. Here, case objectives may focus on the appointment of a legal guardian or on planning a long-term placement.

By law and social custom, natural parents, unless they refuse to participate in planning, have the right to decide on case objectives. They are asked, "What are your plans for the future living arrangements of your child?" Children who are old enough to voice an opinion participate in reaching this decision. Efforts to verbally assess a client's motivation to work towards objectives often are not productive. Ongoing client involvement in case-planning activities will attest to motivational factors. Thus, clients are taken at their word, and the worker assumes responsibility for giving parents the opportunity to realize their objectives. When clients do not participate in case planning, workers must identify objectives by pursuing the alternative most likely to maximize the child's chances for permanency.

Analysis of Assessment Data

Assessment data are analyzed and the results used to establish problem-solving goals. In analyzing Sharon Carr's log, Ann Tripp began by scanning the entries in the activities column and grouping these into categories which describe how the client spent her time. Five such groupings emerged; these were (1) sitting alone and thinking, (2) personal endeavors (things that she did for herself), (3) interaction with family members, (4) interaction with friends, and (5) household management.

Next, the worker looked for consistent relationships between activity categories and the client's evaluation of these activities (comments column), which allow the identification of behaviors which define the client's problem (those activities which are repeatedly evaluated in a negative manner) as well as those that signal client strengths (activities continually evaluated in a positive manner). If the activities in any single category are evaluated differently, a search begins for correlates of positive or negative evaluations. Do these vary systematically in relation to the time of day, to the presence of certain persons, or to the situation in which the recording and evaluation took place? (Some detailed assessment data from the Carr case are presented later in this chapter.)

Careful attention to these relationships is critical for setting goals and for identifying appropriate interventions. For example, if all Sharon Carr's evening activities fell into the two categories of sitting alone and thinking and interaction with friends, and if the former were evaluated negatively and the latter positively, a problem-solving goal might be "to increase the frequency with which she engages in activities with friends." Intervention to achieve this might, depending upon the client's skills, involve her in an assertiveness training group (if she lacked skill in meeting others) or given such skills, on arranging for her to participate in activities at a community center.

Since "sitting alone and thinking and engaging in activities with friends," occur in the same time frame, and since one cannot simultaneously engage in both, increases in time spent with friends should reduce the amount of time spent in isolation, resulting in a net gain in positive evaluations.

Initially, the suggestion that any given intervention will reduce or eliminate a problem is hypothetical. One of the reasons why client progress in problem-solving programs is monitored is so that interventions can be modified if the data do not support the initial hypothesis. Careful analysis of assessment information increases the chance that initial hypotheses will turn out to be correct.

Establishing Goals

Most case plans contain three major categories of information, beginning with a statement of case objectives. Next, the conditions necessary to attain objectives—expressed as goals in which the changes in family life which reduce or elimiante problems—are described. Last, the processes by which these conditions will be brought about (approximations or steps in which worker, client, and others will engage to bring about goal attainment) are explicated.

Goals should be *specific,* identifying exact behaviors in which clients and professionals must engage to realize goals, the frequency and duration of tasks to be performed, and the conditions or situations in which task-oriented behaviors are to be displayed. When behaviors, situations, and frequency are unvarying over time, the weight of specificity can be placed directly on the goal statement. For example, "Sara Smith will visit with her child (expected behavior) in the foster home (situation) every Saturday afternoon (frequency) from 2:00 p.m. to 4:00 p.m. (duration). Harry Jones, child welfare worker, will provide transportation for these visits (worker task).

When behaviors, situations, and frequency vary over time, the goal can be written in more general terms and the weight of specificity carried by the process information, which is reported along with the goal statement. "To increase the frequency with which Sara Smith visits her son who is in foster care until mother and son are visiting for four consecutive days," is illustrative of a goal phrased in more general terms. Frequency is not defined, nor are the location or duration of visits spelled out. The process by which this goal is to be attained is then described as a series of steps in which the specifics missing from the above are reported. For instance, "for one month, from August 20 to September 19, Sara Smith will visit her son in the foster home on Saturday afternoon from 2 p.m. to 4 p.m. In the second month she will visit with her son in her own home each Saturday from 1 p.m. to 5 p.m. In subsequent months the duration and frequency of visits would be increased and their location varied until the final goal of a four-day visit is achieved.

When goals describe behavior that is to occur at a single point of time, neither frequency nor duration are relevant items of information. "Alice Washington will sign up for food stamps at the West Side Distribution Center within ten days," is an example.

A further exception to the requirement for specificity can be noted. This directs attention to situations where problem-solving services are provided by a community resource. Ideally, all of the steps to be followed in a treatment program should be spelled out. However, when services are offered by others, this information may not be accessible. And so, a goal might state that "to increase Len Wylkes's child-care skills, he will attend parenting classes at the Rule Community Center every Saturday afternoon from 1 p.m. to 3 p.m. and participate in a program of activities according to the instructions of Sonia Garcia, program director." There is no specific information describing the process that will be followed to increase his skills. While less than optimal, case planning must proceed in this manner when specific information is not at hand.

Goals should be *descriptive*, directing attention to observable and measurable criteria, the presence of which signify goal attainment. And they should be written in *positive language*, describing behaviors to be increased, rather than focusing on what is to be decreased or eliminated. It is generally easier to reduce or eliminate undesirable behaviors by increasing desirable ones, and unless clients have recourse to helpful alternatives, the chances are good that they will resort to problematic approaches when confronted with difficult situations. For example, a client who is admonished not to use physical punishment with a child who has been abused must acquire skills at noncorporal methods of discipline if he or she is to honor this admonition. With Sharon Carr, it would make little sense to write a goal stating that she will no longer be depressed. Rather, Ann Tripp's task is to identify behaviors that are incompatible with those to be decreased and to write the goal in terms of increasing those behaviors least likely to result in negative evaluations by her client.[1] One of the measures to eliminate Sharon Carr's depression focused on increasing the frequency with which she interacted with friends, since she identified this as a rewarding experience. Time spent in this manner would reduce the amount of time spent sitting alone and thinking, which was correlated with depression. Many of the problems that child welfare staff confront must be attacked indirectly, by decreasing incompatible behaviors and by creating changes in the conditions that facilitate and maintain problem behaviors.[2]

Describing behaviors to be increased directs attention to the interventions necessary to bring about change. To attain the goal of increasing the time Sharon Carr spends with friends, Ann Tripp had to consider whether the client knew where to go to meet others, whether she had the skills necessary to approach strangers in different social situations, and whether child care was available. Descriptive terminology also helps to keep goals at a realistic, attainable level, rather than an idealized one. If vague, nondescriptive terminology is used in formulating goals (for example, "Laura Young will increase her understanding of her child's emotional needs.") outcome criteria are unclear. What is the yardstick for evaluating "increased understanding of emotional needs?" Such vagueness makes identifying methods of attaining goals a difficult, if not impossible, task.

A fully described goal may be an incentive for clients, who are thereby informed of precisely what they must do, and the situation, frequency, and duration of such activities. Furthermore, they are aware of what will be done for them, and are afforded protection against arbitrary demands for change that often occur when evaluative criteria are not clear.

The majority of families have multiple problems, so that several goals must be established to reach overall case objectives. It is often the case that pursuing certain goals is contingent upon completion or near completion of others. For instance, if eliminating drug use, finding work, and locating new housing are required, fully descriptive goals for the latter items need not be written until evidence shows progress in eliminating drug dependency, assuming that the dependency precludes holding down a job. When this occurs, the case plan indicates the importance of finding work and locating new housing as conditions for realizing objectives. However, specific goal statements and information describing the process of attaining these are not initially formulated. Rather, the plan notes that this will be done when evidence shows that substance abuse has been controlled.

Analysis of assessment data is only one of four ways in which goals are identified. Some goals are common to all cases at a given stage of service delivery, others to all cases within a given area of service. The discussion of including assessment goals in all initial contracts with clients illustrates the former. Assessment is necessary whether a case plan is drafted by protective service or foster care staff or an adoption staff who are concerned with resolving post-adoption difficulties. Goals to facilitate parent-child visits are found in all foster-care plans when restoration is an objective, and goals to complete the legal requirements of the adoption process exist in all adoption case plans. The court is another source of goal identification. A judge may order parents to submit themselves for a psychiatric evaluation or require them to participate in a particular therapeutic program. Before reviewing issues related to the identification of problem-solving resources, additional comments regarding process information are in order, as is a discussion of time limits and consequences.

Process Information

This term applies to a series of steps, or approximations, that client, worker, and others involved in problem-solving programs will take to achieve goals. Approximations bridge the gap between a client's present situation and the situation envisioned when goals are met. The selection of steps begins with an identification of client assets (their current strengths relative to the problem at hand) and proceeds by building on these in an incremental manner until goals are accomplished. A visiting schedule with monthly changes in the location, frequency, and duration of visits illustrates this. The clients' visiting patterns when the goal is first developed are their immediate strength, or the starting point for describing the process of attaining the final goal.[3] The worker then delineates the remaining steps, and through the use of supportive methods reinforces the client for progress at each step.

There are several reasons why steps should be identified and put in writing. First, informing clients of what they must do to realize goals, as well as what will be done to assist them, provides an objective basis for clients to decide whether to participate in problem-solving programs. As already noted, the specificity of this information may be an incentive for ongoing client involvement. Putting steps in writing provides clients with a checklist on which they can mark off task completion, and it reduces the margin for misunderstanding what must be done, where, and with what frequency. With the checklist the client has a visible reminder of daily or weekly activities. Since client progress is monitored, if case planning breaks down, the worker is able to identify the point at which difficulties were encountered. For example, if the client whose visiting schedule was increased from two hours per week to a four-day visit proceeds through a series of steps and then stops at the point of visiting for six hours once each week, a worker might hypothesize that the next step (eight hours per week) was too large an increase. Perhaps six hours exhausts the client's repertoire for positive interaction with a child. If the point of breakdown is identified, the worker is able to observe parent-child interaction and test the hypothesis regarding skill deficits and take corrective action, moving the case toward goal attainment. Steps should be small, affording the client the opportunity to experience success. It is safer to increase visits in one-hour increments than in two- or three-hour jumps. If clients proceed comfortably through each of the beginning steps in a case plan, the plan can be accelerated and goals attained earlier than expected. In general, it is easier to accelerate than it is to decelerate the approximations in a case plan.

Time Limits.   These are set for attaining specific goals and realizing overall objectives. Informing clients of the approximate duration of their involvement with social services may increase the likelihood of ongoing involvement. Time limits are important for the worker who is informed of the exact changes that are to be observed at specified times, allowing for review and, if necessary, modification of plans if anticipated changes are not evidenced. And time limits are of special importance to foster-care workers who must consider alternatives for permanency with due regard to the relationship between permanency options and the length of time the child is in care.

Time limits may be derived from the worker's experience, which suggests the approximate length of time needed to conduct an assessment or to resolve any problems for which he or she will assume responsibility in direct intervention. Limits may also be derived from empirical literature and the suggestions contained therein for the duration of treatments, and from collateral resources, who will assume responsibility for problem solving. Time limits for attaining overall objectives are identified by referring to that goal whose resolution requires the greatest time investment.

CONSEQUENCES.   These express the worker's agreement to support client objectives as well as the worker's intention to pursue permanency-planning options should parents withdraw from the planning process. Consequences, then, describe positive and negative sanctions of participating or not particiapting in the case-planning process. The description of consequences in the assessment contract with the Carr family illustrates this.

Understandably, workers may be uncomfortable outlining negative sanctions. That they do so is imperative, however, since the actions described are often necessary if the goals of assuring permanent homes for children are to be realized. Also, clients have the right to know what actions will be taken if they choose not to continue with a case plan.

Identifying Resources

In the best of all possible worlds workers would have a full armamentarium of services to offer clients. Moreover, they would have information concerning the effectiveness of a given intervention with a given problem as well as information about the populations most likely to benefit from certain treatments. If we knew that social isolation of a single parent triggered an abusive act and that there was a 75 percent probability of reducing or eliminating isolation by having a parent participate in "stress-away" therapy for six months at weekly intervals of one hour's duration, decisions regarding the selection of treatment programs would not be difficult.

In our less than ideal world we encounter problems. Services are in short supply in most areas of the country, and studies comparing the relative effectiveness of different approaches to helping abusive and neglectful families are few. So even if services were plentiful, the lack of comparative data is a barrier to program selection. Particularly troublesome is the dearth of information descriptive of the procedures followed in many counseling programs. For this reason, knowledge that program "A" had been effective in eliminating substance abuse would not be a sufficient basis for assuming that another program of the same name would achieve similar results. Despite these limitations, programs must be selected. The following guidelines direct attention to areas that workers concern themselves with when selecting treatment programs. Information gathered from community professionals should be put in writing to serve as a resource directory for others.

SELECTION OF TREATMENT PROGRAMS.   Whether resource persons are *able* to work toward the goals established for a case plan and whether they are *willing* to do so must both be determined. Ability refers to the presence of specific problem-solving skills, asking questions such as, "Does the resource person have the skills to reduce or eliminate substance abuse?" Willingness refers to issues of timing and to the possibility that resource staff may not accept the goals set by a child welfare worker. For instance, a community health counselor may be able to assist a client to increase self-assertion skills, but be unwilling to offer this service apart from a broader program which seeks to modify client attitudes toward self and others. While the latter may be useful to the client, the change objective of the resource person may be far in excess of what is deemed necessary to restore a child from foster care or to dismiss protective services. An extension of time limits necessitated by programs with broader change objectives may not be acceptable. Thus, resource persons are asked if they are *able* to help clients realize the goals established in a case plan, if they are willing to work toward the goals defined by the worker, and if they will restrict their change efforts to attaining identified goals in as expedient a manner as possible.

The importance of clarifying the objectives and goals of each case with community personnel and the willingness of resource persons to accept the clients' and workers' objectives and goals and to restrict their activities accordingly cannot be overstated. Unless responsibilities are clearly defined, each of several resource persons may give the client conflicting advice about the same problems. For example, the advice given by a counselor whose orientation is psychodynamic may differ markedly from the advice given by one whose approach to problem solving derives from sociobehavioral theory. The conflicts that can result for the client from discrepant advice can only impede progress toward the solution of problems. In the absence of mutual agreement on the conditions that constitute goal attainment, different "agendas" may be in operation. While the child welfare worker is striving to restore or strengthen family life by focusing on bringing parental standards up to a defined minimum, the resource person may be seeking to structure programs based on long-range predictions as to what is in the child's best interest and so endeavoring to improve the overall quality of life for the clients. This is not to suggest that improving the overall quality of a client's life is not important. It is questionable, however, whether trying to attain such ends falls within the mandate of public child welfare agencies.

In addition to a concern with whether any single change objective should focus on minimum standards of parenting or aim for far-reaching improvement in family life, workers are frequently confronted with making decisions as to whether all or only some of the problems presented by a family must be resolved to realize case objectives. Since the overriding objective of child welfare services is to achieve permanency for children, either in their own homes or in substitute care situations, it is reasonable to argue that workers should center their activities on a subset of all family problems—specifically, on those that directly affect the child's well-being.[4] A useful guideline in reaching critical decisions as to what problems must be dealt with is to ask whether the child will be endangered, and if so in what ways, if any given problem is not resolved. It is important to remember that clients can be referred for assistance with problems that do not directly affect their children and that they can continue with counseling programs that aim for improvement in the quality of life after child services are dismissed.

Information on the *methods* professionals use to resolve problems is important. It behooves workers to familiarize themselves with the professional literature and the evidence reported therein regarding the effectiveness of different approaches to problem solving. Thus, if a counselor reports that she treats alcohol problems with psychoanalytic or transactional methods, the worker is better able to evaluate the likelihood of either approach furthering goal attainment. Workers learn to be consumers of research, to acquire the skills necessary to evaluate the methodology used in any study, thereby permitting an objective assessment of the conclusions drawn by the reporter.

Whether identified methods are those of an individual counselor or reflect agency policy regarding treatment should be determined. In many community mental health settings workers practice with relative autonomy. For this reason, a treatment approach described by one worker cannot be presumed to reflect all practice within the agency.

Process information, particularly with reference to the tasks in which clients will have to engage to achieve goals, is important. While specific elements of process are subject to modification as programs progress, task explication is essential for an evaluation of the *feasibility* of a treatment plan. Questions regarding feasibility ask, "What does this program require of the client? Is he or she expected to go to weekly counseling sessions and if so does this fit in with his or her work schedule? Is transportation available and at what cost? Are there child-care services for the nonworking parent who does not have the resources to hire a babysitter? Does involvement in the program require specific skills and if so does the client possess these?" (For instance, will the client be required to complete reading assignments or to do extensive record-keeping for the counselor?)

Whether the resource person works with the entire family unit or only with certain family members should be learned. All too frequently parents and children are treated separately with insufficient attention to patterns of parent-child interaction and the affect of environmental variables on problem behaviors. This is not to deny the need for individual treatment in certain situations. It suggests, however, that workers must be cautious in choosing programs that do not involve the entire family. Family members frequently play a role in the onset of problematic behaviors as well as in their maintenance. Change efforts that do not account for the contribution of different family members— despite the fact that one person may be singled out as the identified patient—run the risk that any changes are not likely to be maintained.

Regardless of the services offered, resource persons must be willing to *work in a cooperative relationship* with child welfare staff (to attend staff meetings and submit progress reports on a preestablished schedule) and to accept the authority of the child welfare worker who is directly responsible for case plans (if not to the court, then to the agency and client) and who must, therefore, coordinate all case management activities. Contracts to coordinate the activities of all service providers are reviewed later in this chapter.

Deciding Who Will Assume Responsibility for Problem Solving

In this regard, the worker has three choices: to take on the role of treatment agent and develop and implement programs to resolve family problems; or to enlist the aid of others in the community; or both. In reaching a decision three factors must be taken into account. First, the worker's skill and training in resolving the specific problems presented by any family; second, whether he or she has the time to assume responsibility for treatment; and last, whether community resources are available and willing to enter into cooperative working relationships with child welfare staff. If community resources are available, able, and willing to work cooperatively, their use is recommended because time constraints—imposed by high caseloads and administrative paper work—frequently prevent workers from taking on a direct intervention role. Without time constraints and given problem-solving skills, workers may choose to assume responsibility for problem resolution themselves.

Difficulties occur when workers have skill deficits and community resources are not available. Some workers tackle this problem creatively, reaching out to the lay community for volunteers who can provide respite care for parents. Volunteers, using their own experiences in parenting, can act as role models to teach basic child-care skills, to help parents increase their skills for positive interaction with their children, and to help parents learn noncorporal approaches of discipline. With consultation from trained professionals, the role that volunteers can play in assisting families and making up for resource deficits can be increased in significant ways.[5]

Workers may also organize support groups composed of parents who are able and willing to "trade off" baby sitting and who can provide emotional supports and social outlets for isolated parents.

When problems require the assistance of persons with extensive professional training and when such individuals aren't available, workers must bring this to the attention of supervisors, agency administrators, legislators, and members of the bench. Those individuals who are responsible for allocating funds for resource development and maintenance must be informed about the resources necessary to assist families with problems and also of the unlikelihood that these problems can be resolved satisfactorily (increasing the possibilities of repeated abuse, for example) unless funds are allocated for the development of needed services. But here a note of caution is in order. Workers should not risk their credibility by overselling programs that are faddish or that, while appealing to common sense, have not been shown to be effective in managing the difficulties they purport to handle.

Documenting Program Choices

In recent years a number of court cases have focused on issues such as a client's right to receive treatment as a balance against the deprivation of freedom that results from coercive intervention and the right to be treated in the least restrictive environment.[6] Thus far, these issues have had little impact on child welfare services. However, the increase in mental health litigation in general and suits brought by foster parents, natural parents, and child advocates in particular hint at the possibility that in the near future child welfare will become increasingly more litigious. This creates an imperative for careful documentation of services provided to clients. The service of choice should be recorded even if the program is not available, thus evidencing a considered approach to program selection. Why a given program was chosen should be documented—whether it was selected because the evidence (the literature or the worker's experience) indicates that particular methods are effective or because it is the only program available. The absence of empirical evidence does not mean that something does not work, per se. It does, however, suggest caution in predicting outcomes and directs attention to the importance of reviewing client progress at regular intervals and giving clients permission to withdraw from programs when evidence of change is not forthcoming.

INTERVENTION ROLES

To select the correct program for any client, workers should be familiar with the range of intervention roles counselors can assume and the advantages and disadvantages of each. Let us review four of these—verbal, instigational, replication, and direct.[7] Bear in mind that counseling is a generic term, embracing a range of methods including techniques developed from psychoanalysis, ego psychology, behavior modification, and transactional analysis, to mention a few. In addition to variations in technique, therapies differ on other dimensions. The framework for counseling may be one-to-one or group, the unit of attention the individual or the family. Services may be provided solely in the therapist's office, almost totally in the client's own environment, or in both. And treatment can be long-term or limited, and the therapist a professional or lay person.

Verbal Methods

Approaching change through verbal interaction between counselor and client is one of the most widely employed treatment modalities. This method requires that clients' have verbal facility and the ability to employ "insights" gained in verbal exchanges to alter their behavior in the natural environment. It is based on the supposition that clients possess necessary skills for translating verbal insight into overt actions. Advantages of this approach are that clients can be helped to clearly conceptualize their difficulties and to sort out the alternatives in a situation and the strengths and weaknesses of each. The client is offered problem-solving skills that may help him or her to reach decisions.

Disadvantages may stem from the counselor's failure to assess whether the client has the requisite skills to translate verbal material into behavioral change. And it cannot be assumed that changes occurring in office settings will generalize to and be maintained in the client's natural environment. Counselors must have skill in developing interpersonal relationships as well as in specific methods for solving identified problems.

Instigation

Verbal exchanges during interviews are central to instigative methods of intervention, as are skills in interpersonal relationships. Instigation differs from verbal approaches in that the former is concerned with activities taking place outside of the interview, in real-life settings, while the latter centers on events that transpire during the interview.

Instigation is characterized by agreements between worker and client regarding "assignments that the client carries out in the natural environment."[8] It is employed during assessment (the log that Sharon Carr agreed to maintain is an example) and during treatment. Illustrating the latter would be an instruction to a client to enroll a child in a day-care program. An instigation, therefore, is an instruction that is given in one situation that is to be carried out in another.

The focus on activities in the client's environment increases the likelihood that change will be applied to and be maintained in relevant situations. Client cooperation is a prerequisite to the success of instigative methods. Clients must agree to complete assignments and to share the results with the worker, who assesses the client's skill and facility with assignments. Counselors reinforce clients through purposeful use of supportive methods, by agreeing to monitor client compliance with tasks, by assisting them if task completion proves difficult, and by arranging reinforcers in the natural environment.

Instigation has the potential for effecting change in a variety of behaviors (private thoughts and feelings and actions are examples) that relate to events that are not accessible to the counselor. In all probability, this method ranks second only to verbal approaches in its use by social workers.

Replications

Replications, or simulations, were discussed in chapter five where their use for gathering information from clients was pointed out. Simulations are also used to alter behaviors, thoughts, and feelings by replicating some part of the natural environment and giving clients the chance to practice new approaches to problem solving. They may be asked to observe and replicate the behavior of models. A parent and child may practice new methods of verbal problem solving or a client learn new or novel approaches to self-assertion.

Advantages of simulations include the opportunity to practice new skills in situations where the client's comfort level may be greater than when beginning practice occurs in natural settings. And actual practice is a closer approximation to real life than is simply discussing events. The emphasis on practice decreases reliance on verbal skills. Client skill and comfort can be readily assessed, and constructive feedback and suggestions for change can be offered, immediately following practice trials.

The possibility that the behaviors displayed in the office may not be representative of those displayed in the natural environment reduces the chances of generalization and is therefore a disadvantage of replications. To increase the chances that behaviors will generalize, clients are usually asked to engage in practice at home, once they evidence comfort with new skills during practice sessions.

Direct intervention occurs in the client's natural environment. Counselors seek to "actively influence" client behavior by demonstration and instruction. Thus, a public health nurse might model certain child-care skills and instruct clients to replicate the demonstration. Direct intervention differs from simulations by taking advantage of natural events. For instance, the public health nurse would not seek to create a situation in which to demonstrate child-care skills but to effect change in a situation where these occur in an ongoing manner. Since change efforts take place in the natural environment, the probabilities of generalization increase. There is less reliance on verbal methods since observation of events, not a verbal description of them, is the source for change activities. Direct intervention is costly in terms of time, and it may be intrusive.

In addition to professional counseling, efforts to work with abusive and neglectful families have resulted in therapeutic innovations and in renewed interest in the use of traditional services such as day-care and homemaker services. Some of these approaches are briefly described.

DAY-CARE SERVICES.   This term "refers to full- or part-time care for preschool children outside their homes on a regular basis during the day, while their parents work or are engaged in other activities which separate them from their children."[9] Day care is offered in a variety of settings, including the homes of relatives or neighbors (where money payments may not change hands), in licensed or unlicensed private homes run by neighborhood residents, or in formal day-care centers and nursery schools. Some programs are custodial, with supervision being the primary service. Some are educational or developmental, where the child is "offered opportunities to develop increasing competence in his or her interactions with the people and things of the world."[10] In addition to providing respite services for overburdened parents and enrichment experiences for children, day-care programs may afford parents the opportunity to acquire new child-care skills.

HOMEMAKER SERVICES.   These services provide assistance with cleaning, meal planning, cooking, child care, and other household management tasks. They can help to relieve stress, teach parenting and household management skills, and offer support to the socially isolated parent. The availability of a homemaker may make it unnecessary to place a child in out-of-home care if, for example, a single parent requires hospitalization or is temporarily ill and cannot care for a child. Also, this service can help to pave the way for restoring a child. Homemakers play an adjunct role for the worker. Their position in the home allows them to observe patterns of parent-child interaction, to document their observations and provide information about family strengths and weaknesses.

PUBLIC HEALTH SERVICES.   Public health nurses can play a critical role in the identification and treatment of abuse and neglect, especially for preschool children who are not seen by any person outside the immediate family. Because public health nurses visit the family home, they are in a unique position to acquire valuable information describing parental strengths and weaknesses, and their special training allows them to offer learning experiences for parents in areas such as nutrition and child care.

LAY THERAPISTS.   In recent years there has been an increased reliance on *lay therapists* to assist families-at-risk. Lay therapy stresses the personal qualities of the counselor rather than his or her professional qualifications. The emphasis is on the person's experiences and the relevance of these to the issues with which they will be dealing. Lay counselors working with abusive and neglectful families are generally parents. They may be matched with client families by factors such as race, age, income, or education. The person's ability to relate with warmth, empathy, and support is viewed as important.

Lay therapists work in the client's home, offering parents ongoing, nurturing relationships. They generally provide assistance with matters like transportation and, as role models, are able to offer instruction in household management and child-care skills. They may be trained to offer counseling, in which case professional supervision is given.

Lay therapy is more economical than professional assistance and can save time for professionals. Clients may perceive a lay therapist as less threatening than traditional counselors. With proper training, lay counselors can gather valuable information in the client's environment, which professionals do not have the time to pursue. Problems result if selection procedures are inadequate, if training is not offered, and if tasks are not clearly identified. Lay therapists, like professionals, must learn the limits of their skills or risk engaging clients in discussions or activities which they cannot manage.

PARENTS ANONYMOUS (PA).   This is a nationwide self-help organization. It is staffed by parents who were abusive and it seeks to assist others who have recently abused their children. PA groups are sponsored by professionals—usually a social worker, psychologist, or psychiatrist. In addition to operating hot lines and making crisis visits to homes, groups focus on teaching parents new methods of relating to their children during weekly group meetings. "They emphasize the importance of providing parents with a nonjudgmental atmosphere in which [they] can share understanding, support, trust and [offer] encouragement."[11]

The advantages of PA groups are similar to those of lay therapy save for the fact that group meetings, rather than work in the client's environment, are the locus for providing help. As such, chances for gathering data in the client's natural environment are reduced and the focus on group activities lessens the chances for generalization of change. Although these groups are sponsored by professionals, they are not necessarily tied to a protective service unit. For this reason, problems in monitoring client participation and establishing accountability may be encountered.[12]

CRISIS-ORIENTED SERVICES. These provide emergency assistance, frequently on a twenty-four-hour basis. Services range from in-person counseling to counseling provided over a telephone hot line. Some family needs may be met through the provision of hard services such as emergency loans and temporary housing.[13]

CRISIS NURSERIES. These services can provide a safe haven for children at times of extreme family stress. They may be used as a form of brief foster care or as temporary holding facility when children are removed from their homes following an emergency investigation. Depending upon staffing patterns, children may receive custodial care or educational, medical, and diagnostic services.[14]

Community education in the use of any crisis service is necessary. If parents are aware of services and if they can be taught to use them at times of stress, the likelihood of maltreatment may be reduced, since a crisis is often a precipitating factor in incidents of maltreatment. Unless services are offered under the auspices of a protective service unit, coordinating networks must be established. Crisis workers must be cognizant of the abuse and neglect reporting laws.

Parent Education has been receiving increased attention because of the presumed relationship between deficits in child-care skills and maltreatment. Basic child-care skills, such as bathing, diapering, and feeding, may be taught, and classes on nutrition, noncorporal methods of discipline, and positive ways of interacting with children may be offered.

SERVICE DELIVERY

In its broadest sense, the term service delivery comprehends all activities occurring between worker and client from initial intake through final case termination. More narrowly construed, the term refers to the provision of problem-solving services that when offered, signal the implementation of a case plan and through which case goals and objectives are realized. It is this latter type of service delivery that concerns us here.

Client progress toward goals is *monitored* throughout the service delivery process using methods employed during assessment, allowing the worker to *evaluate* the effects of intervention on reducing or eliminating client problems. Evidence that Sharon Carr's feelings of depression have been reduced or eliminated should be revealed in her log, indicated by an increase in activities identified as positive and in continuing favorable evaluations of these activities, as well as in her verbal reports. Whether family members are participating in household management tasks should be observed by the worker during periods of observation. When treatment services are provided by collaterals, they assume responsibility for monitoring client progress and supplying pertinent data to child welfare staff. By continually reviewing data that they gather, as well as that supplied by clients and other professionals, workers have an overview of progress in attaining all case goals, thus permitting an evaluation of progress toward final objectives. Careful scrutiny of monitoring data allows for modification of ineffective interventions. Monitoring and evaluation are central to establishing accountability. The Carr case will be used to illustrate these processes.

Intervention: The Carr Family

The initial contract with the Carrs was amended to include four problem-solving goals which were established on the basis of the worker's evaluation of assessment data. Analysis of Sharon Carr's log showed that engaging in household tasks and sitting alone and thinking accounted for 78 percent of all of her entries in the activities column of her log. Both these activities were evaluated as either negative or neutral. In fact, 84 percent of all of her evaluations were of this sort, with only 16 percent being positive. Interaction with friends (accounting for approximately 5 percent of all activities) received uniformly positive evaluation while evaluations of time spent in personal endeavors (approximately 10 percent of her recordings) and in interaction with family (18 percent) were mixed.

The suggestion that Sharon Carr's depression might be reduced by increasing the amount of time that she spent with friends was indicated by her positive evaluations of these activities and reinforced by her comments, recorded in the column headed "what did you want," almost all of which expressed an interest in spending time with other adults.

Direct observation during dinner time confirmed Sharon Carr's verbal report that she received no assistance with household chores. Thus, enlisting the aid of the children was seen as an important goal for several reasons: first, to reduce the mother's general feelings of being overwhelmed; second, to reduce the actual percentage of her time spent in household management tasks, thereby freeing her to spend time with friends, and last, because the worker hypothesized that Sharon Carr's feelings about the time that she did spend engaging in chores might improve if these activities were approached cooperatively by all family members. (Data from before and after intervention are graphically depicted on pages 236 and 238.)

Information on Nita's school problems was gained entirely through verbal exchanges with Ann Tripp. The young woman explained her truancy by stating that going to school was "boring" and that she would "only have a bunch of kids like her mother—so who needs to go to school?"

The four problem-solving goals were established as follows: The first was to "increase the frequency with which all family members engaged in and completed household chores." The second and third were proposed to eliminate Mrs. Carr's depression. One sought to enlarge her circle of acquaintances and to increase the frequency with which she interacted with friends through involvement in identified activities at a local women's center. The other was to enroll the twins in a day-care program, giving the client free time during the day. The fourth goal concerned Nita's school problems. Nita agreed to work with a vocational counselor who would assist her in the identification of career options and develop a plan whereby she could acquire the educational or technical skills needed to pursue a career of her choice.

Responsibility for attaining the goals of the Carr contract was divided between Ann Tripp, members of the Carr family, and two counselors from a community center. Tripp agreed to develop and implement a plan to meet the goal of involving all family members in household management, to develop a means of monitoring family compliance with this program, to coordinate the activities of other service providers, and to share evaluation information at weekly meetings with the family. Sharon Carr and Nita agreed to initiate contact with their respective counselors at the women's center, to cooperate with their counselors in the process of developing programs, and to follow through with program requirements. Sharon Carr agreed to continue recording in her log. Mother and daughter signed consent-to-release-information forms, permitting the exchange of data between Ann Tripp and the counselors. One counselor agreed to assist Sharon Carr in identification of appropriate activities at the center, to monitor her involvement in selected programs, and to help her to resolve any difficulties she encountered while participating in center activities. A career counselor agreed to assist Nita in attaining her goal. Mrs. Carr agreed to enroll the twins in a day care program identified by Tripp.

To assure that the activities of all professionals were goal-oriented, a coordination contract was entered into between Ann Tripp and the counselors at the women's center. This contract is reviewed next, followed by the plan that Tripp developed for the division of household responsibilities. Finally, the outcome of intervention with this family will be discussed.

CONTRACTS.   Contracts to coordinate the activities of multiple service providers, outlining the specific tasks of each party, are necessary to guide collaborative efforts.[15] If no such framework is created, problems can arise to hinder goal attainment. One is duplication of services, where several persons provide conflicting advice relative to the same problem. Failing to exchange information needed for decision making and timely court reporting is another.

The document shown in figure 8.2 illustrates the use of contracts as a framework for coordination. Ann Tripp and both counselors at the center entered into this agreement. The objective, noted in the opening paragraph, was to create a framework for collaboration. The tasks of all three parties are described in the succeeding paragraphs.

Both counselors have agreed to assist their clients in the identification of options (for Sharon Carr, the concern is with activity groups; for Nita, career choices), to assess their clients' skill at pursuing options, to facilitate client acquisition of requisite skills, and to monitor client progress. The paragraphs that deal with the responsibilities of both counselors note that each will pursue goals in accordance with their professional training, emphasizing the fact that diverse skills, generally beyond the training of any one person, are needed to help clients. Ann Tripp assumed responsibility for problem solving in areas not addressed by others. Additionally, she is responsible for gathering, summarizing, and reporting data and for convening and chairing meetings.

Two of the most important elements of coordination contracts are noted in the final paragraph. These agree that each party will restrict its activities to those tasks spelled out under its name and give priority to meeting these obligations. Additional areas of importance are seen in the agreement by both counselors to report any barriers they encounter that might hinder fulfillment of their responsibilities to the caseworker, to attend meetings to develop ways of removing barriers, and to submit reports to the worker on a regular basis.

PLAN TO DIVIDE HOUSEHOLD RESPONSIBILITY.   A plan to share household tasks among family members was developed by Ann Tripp and attached to the contract. As depicted in figure 8.3, meeting this goal required the Carrs and their worker to move through a series of steps beginning with the identification of household chores and ending with implementation of the plan. The requirement for a clear description of the components of each chore (step 2) and Tripp's agreement to help negotiate responsibility for unassigned tasks (step 5) were included to avoid family disputes arising from differences of opinion as

FIGURE 8.2   Coordination Contract

This contract is entered into between Ann Tripp, Child Welfare Worker for the New City Public Welfare Department, Kelly Bryce, Supervising Counselor at the Hillside Women's Center and Alice Pierce, vocational counselor at the Hillside Women's Center. The objective is to establish a framework for coordinating service delivery efforts for Sharon Carr (mother) and her daughter Nita Carr.

1. *Kelly Bryce, Supervising Counselor:*   agrees to assist Sharon Carr in identifying activities of her choice and to assess whether she has requisite skills for participating in selected programs. If skill deficits are identified, Kelly Bryce agrees to arrange for skill training. She also agrees to monitor client involvement in group activities, including attendance, level of participation and client satisfaction with her involvement. Should the client experience any difficulties while participating in group activities, Kelly Bryce will assist her in resolving these by developing a problem solving plan. All activities will be carried out by Kelly Bryce in accordance with professional training.

2. *Alice Pierce, Vocational Counselor:*   agrees to assist Nita Carr in the identification of suitable career options. This includes assessing Nita's career interests, her current skills and those she will have to acquire to pursue identified career goals. For each career alternative, Alice Pierce agrees to develop a plan for the acquisition of requisite educational or technical skills. Assessment and planning will be carried out in accordance with Alice Pierce's professional training. She agrees to monitor Nita's involvement, including her attendance at counseling and testing sessions.

3. *Ann Tripp, Child Welfare Worker:*   will be responsible for assisting the Carr family in resolution of those difficulties not addressed by either Kelly Bryce or Alice Pierce. She will gather and summarize information on client progress in working with Kelly Bryce and Alice Pierce and report this to the court for regular review hearings. If difficulties are encountered in completing the goals of this contract, Ann Tripp agrees to convene and chair meetings and to cooperate with others in developing methods of resolving difficulties.

While it is recognized that work with either client may extend beyond the assigned tasks, all parties agree to (1) not extend their work into any area specifically assigned to one of the other parties, and (2) give priority to fulfilling those objectives for which they were brought into this case. Furthermore, if barriers are identified that threaten contract goals, both Kelly Bryce and Alice Pierce agree to report this as soon as possible to the child welfare worker. All parties agree to attend any meetings should this be necessary. Summaries of client progress will be submitted to Ann Tripp every 30 days. This contract is in effect for a period of 60 days.

Signed:

_____   _____
Ann Tripp, Child Welfare Worker   Date

_____   _____
Kelly Bryce, Supervising Counselor   Date

_____   _____
Alice Pierce, Vocational Counselor   Date

FIGURE 8.3 Plan to Divide Responsibility for Household Chores

The objective of this plan is to divide responsibility for completion of household chores. To accomplish this, Ann Tripp and members of the Carr family agree to the following:

(1) to list all household chores and the frequency with which they must be undertaken and the time of day by which they should be completed;

(2) to describe each of the steps involved in chore completion—for instance, all of the tasks which must be completed in cleaning up after dinner or straightening the living room;

(3) each family member, except the twins, will write down the amount of time they have to complete chores on a daily basis. Using the chore list, each will identify tasks they are willing to undertake;

(4) Ann Tripp will assist Sharon Carr in identifying tasks appropriate to the twins' age;

(5) Ann Tripp will assist the Carrs in negotiating responsibility for any tasks that remain after chores are assigned by prefernce.

(6) all of the above steps are to be completed within two weeks of the signing of this contract; this will occur during scheduled weekly meetings at the family home;

(7) in the first week following completion of the above steps, each family member agrees to undertake and complete the assigned tasks and to record task completion on a checklist provided by Ann Tripp.

to what constitutes chore completion and who will assume responsibility for undesirable tasks. Negotiation training provides the opportunity for family members to acquire problem-solving skills they can use at a later time without worker intervention.[16] Respect for individual preferences is shown in step 3, where it is noted that family members should identify tasks they are willing to undertake. Data on frequency with which chores had to be done, the time of day by which they should be completed (step 1), and the descriptive information called for in step 2 should enable the process of individual selection. Identification of age-appropriate tasks for the twins serves two purposes. It acknowledges that they are able to contribute to goal attainment, and it provides a framework for the caseworker to teach her client what she can expect from children their age.

The checklist shown in figure 8.4 illustrates the method by which compliance with meal preparation chores was monitored. Listing chores by person and by day and setting a time limit for completion reduces the likelihood of disagreement over who was responsible for any task and when it was to be done. Checking off chores following completion is yet another way to avoid discussion about compliance, and produces monitoring information. Whether the Carrs were able to resolve disagreement in mutually satisfactory ways was not known. Ann Tripp's instructions to the family to call her should difficulties arise, rather than to attempt resolution on their own, and her agreement to mediate any differences, are efforts to avoid failure of this goal

FIGURE 8.4   Chore Checklist: Meal Preparation

	M	Tu	W	Th	F	Sat	Sun
Mother:							
Shopping							
Prepare Menus							
Prepare Meals							
Nita:							
Set Table							
Wash & Stack Dishes							
Clean Counter Top							
Barry:							
Clear Table							
Dry Dishes							
Replace Dishes in Cabinet							
Sweep Floor							
Empty Trash							

The above applies to all family meals with the following exceptions:

1) Sharon Carr will assume responsibility for all tasks involved in preparing breakfast on school days.
2) Persons preparing a meal for themselves will execute all clean-up tasks created by meal preparation.

    Cleaning up is to be completed within one hour of the end of any meal. A checkmark is to be placed next to the chore each time that it is completed, by the person completing the task. Sharon Carr will review the checklist within 15 minutes following chore completion.

    If any problems are encountered in complying with this plan, family members agree not to attempt resolution on their own. Rather, they are to contact Ann Tripp as soon as possible. She agrees to meet with the Carrs at the earliest possible time following such a report and to assist them in resolving any difficulties.

    Ann Tripp also agrees to telephone the Carr home every other day for 10 days, to monitor compliance and to review any issues the family wishes to discuss. Finally, she will review the charts at weekly meetings with the Carr family.

because of family quarrels. This latter point highlights the fact that assessment is continuous throughout the period of service delivery. In addition to the possibility that issues not identified during initial assessment may emerge, the requirements of any approach to problem solving may give rise to new difficulties. The process may require skills absent from an individual's repertoire and changes may occur more quickly for some family members than for others.

Intervention with the Carrs lasted fifteen weeks. The twins were enrolled in day care and excellent progress was made in reducing Sharon Carr's depression and increasing the family members' chore completion. Progress in selecting career options for Nita did not proceed as hoped and her school attendance, while improved, was not perfect.

OUTCOME: SHARON CARR'S DEPRESSION.   Ann Tripp reviewed Sharon Carr's log at regular ,intervals throughout the period of service delivery, summarizing and analyzing the information as she had done prior to intervention. These data, when contrasted with that collected during assessment (baseline data), evidence clients progress toward goals. The results of this analysis appear in figure 8.5, where the percentage of log entries in the five categories concerning Sharon Carr's

FIGURE 8.5 Percent of Log Entries in Each of 5 Activity Categories

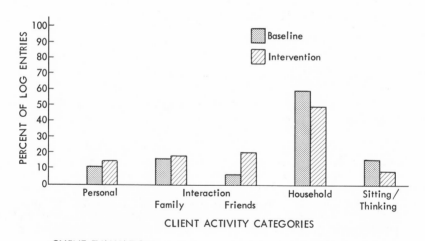

CLIENT EVALUATION
OF ACTIVITIES

	B	I
	%	%
Positive	16	46
Negative	36	20
Neutral	48	34

activities are shown for baseline and intervention phases. Also included is the percentage of positive, negative, and neutral evaluations made by the client.

The significant increase in activities with friends (from 5 percent during baseline to 20 percent at the end of intervention) supported the reports from Sharon Carr's counselor which showed an almost perfect record of attendance at the center and a high level of participation in all activities. The data bear out the worker's hypothesis that increasing the amount of time spent with friends through involvement in the center's program would decrease the number of entries recorded under the heading of "sitting alone and thinking." Especially significant are the changes in the client's evaluations of activities. The balance between positive, negative, and neutral assessments shifted. During assessment almost one-half had been neutral, and now we see an almost equal percentage of positive evaluations and a marked decrease in negative ones from 36 percent to 20 percent.

COMPLIANCE WITH CHORE COMPLETION PROGRAM. This was reflected on the checklist maintained by the Carrs. Ann Tripp calculated the average number and percentage of chores completed by all family members for each of the fifteen weeks. The data in figure 8.6 show the percentage of tasks completed ranged from 50 percent in the first week to over 90 percent at the end of fifteen weeks, compared with baseline data of zero from worker observation and client verbal reports. These results were confirmed through ongoing observation by Tripp following the same format as during assessment.

NITA'S CAREER AND SCHOOL GOALS. Nita maintained four out of seven appointments with the vocational counselor. She took a battery of vocational tests and engaged in discussions of career options. However, she did not read job information pamphlets given to her, nor did she follow through with instructions to contact schools whose programs might be useful to her. She continued to miss an average of one day of school per week. Ann Tripp had little success in discussing these issues with the young woman. Her efforts to confront Nita with the consequences of her behavior were met with statements such as, "I'll go to my next appointment, I'll contact the schools" and so forth. She would not report how she spent her time when truant from school.

In sum, three out of four goals were attained by the end of the contract period. The twins were attending day care, Sharon Carr's feelings of depression were significantly reduced, and family members were sharing responsibility for household chores. The worker recommended that the case be kept open for an additional sixty days in order to continue work with Nita and to follow-up with assistance, if necessary, to help the Carrs maintain changes. Family members agreed, and

FIGURE 8.6 Percentage of Chores Completed: 15 Weeks

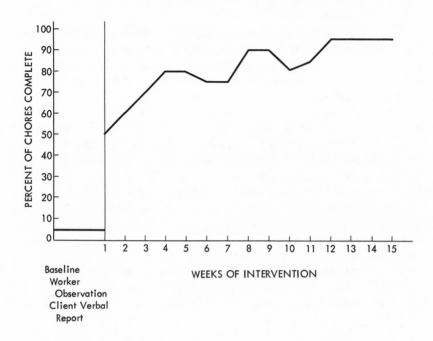

Tripp filed her report for the court review hearing. The data just reviewed, along with a narrative summary, were presented to the court as evidence of client cooperation with and progress in case planning. The court accepted the caseworker's recommendations that the case be continued. We will return to the Carrs in the next chapter where follow-up and termination are covered.

Pursuing Options for Permanency

Some parents do not participate in case planning; others begin only to withdraw at some point in the planning or implementation process. In certain situations, current technology is not sufficient for resolving family problems. So despite a worker's best efforts to maintain children at home or to reunite them with their biological parents, objectives are not always realized. When this occurs, child welfare workers must take action to pursue alternatives that will provide continuity in care for children. The Quigley case illustrates one approach to attaining permanency.

THE QUIGLEY FAMILY

One-year-old Ronald Quigley was placed in foster care following six months of protective service supervision at home that was precipitated by a report of suspected abuse. Particulars supporting the initial petition were not revealed in the case record. Since the child had been left at home, it is reasonable to assume that there was no serious harm nor evidence of imminent danger. Out-of-home placement was recommended by the protective service worker and supported by the judge because Ronald's parents failed to participate in case planning. Marie, a four-year-old sibling, had been in continuous placement for three years at the time of Ronald's placement. The circumstances of Marie's foster parents precluded Ronald being placed in their home.

From the case record we learn that Marie's placement followed the arrest of both parents for possession of narcotics, for which they were placed on twelve months probation following suspension of their sentence. Records obtained from the FBI revealed that the father, Ward Quigley, had an arrest record dating back twenty years to his fourteenth birthday. The mother, Hilda Quigley, had no prior arrests. Contact between Marie's caseworker and the Quigleys had been sporadic, as were visits between the youngster and her parents. Exact information was not available. Hilda Quigley visited Ronald in the foster home three times in the first nine months of his placement and kept two out of seven appointments with the worker. The father did not participate, and neither parent visited their daughter during this time.

In the tenth month of Ronald's placement a probation officer telephoned Gordon Jackson, the child welfare worker, informing him that Hilda Quigley had been arrested for petty theft and possession of narcotics. She was released on bail, pending trial. Two days later she telephoned the worker, informing him that she and her husband had been divorced six months earlier and that she had been awarded custody of both children. She made an appointment with Gordon Jackson which she did not keep. A telephone call to the probation officer revealed that the mother had not appeared for her probation hearing. The possibility that she had "skipped town" was suggested by a neighbor's report that she had been seen leaving her apartment with suitcases. There was no forwarding address and Ward Quigley's whereabouts could not be determined. Gordon Jackson checked county records to verify Hilda Quigley's claim that she and her husband had been divorced; however, no supporting documents were found.

Approximately four months later Ward Quigley reappeared. He telephoned Gordon Jackson to say that he was "back for good, had a job and wanted his son returned to his care."[17] He did not know where his wife was and professed ignorance of the divorce action.

The transcript from two tape recorded interviews shows that the worker agreed to help the father reach his objective of having his son restored. Initial goals were for him to submit to weekly urinalysis tests for a period of nine months to establish nonuse of drugs, and to visit his son regularly in the foster home, thereby allowing for worker assessment of parent-child interaction. A contract to this effect was signed.

A three-week period of compliance with the conditions set forth in the contract was followed by two weeks during which Gordon Jackson could not locate his client. At the beginning of the sixth week, Ward Quigley telephoned the welfare office, explaining that he had gone to Reno, Nevada to look for his wife following a report he had received that she was living and working there. His search was not successful. He asked for and received another opportunity to work toward his objectives. The worker pointed out that Ward Quigley was creating a case against himself, since his disappearances would support a termination action based on noninvolvement, as stipulated in the contract.

Ward Quigley adhered to the contract for two more weeks, then once again dropped out of sight. Several weeks after the last contact with his client, Gordon Jackson received a telephone call from the sheriff's office informing him that Ward Quigley had been found "comatose" in a parked automobile. He was hospitalized for an overdose of heroin and treated in the county detoxification unit for three days. Police and hospital records were forwarded to the District Attorney's office for a decision to prosecute.

Issues in the Quigley Case

When the Quigley case was presented at a staff meeting, a field student placed in the child welfare agency commented: "Why even bother trying? He'll never do it." That was everyone's best guess, and not without reason. Insofar as past behavior is any indication of future action, there was little reason for optimism. However, regardless of anyone's opinion, the worker had two very good reasons for giving the client another chance. First, he does have a right to try, and the worker has a professional obligation to give him the chance. People do change; whether Ward Quigley would remained to be seen. The second reason recognizes that, for the children, permanent planning options were closed. They would remain so (excluding total abandonment) until such a time as systematic efforts were made to involve natural parents in planning and these efforts and the parents' response to them were documented. It is not uncommon for parents to drift in and out of the lives of children in foster care—occasional contact prevents a charge of abandonment.[18] However, careful documentation of all worker efforts to locate parents and to involve them in case planning (even if this documentation consists solely of a log of failed appointments), a list of search efforts, and a contract describing the case plan suffice to sustain a termination petition in some jurisdictions. Workers draft contracts and give them to clients even if they are not willing to sign them, which shows an intent to offer services.

SEARCHING FOR MISSING PARENTS.   This is an important part of child welfare work. It takes time and creativity to identify methods for locating them. Useful approaches used by workers include the following: letters are sent to parents by registered mail (return receipt requested) at all previous addresses, in care of relatives, friends, employers, or to general delivery if they may be residing in another city; letters requesting a records check for addresses are sent to public utility companies, welfare departments in other states, the state unemployment office, registry of motor vehicles, state police, local law enforcement agencies, the FBI, state prisons, and state hospitals, if there is reason to believe that parents may have come into contact with any of these agencies and institutions; finally, letters are addressed to parents in care of the Social Security Administration in Washington, or to community colleges or universities that the parent has attended with a request that they be forwarded, which will be honored.[19]

A CONFERENCE WITH ADOPTION SERVICE.   Ten days after Ward Quigley's arrest and hospitalization, Gordon Jackson and his supervisor met with the adoption staff from the unit to discuss whether the facts of this case supported a petition to terminate parental rights. Also, Ronald's foster parents were moving out of state and his caseworker wanted to know whether a preadoptive home was available so that placement in a new foster home could be avoided. If termination seemed likely, Marie's foster parents were to be approached with the idea of her adoption.

Prior to the meeting, Gordon Jackson submitted a case summary to adoption personnel in which the information deemed necessary to reach an initial determination was reported. The contents of this summary represented only a small percentage of all the documentation available in the case record. The categories of information presented and their relevance to the decision at hand are reviewed next.

SUMMARY INFORMATION.   The court's authority to take action on behalf of a child must be established. The basis upon which the court assumed *jurisdiction* at the initial dependency hearing is sufficient for this purpose. Thus, the child's legal status (that the child is a dependent of the court) is reported and the section of the code under which dependency was taken is noted. State statutes may specify minimum *time limits* for termination action. Consequently, adoption workers must be informed of the *length of time* the child has been a dependent. Time requirements vary from state to state and within states for different sections of the code. For example, in California an abandonment petition may be filed after six months during which there has been no contact between parent and child. Termination on the basis of substance abuse requires that the child has been in continuous care for a minimum of one year.

The *legal and social relationship* of caretaking adults to the child in question must be shown. When a child is born to legally married parents, the rights of both must be terminated. The relationship between termination and the right of unmarried fathers is reviewed later in this chapter. The child's custody, which may or may not be vested in legal parents, must also be established.

The *basis for the involvement of social services* is reported. Here the information goes beyond simple identification of the section of the code under which dependency was assumed, by informing others of the evidence that supported the initial petition (X rays indicating physical abuse, for example), the general types of services provided (such as foster care or protective services) and specific information about the problem-solving services that were offered. For instance, homemaker services rendered to relieve a single parent of full-time responsibility for child care, and the outcomes of service delivery are summarized. Additionally, all the documents contained in the case record are listed—the social history, worker's contact log, signed contract, reports from collaterals, and so forth.

CURRENT INFORMATION. The exact information that is felt to support the termination petition is described. A casework log, listing chronologically attempts to locate missing parents and their results, plus all of the parents' appointments with the worker and their appointments to visit their child, and the number and percentage of these that were maintained and failed, may represent the major evidence to support an abandonment petition.

Certain allegations, such as substance abuse, are difficult to prove because real evidence is not easily obtained. A worker's statement to the effect that he or she observed parents under the influence of drugs or alcohol is not likely to be admissible in court, and clients are not apt to voluntarily submit themselves for medical tests while intoxicated or under the influence of drugs.[20] While evidence in the form of urinalysis tests (for drug abuse) or breathalizer tests (for alcohol use) are generally acceptable, documentation of this sort may not be available unless the parent was arrested. Even with current evidence, it is important to establish a pattern of use because the court is concerned with the probability of continued abuse and a single episode does not permit such a hypothesis. For this reason, past behavior, such as Ward Quigley's history of arrests and incarcerations for drug-related incidents, is especially pertinent.

Adoption staff agreed that the evidence regarding Ward Quigley's current and past use of drugs was, in all likelihood, sufficient to sustain a termination petition. It was less clear if the facts would support a similar action in regard to the mother's right, since there was no evidence of a long-standing pattern of use. Her absences and lack of contact with the children would, it was decided, support termination based on abandonment. The adoption worker agreed to arrange a meeting with agency counsel for a final determination on the acceptability of the case and to begin a search for a preadoptive home for Ronald. Gordon Jackson assumed responsibility for meeting with Marie's foster parents to inquire about their interest in adopting her.

PREPARING A CASE FOR ADOPTION PRETRIAL.[21]   What happens next is that the information just reviewed is presented to counsel for review and an initial determination is made of whether there is sufficient evidence to proceed with the petition. Legal staff will direct the adoption worker to remove essential documents from the case record and may instruct the worker in other necessary tasks. For example, documents to be presented at court, such as school records, police reports, and social service reports, may have to be certified for accuracy before they are admitted to court. An interview with natural parents may be required. If termination is proceeding based on a voluntary relinquishment, it is important to determine that the parents understand the legal ramifications of such a decision.[22] When the proceeding is involuntary, the parents may be asked to describe their experiences with social services so that any discrepancies between their perception of events and those reported by child welfare staff can be identified.

If the case appears legally sound, a meeting may be called for all service workers who will testify at the hearing, their supervisors, and the agency attorney. Such a meeting provides a forum for reviewing the merits of the case and for clarifying any ambiguities that exist in the record. The attorney may direct staff to produce additional information. For instance, a counselor may be asked to delineate the precise grounds for a diagnosis or to supply exact data concerning contact with clients. If parental whereabouts are unknown, a search is instigated, search efforts are published, and the petition prepared.

Adoption workers *search for biological parents* even though this may duplicate the efforts of other staff. It is necessary to show the court that an exhaustive search has been made. These efforts are published in the newspaper, which in turn prepares a "declaration of search efforts" that is presented to the attorney along with the petition. The petition is then signed and filed, along with supporting documents, and a court date awaited.

Once a date has been set notices are sent to five branches of the military (Army, Navy, Marines, Coast Guard and Air Force) inquiring into whether either parent is in their service and, if so, asking that they be notified of the court hearing date. An affidavit is submitted at court attesting to this action and all persons who must appear at the hearing are notified of the date.

If the parents are located, they are served with a summons.[23] Should they move to avoid being served, the worker must notify the court and ask that the case be held over for a later date. A new search must then be conducted.

The search for natural parents has become complex since 1972 when the United States Supreme Court ruled, in the case of *Stanley* vs. *Illinois,* that the consent of unwed fathers as well as mothers was required by law.[24] Prior to that time, if a child was born to an unmarried woman, only her consent to the adoption was necessary. The Stanley case has created a great deal of confusion as to whether it is necessary to search for all spouses, regardless of the length of their relationship with the mother and child, and left unanswered the question of how exhaustive a search is necessary to satisfy the law.

Efforts to provide guidelines to reduce ambiguity take two forms. Some states have enacted legislation addressing the rights of unwed fathers. Illinois, for example, requires consent from both parents of an illegitimate child. However, "failure to demonstrate interest in the baby within thirty days after birth constitutes grounds for termination of parental rights due to unfitness."[25] The second approach is illustrated in the Uniform Parentage Act which describes a procedure for identifying the father and allows for "speedy termination of his potential rights if he shows no interest in the child."[26]

THE INITIAL COURT HEARING. Just prior to the initial hearing, subpoenas are generally issued to all parties whose testimony will be required. A pretrial conference of all persons whose testimony will be used may be called. The exact information that each will provide is put in writing and given to legal counsel. If natural parents and children require their own attorneys, this is arranged prior to the proceedings. If the documentation presented to the court is thorough, and the proceedings are not contested, the petition may be granted at this time by "default."[27] In addition to contesting the proceedings, biological parents have the right to appeal the court's decision.

All records that pertain to the court action are filed with the state. If an adoptive home has not been found, the process of identifying an appropriate placement gets under way. Following termination and preadoptive placement of the child, the court issues an interlocutory (temporary) decree which usually is valid for six months. During this period adoptive parents or the agency can terminate the placement. If this initial period is successful, a final decree is granted and a new birth certificate issued in the name of the adoptive parents.[28]

Conclusion of the Quigley Case

The adoption worker followed the procedures just reviewed. Hilda Quigley was not located and Ward Quigley did not appear at the hearing. Parental rights were terminated on the basis of drug abuse (Ward Quigley) and abandonment (Hilda Quigley). A preadoptive home for Ronald had been found prior to the hearing, and he was placed in that home with the understanding that the petition might not be granted.

Marie's foster parents were not willing to formalize their relationship by becoming adoptive parents or legal guardians. While she could have been removed and placed in a preadoptive home, this was not recommended because of the length of time she had been with her foster parents and because of the quality of their relationship. A contract for long-term foster care was drawn up and signed by Marie's foster parents and the agency.

SUMMARY

Case plans are developed following an affirmative intervention decision.

A case plan contains three major categories of information: the client's objectives in working with the child welfare agency; goals that must be attained to realize objectives; and the processes that client, worker, and collateral resource will engage in to realize goals.

Objectives selected by the client are identified in relation to the range of possible outcomes in any area of service.

Child welfare workers develop goals based on analysis of assessment data. Goals describe expected changes in client behavior that will signal the resolution of identified problems.

Process information describes specific actions to be taken by client, worker, and collateral in order to realize goals; the frequency of and duration of these actions; and the situations in which behaviors are to be displayed.

Time limits, derived from worker experience, the empirical literature, and information provided by collateral resources, are set for attaining goals and realizing objectives.

Consequences express the worker's agreement to support client objectives given ongoing involvement in the processes described in a case plan and describe the alternatives workers will pursue to find permanent homes for children should parents withdraw their participation.

Problem-solving services may be provided by workers with appropriate training, other professionals in the community, and community volunteers.

In selecting community treatment programs workers must determine whether resource persons are able to assist in the resolution of client difficulties, whether they are willing to accept the goals defined by child welfare staff, and whether they are willing to enter into cooperative working relationships with child welfare personnel.

Workers must identify the problem-solving methods used by collateral resources and evaluate the efficacy of these methods for achieving case goals.

Workers must evaluate whether the requirements of a treatment program are feasible by considering whether the client has the skills required for participation and also by regarding the relationship between program requirements and the client's work schedule, the availability of transportation, and child-care services.

Workers carefully document the service of choice as well as the reasons for selecting any given approach to problem solving.

Familiarity with the range of roles counselors can assume during intervention and with the advantages and disadvantages of each enables the selection of treatment programs.

Verbal methods rely on the client's ability to translate "insights" gained through verbal exchanges in an interview into overt actions in his or her natural environment.

Instigative methods rely on the client's ability and willingness to engage in activities and assignments defined by the worker that are to be carried out by the client in his or her natural environment.

Change through simulations is approached by replicating some part of the client's natural environment and by providing the client with the opportunity to practice novel approaches to problem solving.

Like simulations, change through direct intervention provides the client with the opportunity to practice novel approaches to problem solving, but takes advantage of events as they naturally occur in the client's environment.

In addition to approaching change through professional counseling, efforts to assist families-at-risk include the use of day-care programs, homemaker services, public health services, parent education classes, and the services of lay therapists.

Broadly construed, service delivery involves all the transactions between worker and client, from intake through termination. In a narrower sense, it refers to the provision of problem-solving services which, when offered, signal the implementation of a case plan.

Workers and collaterals monitor client progress in problem-solving programs and evaluate the effect of interventions in reducing client problems.

Careful monitoring and evaluation allow for modifications in ineffective treatment programs, and these data contribute to establishing accountability.

Written contracts provide a framework for coordinating the activities of all service providers. Such agreements include: a description of the tasks that the child welfare worker and each resource person will undertake to assist the client; information relative to the coordinating tasks of the child welfare worker, including gathering and summarizing information, filing court reports, and chairing meetings, if necessary, to resolve any difficulties encountered during service delivery; an agreement by collateral resource persons not to extend their work into any area specifically assigned to another and to give priority to meeting goals for which they have assumed responsibility.

When parents do not participate in case planning, workers must take action by pursuing alternatives that will provide continuity in care for children.

Permanency options, such as adoption and legal guardianship, may be closed unless efforts are made to provide services to natural parents and these efforts and the response of parents are carefully documented.

To determine whether the facts of a case can support a petition to terminate parental rights, case data are summarized and presented to legal counsel. Pertinent information must establish: the grounds for court authority over the child; the length of time that the child has been in foster care; the legal and social relationship of caretaking adults; the basis for the involvement of social services; and current information including service delivery data and other evidence which will be presented to support a termination petition.

Legal staff may direct workers to gather additional supportive data and to interview biological parents.

When parental whereabouts are unknown, a formal search must be undertaken and efforts, such as publishing notices in newspapers, must be verified for presentation in court.

If parental whereabouts are known, they are served with a summons stating the date, time, and place of the hearing and summarizing the allegations of the petition.

Subpoenas are issued to all persons whose testimony may be required at a court hearing.

If the court proceedings are not contested, the termination petition may be granted at the initial court hearing.

Following termination of parental rights and preadoptive placement of the child, the court issues a temporary decree, usually for a six-month period of time.

If the preadoptive placement is not terminated during this time, either by the agency or the adoptive parents, a final decree is granted and a new birth certificate in the name of the adoptive parents is issued.

NOTES

1. There are two kinds of incompatability. Physical incompatability refers to competing behaviors—those that cannot be performed at the same time as the problematic ones. A parent who is supervising his child at play cannot simultaneously be guilty of supervisorial neglect. Functionally incompatible behaviors, while not the opposite of undesirable ones, can be structured to compete with them, thus allowing for the hypothesis that increases in one class of behaviors will result in decreases in another. Increasing the amount of time that Sharon Carr spends interacting with friends in order to decrease the amount of time that she spends alone is an example. See, Eileen D. Gambrill, *Behavior Modification: Handbook of Assessment, Intervention and Evaluation* (San Francisco: Jossey-Bass, Inc., Publishers, 1977), p. 155.

2. A client who is learning noncorporal methods of discipline might also be taught to identify internal cues such as feelings of anger or resentment toward a child that are likely to elicit a harsh physical reaction, and to respond with appropriate disciplinary action before anger escalates to the point where probabilities are high that extreme physical force will be used.

3. Client assets can be identified through discussion, direct observation, simulations, and data gathered from self-reports and the reports of others. For example, clients may be asked to describe the process they would follow in applying for an AFDC grant, and to reveal their degree of comfort or discomfort with each step. The last step clients can complete in comfort is their strength vis-à-vis applying for a grant. Or worker and client can engage in role playing, the worker taking the part of the eligibility person, the client that of applicant. This allows the worker to observe and evaluate client skills in an interview simulation and to intervene by arranging for clients to acquire skills that they do not have.

4. K. T. Wiltse, "Current Issues and New Directions in Foster Care," in *Child Welfare Strategy in the Coming Years* (U.S. Department of Health, Education and Welfare, Children's Bureau, DHEW publication No. (OHDS) 78-30158, 1978), pp. 61–62.

5. Several programs that make use of community volunteers to assist families are described in, Sheila Maybanks and Marvin Bryce (eds.) *Home Based Services for Children and Families: Policy, Practice and Research* (Springfield, Ill.: Charles C. Thomas, Publisher 1979).

6. Carol M. Rose, *Some Emerging Issues in Legal Liability of Children's Agencies* (New York: Child Welfare League of America, 1978).

7. This section draws on material from, Eileen D. Gambrill and Theodore J. Stein, *Supervision in Child Welfare: A Training Manual* (Berkeley: University of California Extension Press, 1978), pp. 136–40.

8. Ibid., p. 138.

9. Dennis R. Young and Richard R. Nelson, *Public Policy for Day Care of Young Children: Organization, Finance and Planning* (Lexington, Mass.: D.C. Heath & Co., 1973), p. 1.

10. D. L. Peters and F. Jeffrey Koppel, "Day Care: An Overview" *Child and Youth Services*, Vol. 1, No. 4 (1977), p. 4.

11. *The Community Team: An Approach to Case Management and Prevention, Child Abuse and Neglect: The Problem and Its Management*, Volume 3, (Washington, D.C.: U.S. Department of Health, Education and Welfare, DHEW publication No. (OHD) 75-30075, 1975), pp. 86–87.

12. Ibid.

13. Ibid., pp. 87–88.

14. P. J. Beezley, "Modern Treatment Options," in *The Child Protection Team Handbook* (ed.) Barton D. Schmitt, (New York: Garland STPM Press, 1978), pp. 272–73.

15. Gambrill, *Supervision*, pp. 151–55.

16. The use of negotiation training to resolve parent-child problems is illustrated in, Theodore J. Stein and Eileen D. Gambrill, *Decision Making in Foster Care: A Training Manual* (Berkeley: University of California Extension Press, 1976), pp. 108–118.

17. The father made no mention of Marie. At a subsequent session, the worker noted that they would have to discuss her future living arrangements once Ward Quigley had the opportunity to begin work towards Ronald's return.

18. Depending upon state law, contact need not be in person. One or two letters or telephone calls in a year may constitute a show of interest, precluding termination based on abandonment.

19. Victor Pike and Others, *Permanent Planning for Children in Foster Care: A Handbook for Social Workers* (Portland, Ore.: Regional Research Institute for Human Services, Portland State University, 1977), p. 92.

20. The worker can describe observed behavior based upon which an inference was drawn, but, the cause of such behavior cannot be established unless the client was observed consuming alcohol or using drugs or through breathalizer or urinalysis tests.

21. The steps described here refer to practice in California. State by state variations suggest caution in generalizing from this material.

22. Most states require that consent be given in the presence of a court or agency representative in order to safeguard against the possibility that parents may have been coerced into giving their consent. Voluntary relinquishments are generally taken after the birth of a child because some parents change their minds after seeing the infant. In addition to biological parent's consent, consent must be obtained from any person lawfully entitled to custody of the child or empowered to consent for the minor, from a court that has jurisdiction to determine custody, and from the minor if he or she is over ten years of age, unless the court determines that it is in the minor's best interest to dispense with consent.

23. A summons is a formal notice reporting the date, time, and place of the hearing. Allegations of the petition are summarized, and the reasons why the child is said to be within the court's jurisdiction, as well as the grounds for seeking termination, are documented.

24. This case involved two unmarried adults who lived together, off and on, for eighteen years, during which time they had three children. When the mother died the children were declared wards of the state for purposes of adoption. Peter Stanley protested, arguing that he had been deprived of his children without a finding of unfitness. The Supreme Court agreed with the father and referred the case back to the Illinois Court for a rehearing. (As it turned out, Stanley was declared unfit and the children remained in the custody of the State of Illinois.) See, *Children's Rights Report*, Vol. II, No. 5 (February 1978) (New York: Juvenile Rights Project of the American Civil Liberties Union Foundation), p. 3.: Donald Brieland and John Lemmon, *Social Work and the Law* (St. Paul, Minn.: West Publishing Company, 1977), p. 386.

25. Ibid., p. 387.

26. Ibid., p. 359.

27. Barbara D. Larsen, *Reach Out—A Program for Children in Need of Adoptive Planning* (Los Angeles: Los Angeles County Department of Adoptions, 1978), p. 12.

28. Brieland, *Social Work and the Law*, pp. 378–79.

9

Case Termination and Follow-up

TERMINATION

Termination is a process that begins at intake, when the objectives of child welfare services are explained. It is here that clients learn that foster care is a temporary service, offered until children can be reunited with their parents; that protective service offers time-limited assistance in the family home in order to stabilize family life and safeguard children; and that adoption services culminate when a child is securely placed with a new family. The time limits set in contracts point out that services are short-term.

Throughout the assessment, case planning, and service delivery phases, workers prepare clients for managing independently, paving the way for cases to be closed by the child welfare agency. When Ann Tripp explained the rationale for maintaining an activities log, she was teaching her client that feelings of depression do not occur in isolation, but rather that they are correlated with other, ongoing events in the client's life which must be identified to reach correct intervention decisions. By providing recording forms Ann Tripp gave her client a tool which she could use in the future should her situation warrant self-monitoring. When she taught the process of analyzing the log, she was instructing Sharon Carr in ways of identifying activities and associated factors such as people, places, and cognitions that led to differing evaluations of her moods. This provided an objective basis for discriminating between problem and nonproblem situations and allowed her client to take a more balanced view of her situation. Describing the process of selecting interventions on the basis of the analysis could facilitate the chance that Sharon Carr would take action on her own behalf in the future.

When workers involve clients in the process of developing case plans, as Ann Tripp did when she formulated a procedure for the Carrs to follow in dividing responsibility for household management, they are imparting skills that clients can later use to resolve basic family difficulties.

Throughout service delivery, clients are taught to accept increased responsibility for problem solving. Initially, a worker may assume responsibility for identifying community resources and arranging appointments for clients. By describing the processes involved and by encouraging clients to observe their goal-oriented behavior, workers act as role models, conveying skills which clients can later use on their own behalf. As clients demonstrate planning skills, they can be asked to identify their strengths in the face of given problems, and, building on identified strengths, to describe the steps that must be taken to realize goals. When workers share evaluative data they point out the ways in which the client has built on his or her own strengths and stress the client's contribution to goal attainment. This continually reassures family members that they have the ability to make further gains on their own. Next, as the evidence of client progress toward goals and objectives mounts, workers decrease the frequency with which they see clients, pointing out the client's ability to act independently.

Some components of service delivery terminate before others. For instance, the goals to be attained in working with a public health nurse or mental health worker may be reached before overall case objectives are realized. Thus the client is able to experience termination in a "staggered" manner and to review the experience with the worker. Since the worker continues to monitor client behavior he or she is able to reinforce family members' ability to maintain change without direct assistance. And the family knows that the worker is there to intervene should this be necessary. Finally, clients are assured that they can contact their worker should difficulties emerge that they cannot manage on their own.

Workers terminate cases when (1) a decision is made not to provide the services of the child welfare agency (the Andres case illustrates this), (2) parents will not accept services voluntarily and there is insufficient evidence or reason to refer the case to court, (3) voluntary clients withdraw from services and there is insufficient evidence or reason to refer the case to court, (4) a case is transferred from one unit in an agency to another unit (for example, from protective services to foster care services) and the case may be closed to the transferring worker, and (5) the evidence gathered during service delivery shows that goals and objectives established in a case plan have been reached. When termination occurs for the last reason, it should be preceded by a follow-up period during which workers maintain contact with the family in order to assure that changes in family life brought about through service delivery efforts are maintained and to assist clients in the resolution of new difficulties that might threaten the child's safety at home.

Termination may occur before all of the family's problems are resolved. Once evidence indicates that parents are able to provide a minimal level of child care, cases may be closed with a referral to a community agency for assistance with unresolved difficulties.[1] The decision to terminate is reached in consultation with supervisors, with members of a service delivery team, and with collaterals who have been active in providing services.

FOLLOW-UP

Workers maintain contact with families during follow-up. Meetings occur on a regular basis, although less frequently than during the service delivery phase. Contact may consist of telephone calls, home or office visits, or some combination of these.

Information gathered during this time informs the worker that changes effected through the provision of services are being maintained in the client's natural environment. The worker offers ongoing reassurance of the client's ability to manage on his or her own by pointing out skills the client has acquired and by supporting the use of these skills. Follow-up allows for corrective action should difficulties be encountered. The duration of this phase, the frequency with which clients are seen, and the method of contact are contingent upon the family's ability to manage independently, the availability of personal support systems, availability of professional services from community resources, and the worker's time. In general, three to six months constitute an ample follow-up period. The importance of this phase is illustrated by a case example.

THE WATSON FAMILY

Steven Watson, age nine and one-half, was returned to his parent's home following three and one-half months in foster care. He had been physically abused by his father, Peter Watson, prior to his placement. Services provided by the child welfare worker before Steven's return had (1) enabled the father to eliminate alcohol consumption, (2) facilitated his involvement in caring for four other children who had remained in the family home, thereby relieving his wife of full-time responsibility for child care, and (3) helped the family resolve some behavior problems of their children at home.[2]

Follow-up

For sixty days following Steven's return to his family home, the worker visited with the Watsons on a biweekly basis, maintaining telephone contact on alternate weeks. No difficulties were identified during this time. At the beginning of the third month, Steven's mother, Gloria Watson, reported that he was beginning to have tantrums (screaming and shouting) and to fight with his younger siblings, although in his father's presence he was said to "exhibit exemplary behavior." Gloria Watson was usually in some other part of the house and would become aware of "screaming and shouting." She said "it seemed that the children would get into an argument over toys or what to watch on television and that Steven would 'bully' the younger children and, when he could not get his way, would scream and shout."

When asked how she dealt with this problem, Gloria Watson said that she would separate Steven from the four younger children and "talk with him about the problem," and that she was spending as much as one-half to a full hour with Steven each afternoon following these "scenes." This "greatly distressed" her because it interfered with completion of her own chores. She said she knew she was "probably supporting this behavior by spending so much time with Steven" but that her only concern was putting an end to the yelling and shouting and that in this she was effective.

Shortly after Steven had been reunited with his parents, the worker had suggested that they identify some activities, possibly at a neighborhood community center, in which the children might engage after school and on weekends, when Peter Watson was working, in order to relieve Gloria Watson of caring for all five children by herself. The worker broached this subject again as one method of resolving the current issue, and the parents agreed to contact the neighborhood center and obtain a list of appropriate activities for the children. The worker agreed to meet with the parents and the children in four days and to go over the list and discuss a procedure for enrolling the children at the center.

Two days later Gloria Watson telephoned the worker and told him that she and Peter Watson were convinced that Steven was "hyperactive," and that they wanted to have a medical consultation. The worker doubted that there was any organic basis for the youngster's difficulties, but thought that if organic causes could be ruled out the parents might be more willing to engage in an appropriate program to eliminate these recent problems. Over the next several weeks Steven underwent a general physical examination, glucose tolerance test, EEG, psychiatric assessment, and psychological testing. None of the physical tests indicated any organic problems. The psychiatrist told the parents that he did not believe that psychotherapy was called for and reinforced the caseworker's recommendation regarding Steven and the younger children.

The parents then followed through on the suggestion that they identify appropriate programs at the community center. Steven subsequently joined the Cub Scouts and enrolled in an arts and crafts class that met twice each week at the center. The worker also suggested that since Steven was positively reinforced by time with his mother, she should set aside some time each week that she and Steven could spend together in a structured activity pleasurable to both. Both Steven and Gloria Watson stated that they had "always enjoyed reading together and talking about what they read," but had never done this on a set schedule. Gloria Watson agreed to spend one-half to one hour in this activity with Steven on those afternoons when he was not participating in community center activities.

The worker remained with this case for ninety additional days of follow-up, reducing this contact to the biweekly in-person and alternate week telephone contacts that had been maintained prior to the onset of the last problem. Steven was still reported to fight "on occasion" with his siblings, but not to an extent that was considered to be a problem. The court dependency was dismissed.

While follow-up activities are important in all cases, the nature of foster care makes them especially so. Parents and children must readjust to each other after a period of separation that in many instances may have lasted several years. While increased visits prior to restoration approximate living together on a full-time basis, they are not an identical experience. Knowing that visits are finite—that they will end with the child returning to the foster home—may cause parent and child to be on their best behavior, or it may cause them to mask problems because they want to enjoy the brief time that they have with each other. Masking problems is not likely to continue following restoration, although there may be a "honeymoon" period during which each will try to please the other, tolerating behaviors that they will later find unacceptable. Consequently, follow-up in foster care cases is of critical importance.

Follow-up With the Carrs

Ann Tripp made biweekly visits to the family home during the first month and one at-home visit in the second month. Telephone contact was maintained on nonvisiting weeks. For two months the children continued with their household responsibilities and Sharon Carr's log and her verbal reports showed an increase in personal activities, in interaction with friends and with family, as well as an overall increase in positive evaluations of activities. Nita's involvement with the career counselor and school attendance did not improve during this time.

Ten days into the third month Ann Tripp received a "frantic" telephone call from Sharon Carr who reported that Nita had disappeared. She had not returned from school the previous day. The mother had contacted Nita's closest friends, her school principal, and her counselor at the women's center. The only information forthcoming was that Nita had not attended school the previous day.

Ann Tripp retraced some of the mother's efforts. She contacted the school and Nita's counselor at the women's center and telephoned local hospitals and the police, but learned nothing. Two hours after Sharon Carr's call, she and Ann Tripp went to the police department to file a missing person report.

The worker continued follow-up work with the Carr family for an additional four months. Nita's whereabouts were not ascertained and she was officially classified as a "runaway." During this time, Tripp focused her efforts on helping the Carrs deal with Nita's disappearance while simultaneously trying to prevent them from losing the gains that they had made in resolving their initial difficulties. In addition to discussing the family's feelings about Nita's behavior, the worker provided them with literature dealing with the phenomenon of runaway youth, and she introduced Sharon Carr to a social worker at a family service agency who was experienced in working with parents of runaway children. Through a combination of these efforts, the mother slowly learned to view Nita's behavior in the context of a growing social phenomenon, somewhat decreasing her feelings of personal blame.

By the start of the third month of the extended follow-up period, life in the Carr home took on a semblance of normality. Progress in maintaining change, which had understandably slipped during the crisis surrounding Nita's disappearance, was regained. Two months later, the court dependency was dismissed at the worker's recommendation, and the case was terminated.

The Quigley Children

Ronald Quigley's adoption was finalized seven months after he was placed in the preadoptive home. Marie remained with her foster parents in accordance with the conditions set forth in the long-term care agreement.

SUMMARY

Termination is a process that begins at intake, when workers inform clients that child welfare services are short-term in nature.

Throughout the process of assessment, case planning, and service delivery, clients are taught skills which will enable them to act autonomously and they are asked to assume increasing responsibility for problem solving.

Workers reinforce clients' ability to act autonomously by decreasing the frequency with which they see family members, by highlighting the ways in which the client is able to act without relying on the worker, and by pointing out the exact ways in which the client is contributing to goal attainment.

Since some components of service delivery end before others, clients can experience termination in a staggered fashion, which allows them to review their feelings about this experience with their worker.

Cases terminate for a variety of reasons, including parental refusal to accept services, parental withdrawal after service delivery has been initiated, transfer of cases to other units in the agency, and proof that goals and objectives have been realized.

Follow-up services may be provided prior to termination to assure that changes in family life are being maintained, and to take corrective action should back-sliding" occur or new problems be identified, and to provide ongoing reassurance to clients of their ability to act independently.

NOTES

1. *Standards for Child Protective Services* (New York: Child Welfare League of America, 1973 revised), p. 37.

2. This case is reported in detail in, Theodore J. Stein and Eileen D. Gambrill, *Decision Making in Foster Care: A Training Manual* (Berkeley: University of California Extension Press, 1976), pp. 171–94.

10

Future Directions

Throughout this text I have used the concept of rights to further the reader's understanding of certain relationships, such as those existing between families and the state and between federal and state levels of government, and to provide a context for understanding changes in the field of practice. Many of the legislative and judicial changes reviewed in chapter four of part one and the effects these have had on direct practice (some of which were illustrated in the case material reported in part two) are the direct result of efforts to establish the principle that every child has the right to be raised in a permanent home, and to develop mechanisms through which this goal can be realized.

Asserting each child's right to continuity in care is only one goal of child advocates and a movement that has come to be known as the Children's Rights Movement. From the perspective of direct practice in child welfare, the changes brought about through child advocacy, most particularly by the "Constitutionalization" of children's rights, have far-reaching implications.[1] The objectives of the Children's Rights Movement, the gains that have been made, and the implications these have for social work practice in child welfare are the primary focuses of this chapter.

We begin with an overview of child advocacy as a context against which issues related to children's rights will be addressed. The chapter concludes with a discussion of changes in the population of children who are served by child welfare agencies.

CHILD ADVOCACY

Child advocacy is a social movement whose objectives are "to identify and promote improvements in conditions which adversely affect the growth and development of children."[2] This definition can be applied to the activities of nineteenth century social reformers, and so the origins of the advocacy movement can be traced back to the late 1800s, when the first Society for the Prevention of Cruelty to Children was founded in New York. Then, as now, child advocates were concerned with improving the conditions that adversely affect the well-being of children. The particular facet of the advocacy movement that addresses itself to children's legal rights is of more recent origins, taking direction from events occurring in the 1960s and 1970s when women, racial and ethnic minorities, gay people, and prisoners began to apply pressure to advance and protect a diversity of rights.

Child advocates include professionals, such as lawyers, social workers, and physicians, as well as lay people. They address themselves to a broad array of issues. In addition to advocating the extension of constitutional guarantees to young people, they lobby for the passage of legislation through which special programs for children will be created and funded, intervene on behalf of children to see that they receive needed services, and engage in other activities in their efforts to advance the "children's cause."[3]

Impetus for the growth of the advocacy movement in the 1970s came from many directions. It came from documented evidence of social neglect of children, including physical neglect and abuse of youngsters in substitute care settings where they had been placed for protection; the drift of children into unplanned, long-term foster care; the absence of educational and treatment programs, the need for which was said to justify depriving young people of their liberty by confining them to institutional settings; the absence of adequate medical care for many children; and evidence of the deleterious effects of assigning pejorative labels to young people.[4] The advocacy movement grew, not only to advance children's rights in specific areas, but also to act as a "watchdog" on social and judicial agencies whose actions often seemed less benign and effective than they professed to be.

CASE ADVOCACY.   Advocates pursue their goals on a case-by-case basis or through class actions. A child welfare worker who is seeking to eliminate restrictive eligibility requirements in order to obtain a needed service for a child is engaging in *case advocacy*. Likewise, a foster parent may advocate a child's right to remain in a permanent family setting by appealing an agency decision to remove a youngster to a new foster home.

CLASS ADVOCACY. Attorneys seeking to expand the statutory grounds under which parental rights may be terminated in order to remove barriers to placing children in permanent homes are taking action to benefit all children in need of permanent homes. This is an example of *class advocacy*. Each type of advocacy serves an important but different function. Class advocacy, because it addresses the common needs of a group of children, is a more efficient approach to change than advocacy on a case-by-case basis. However, the benefits for the individual child depend on the specific characteristics he or she shares with other members of the class. The case advocacy approach permits action addressed to meeting the unique needs of an individual child.

It is important to maintain a distinction between advocacy and the provision of direct services. The latter is concerned with making use of available resources to benefit children in specific ways—for example, a worker assisting a parent to enroll a child in a day-care program to achieve the goal of preparing the youngster for entry into public school. Advocacy is concerned with accountability—with seeing to it that the day-care program is indeed providing the child with educational opportunities, as opposed to offering strictly custodial care.[5]

THE CHILDREN'S RIGHTS MOVEMENT

Historically children's rights have been viewed as synonomous with those of their parents. The process of recognizing that children have rights which in certain circumstances can be viewed independently of parental interests has been a slow one. It evolved since the eighteenth century, when children were regarded as chattels (and the term "children's rights" would have been a non-sequitur) to the neglect laws of the nineteenth century, stating that there are situations in which the state has a responsibility to intervene in parent-child relationships to protect youngsters from harm.[6]

Proponents of the children's rights movement present a twofold position on this subject. On the one hand, they press for the extension of many adult rights to children. For example, they argue that youngsters have a right to receive medical treatment without parental consent and the right to legal counsel in any situation where their interests are affected. On the other hand, they seek a "legally enforceable recognition of children's special needs and interests."[7] These conceptually distinct positions are reviewed separately.

Constitutionalization of Children's Rights

Legally, the concept of rights refers to "enforceable claims to the possession of property or authority, or to the enjoyment of privileges or immunities."[8] Rights in American society are ascribed primarily to adults. Children, because they are dependent and immature and so require protection and guidance, are legally classified as "infants or minors" until reaching the age of 18 or 21. The legal view of children is expressed in the doctrine of *parens patriae*, which has provided the justification for restricting the rights of children in juvenile court proceedings. The view of the children embedded in this legal doctrine reflects a larger social perception of the rights and responsibilities of young people, and advocates of constitutional safeguards for children have directed their activities to a broader range of issues than those involving courtroom procedures.

Beginning in the 1960s court challenges have resulted in the extension of certain constitutional rights to children. First Amendment guarantees of freedom of speech were extended to young people in 1967 when, in the case of *Tinker v. Des Moines Independent Community School District*, the United States Supreme Court ruled that children are "persons" under the Constitution whose right to freedom of speech or expression is not "shed at the schoolhouse gates."[9] In 1976 the Supreme Court struck down a Missouri state law that required minors to obtain parental consent prior to having an abortion, arguing that "children as well as adults have a 'right to privacy'." The Court noted that a minor's right to privacy outweighed "any parental interest in the abortion."[10] Decisions extending constitutional rights to children have been equivocal. For instance, in 1977 the United States Supreme Court refused to extend the prohibition against "cruel and unusual punishment" to schoolchildren, arguing that this prohibition was meant to protect prisoners, not to safeguard children from corporal punishment in the schools.[11]

Of special import for practice in child welfare are those cases that have resulted in the extension of certain *due process* rights to juvenile court proceedings. The essence of due process is that a "person should always have notice and a real chance to present his or her side on a legal dispute and that no law or government procedure should be arbitrary or unfair."[12]

Based on the assumption that all parties to juvenile court proceed-

ings were concerned with the best interests of the child, such proceedings have not typically been viewed as adversarial. Hence, due process
safeguards were not seen as essential to protect children's interests.
The assumed benevolence of the court was challenged in 1967 on behalf of a fifteen-year-old boy named Gerald Gault (in re Gault), who was
charged with making obscene telephone calls to a neighbor. Neither the
youngster nor his parents were given advanced notice of the charges
against him, and he was not informed of his legal rights.[13] The boy was
sentenced to six year's confinement for a crime which, if committed by
an adult, bore a maximum penalty of a "small fine or two months in
jail."[14] The United States Supreme Court ruled that certain due process
rights (the right to receive notice of a hearing in order to prepare a
defense, the right to counsel, the prohibition against self-incrimination,
and the right to confront and cross-examine witnesses) had to be extended to juveniles at the jurisdictional hearing in delinquency proceedings. Additional safeguards have been extended to juvenile court
proceedings but, once again, decisions have been equivocal. In 1970
the principle of "proof beyond a reasonable doubt" was established as a
requirement at the jurisdictional phase of the hearing (in re Winship).
However, the following year the Court refused to recognize that
juveniles are constitutionally entitled to a trial by jury (McKeiver v.
Pennsylvania).[15]

The constitutional guarantees extended thus far have not, by and
large, affected neglect and dependency hearings. They are concerned
with situations where the child's liberty, not custody, are at stake.
However, the likelihood that dependency hearings will be affected by
the extension of due process guarantees is suggested by several trends.

First, as the American Civil Liberties Union argues, the distinction
between loss of liberty (the issue at hand in delinquency hearings) and
the question of a child's custody, which are the concern in dependency
proceedings, may have little practical meaning.[16] The importance of
providing children with independent counsel in some custody cases
has already been recognized, as well as in cases in which the state seeks
to compel medical treatment, or education, or to commit youngsters to
mental hospitals.

Cases that have pitted children's rights against those of the child
caring agencies to make unilateral decisions for youngsters in their care
also reflect this trend and are of particular importance to child welfare
personnel. These cases have challenged the doctrine of in loco parentis
under which "persons and institutions caring for children are said to
occupy the legal position of the child's parent and, as such, to be
immune from suit." They have been successful in asserting a child's
right to contest treatment, to receive treatment and to be free of arbitrary punishment.[17]

Foster parents have challenged the position of child-caring agencies that suggest they have no "standing" with regard to the children in their care. While court decisions vary, many, in arguing for the validity of the concept of psychological parenthood, have supported foster parents in their claims to consideration when decisions affecting the welfare of children in their care are made. Courts have recognized that foster parents have a right to a hearing before children are taken from their homes and a right to appeal decisions that result in the removal of children from their homes.[18] In 1974 the Supreme Court of California observed that:

> a person who assumes the role of a parent, raising the child in his own home, may in time acquire an interest in the companionship, care, custody, and management of the child ... and acquires the interest of a "de facto parent." [the court defined de facto parent as] "that person who, on a day-to-day basis, assumes the role of parent, seeking to fulfill both the child's physical needs and his psychological need for affection and care." [they concluded that] ".... they [the foster parents] should be permitted to appear as parties to assert and protect their own interest in the companionship, care, custody and management of the child."[19]

Children's Bill of Rights

The second thrust of the Children's Rights Movement seeks to establish a children's charter or a bill of rights in which children's special needs and rights are delineated and through which their rights could be enforced. This facet of the Movement dates back to the 1930 White House Conference on Children and Youth, where the first such charter was formulated. Subsequent efforts to develop a bill of rights for children have been advanced by the United Nations, The National Commission for the Mental Health of Children, the National Association of Social Workers, and others.[20]

The coverage in these documents is far-reaching, ranging from pragmatic issues such as a child's right to an education and medical treatment to expressing broad social ideals such as the principle that all children have a "right to continuous loving care or to grow up in a sympathetic community."[21]

The items covered in these documents reflect a praiseworthy concern for the special needs of children, but they fail to distinguish between enforceable issues, such as insuring children's education or access to medical services, and issues that concern a child's right to loving care, which cannot be enforced by a court of law.

IMPLICATIONS FOR PRACTICE. Concern with advancing and safeguarding the rights of children and their natural and foster parents is creating a legal framework around social work practice in child welfare. Many elements of this framework have been established in recent years, attesting to the momentum of the children's rights movement and the gains it has made. Various components of this legal framework have been covered in previous chapters. Before addressing their implications for day-to-day practice in child welfare, a summary review is in order.

The passage of the Child Abuse Prevention and Treatment Act and the requirements for mandatory reporting of maltreatment have established a formal mechanism for community monitoring of parental behaviors and greatly expanded the legal mechanisms for responding to reports of parental misbehavior vis-à-vis their children. The neglect statutes handed down from the nineteenth century are largely a reactive mechanism for state intervention into family life. The child abuse reporting laws, while retaining the right to react in instances of maltreatment, are, to a great extent, proactive. Provisions for educating the lay community about abuse and neglect, requirements that lay persons as well as professionals report suspected cases of maltreatment, the codification of penalties for not reporting, and the abrogation of privileged communication between patient and physician and between husband and wife create an explicit framework for the state to monitor parent-child relationships that would, in times past, have been found an unacceptable intrusion into family privacy.

The mechanisms for reporting and the statutory mandate to intervene in family life whether or not parents want assistance are perhaps the strongest statements to date of how far the state is willing to go to safeguard a child's right to be protected from physical harm. However, while expanding the framework for coercive intervention, efforts to limit the conditions under which the state can intervene in parent-child relationships (providing a balance against unwarranted and excessive intrusion), can be seen in attempts to identify reportable conditions, to provide reporters with examples of these conditions, to limit coercive intervention to those situations where there is reasonable evidence of harm to a child, and by establishing stringent evidentiary requirements.

Likewise, efforts to identify minimum standards of parenting, to limit court intervention to those situations where parental behavior falls below an identified minimum, and to require a showing of the exact ways in which a child is being harmed reduce the likelihood that intervention will occur solely on the basis of parental conduct or condition and further establish safeguards for a family's right to privacy. Alaska's new Children's Code is perhaps the best example to date of the codification of such safeguards.

While the elements of a legal framework for practice are most evident in protective services, they are also apparent in the areas of foster care and adoption. This is especially true in regard to mechanisms that have been established to facilitate the placement of children in permanent homes, supporting the claim that this is each child's right. These mechanisms are broad and vary in nature. They include monitoring systems, such as required judicial review of the cases of children in out-of-home care, which is expected to halt the drift of children into unplanned, long-term placement; the enactment or modifications of laws permitting the termination of parental rights; the growing use of subsidies to facilitate adoptions; efforts to modify statutes in order to facilitate the adoption of children across state lines; and legislative efforts to establish time limits for case planning, particularly for pursuing adoption for children who cannot be restored to the biological parents. One critic notes that, "the growing concern of the state for the welfare of children has shifted the focus from the rights of natural parents to those of the child."[22]

What are the implications for day-to-day practice in child welfare? It is axiomatic that the interface between child welfare and the law is enlarging, and evidence suggests that this trend will continue. Therefore, consulting with legal personnel and appearing in court will become normal aspects of practice.

The due process safeguards reviewed earlier in this chapter are already affecting neglect and dependency hearings, and it is probable that this trend will continue. As juvenile court proceedings become more formal, "uncorroborated admissions, hearsay testimony and untested social investigations [will no longer be acceptable] as the basis for adjudication." Workers will be expected to present substantive, factual testimony in court.[23] Therefore, guidelines for gathering and recording data during assessment and investigation, case planning, and service delivery will stress the acquisition of factual, rather than impressionistic, information and will emphasize recording in a descriptive, as opposed to an inferential, manner. Workers will have to become familiar with legal rules regarding evidence in order to determine what to look for during investigations and what will be admissible in court. If the American Bar Association's guidelines for presenting information to the court are adopted, the use of summary labels, without a descriptive account of the observed facts from which the labels were drawn, will not be permitted in court.[24]

The informal, nonadversarial nature of juvenile court proceedings has permitted members of the bench to exercise a great deal of personal discretion in reaching decisions and has allowed workers to base their recommendations to the court on subjective impressions. As hearings become more formal and as judicial and casework decisions are challenged by attorneys representing the respective interests of children and their natural and foster parents, the measure of personal discretion and subjectivity will no doubt be curtailed. There will be an emphasis on specifying the grounds for any recommendation or decision as objectively as possible. Workers will have to consider that each party to a case may have special, perhaps conflicting, interests in the decisions that are reached and to take these respective interests into account in formulating recommendations. Child welfare staff will have to be prepared to defend their choices as they are called upon to testify in court more often.

Although the present thrust to formalize courtroom procedures is focused primarily on the jurisdictional, or fact-finding, phase of juvenile court hearings, the procedures to be followed at disposition and during review hearings are being affected. This is most evident in the movement to require workers to formulate and present written case plans to the court for each child, and most particularly with reference to the information to be presented in these plans. The specifications for case-planning information that are called for in the Adoption Assistance and Child Welfare Reform Act of 1979 illustrate the direction that is being taken.

> The term "case plan" means a written document which includes at least the following. . . . a plan of services that will be provided to the parents, child and foster parents in order to improve the conditions in the parents' homes, facilitate return of the child to his own home or the permanent placement of the child and address the needs of each child while in foster care, including a description of the appropriateness of the services that have been provided to the child under this plan.[25]

Some of the recommendations that have been formulated by the National Council of Juvenile and Family Court Judges in order to give direction and substance to review hearings are of special importance for practitioners. Discussing case planning and referring to the problem-solving goals that are established in a case plan, the council states that goals must be specific, not broad, and that vague treatment orders, such as a directive to a parent to participate in mental health counseling, should not be acceptable. All treatments that are proposed in a plan should address an identified family problem, and the ways in which the treatment modality is expected to resolve the problem should be "clearly defined." Council recommendations stress that the child's parents or guardians should be involved in developing plans and that "professional jargon" should be eliminated in favor of "lay language" to ensure that all parties understand the implications of the plan.[26]

The case management procedures used by the workers whose cases were presented in the preceding chapters illustrate one approach to meeting the imperatives a legal framework imposes on social work practice in child welfare. In general it can be said that the development and implementation of new approaches to practice constitute a response to the increased importance of the rights of those persons most directly affected by the procedures and practice employed by child welfare and court personnel. These procedures and practices give teeth to the idea that the rights of children and their caretakers are to be respected and safeguarded by providing objective grounds for challenges to court and agency decision-making procedures.

The implications of extending constitutional guarantees to children are more clear than those that devolve from a Children's Bill of Rights. Many of the issues incorporated in the various children's charters are stated at a level of abstraction that renders their implementation extremely difficult, if not impossible. That fifty years have passed since the first charter was developed clearly indicates the difficulties inherent in implementing many of the principles these charters contain. Also, implementing a bill of rights for children leaves a number of questions unanswered, such as; "To what extent is the state willing to intervene in family life to monitor parental behaviors in order to assure that children are receiving the extensive rights covered?" "What is the standard for evaluating whether children are receiving 'continuous loving care'? Of perhaps greater significance in a pluralistic society are questions of whether any such standard could be developed that would take into account divergent styles of child rearing. Whether our society is willing to commit the monetary resources necessary to develop the wide array of services—medical, educational, and social, for example—needed to fulfill the tenets of a bill of rights for children is questionable. Evidence to date does not suggest reasons for optimism. The Comprehensive Child Development Act of 1971, through which a wide array of programs to meet the developmental needs of children would have been established, was vetoed by President Richard M. Nixon, and the chances for passage of such legislation in the near future are slim. Likewise, Congress has appropriated little money for the National Center for Child Advocacy, severely restricting their ability to pursue the objectives of "identifying and promoting improvements in conditions which adversely affect the growth of children."[27]

A very difficult set of questions focuses attention on the relationship between a child's age and the child's ability to make the judgments required to exercise rights independent of adult guidance. There is little argument that age criteria are frequently arbitrary. When the voting age was lowered from twenty-one to eighteen it was not because factual data emerged showing that eighteen-year-olds were capable of a level of maturity not previously found in this age group. And the fact that certain constitutional rights have been extended to juveniles in recent years acknowledges that young people are able to exercise greater judgment than they have previously been given credit for. However, there are no easy answers to questions such as what legal rights can be exercised by a fourteen-year-old but not by a twelve-year-old? Nor do we have formulas that can be easily applied in order to answer such questions.

The fact that there are limits to implementing the principles set forth in a bill of rights for children should not mean that they are rendered meaningless. Rather, as the Presidential Advisory Committee on Children and Youth suggests, advocacy for a children's charter should be seen as an "indication of the state of public conscience and the intensity of social concern."[28] The tenets set forth in children's charters are perhaps best viewed as establishing a set of long-range social goals for children.

The Children's Rights Movement reflects the zeitgeist of our times. While it is not possible to predict the exact gains that will be made by advocates of children's rights, it is not likely that the trend to accord greater rights to young people will be reversed.

THE CHANGING POPULATION OF CHILDREN

The final issue addressed in this chapter draws attention to the children who are served by child welfare agencies and concerns the suggestion that these youngsters are older than those served in the past.[29] Evidence on this point is equivocal; for example, Shyne reports that the median age of the children being served by child welfare agencies in 1977 was 9.2 years compared to a median age of 9.9 years in 1961.[30] Nevertheless, there may be a trend taking place that is not reflected in our most current national statistics.

There are good reasons why the ages of children receiving the services of child welfare agencies might be on the increase. The Juvenile Justice and Delinquency Prevention Act of 1974 requires that states receiving federal monies cease to place status offenders (youngsters who have engaged in acts that would not be the concern of the law if committed by adults) with youths who are charged with delinquent behaviors. This has led to the diverting of some of these youths from the juvenile justice system to child welfare agencies.[31] The movement toward deinstitutionalization places a burden on child welfare agencies to develop substitute care and treatment services for a population of children who, in the past, were served in institutional settings where the burden for child care and treatment was placed on institutional staff, not on child welfare workers in public agencies.

Also, there seems to be an increased willingness on the part of parents to turn their hard-to-handle adolescents and preadolescents over to public social services and of the schools to abdicate responsibility for children by "suspending and pushing" troublesome youth out of school.[32] In 1974 the Children's Defense Fund reported that "two million youth in the United States are permanently out of school."[33] Given the scarcity of opportunities for children outside of educational settings, it is reasonable to hypothesize that these young people constitute a group at risk of running afoul of the law. In 1976 teenage unemployment rates were more than eight times the rate of unemployment for majority males, with ethnic minorities the hardest hit group.[34]

In many ways the juvenile court and public child welfare agencies are becoming institutions of last resort for problems that families seem unable or unwilling to cope with and that communities and other public institutions are reluctant to address. These difficulties may, in part, be a direct result of our unwillingness to recognize the multiplicity of problems facing all families in our society and to respond with a wide array of supportive services.

As currently construed, child welfare systems are ill-equipped to provide adequately for large numbers of older children. There is a shortage of foster homes, in general, and a lack of homes that can provide for the older child who is said to have "more complex problems" and to be more seriously disturbed than younger children.[35] Whether some or many of these youngsters are seriously troubled or whether problems are inferred from knowledge of their status is not clear. Sari, referring to runaway youth, has observed that

> Runaways are characterized as seriously disturbed problematic youth when, in fact, two-thirds are over the age of fifteen, stay away from home no more than two days and spend the time with a relative or family friend less than ten miles from their home.[36]

Assuming, however, that at least some percentage of these children do have behavioral or emotional difficulties, it must be recognized that our limited ability to deal with troubled youth within a traditional foster family situation was instrumental in providing substitute care in institutional settings.

Central to any approach to dealing with older populations of children will be the development of new resources, most notably group care facilities. The number of such facilities can be expected to increase and it is reasonable to expect that the trend toward training for foster parents to equip them with skills to manage the behavior problems of older children will continue. Changing expectations for foster parents will give impetus to the movement to professionalize their role—to develop career ladders and establish pay scales to compensate them for providing special services. Case planning for emancipation, rather than for restoration or adoption, can be expected to increase.[37] Finally, insofar as the extension of constitutional rights is age-related, we may expect that additional rights will be extended to juveniles, adding further formality to juvenile court procedures and placing greater emphasis on carefully considering these claims in all aspects of case planning and service delivery.

CONCLUSION

It is a time of transition for the field of child welfare. The uncertainties of a transitional period can evoke anxiety as we let go of the familiar and search for answers to difficult questions—yet they can also elicit excitement for participants in this process of change.

The explication of clear guidelines for decision making and case planning should reduce much of the ambiguity and frustration that has characterized practice in the past and is a logical outcome of striving to attain social ideals for children without having clearly articulated methods for realizing them. As procedures are refined and their use institutionalized, workers can expect to see their efforts on behalf of children bear fruit as increasing numbers are placed in permanent family settings.

The lesson of recent years is that we know less about the conditions that facilitate optimal child development than we thought we knew and that our actions, despite the best intentions, are not always benign. The pendulum is swinging away from idealistic to realizable standards for judging parents and to attaining realistic goals for children. By recognizing our limits and by building incrementally on what we do know we may, in the final analysis, be able to serve the best interests of children and their families.

SUMMARY

Child advocacy is a social movement whose objectives are to identify and promote improvements in conditions which adversely affect the growth and development of children.

Child advocates include professionals and lay persons seeking to advance children's legal rights, to obtain needed medical and social services for children, and to monitor and hold accountable the social and judicial agencies that exist to serve children.

Advocates pursue their goals for children on a case-by-case basis and through class actions.

Case advocacy is appropriate when the unique needs of an individual child must be advanced.

Class advocacy is an efficient approach to addressing the common needs of a group of children.

Proponents of children's rights press for the extension of adult rights to children and seek legally enforceable methods of assuring that children's special needs and interests are met.

A range of Constitutional guarantees, including freedom of speech, a right to privacy, and the right to certain due process protections at the jurisdictional phase of juvenile court hearings, have been extended to young people.

The extension of due process rights has not, by and large, affected neglect and dependency hearings.

That they will do so in the future is suggested by court decisions in which children and their foster parents have successfully challenged the doctrine of *in loco parentis,* which has provided immunity from suit to child caring agencies.

The absence of full constitutional protections for youths reflects uncertainties on the part of judicial decision makers as to how much freedom children can exercise independent of adult guidance and wariness of creating mechanisms that will pit children against their adult caretakers.

Whether the special needs of children can be advanced as legally enforceable rights is questionable. However, identifying certain needs and formulating them in a bill of rights for young people can raise the public conscience and establish a set of long-range social goals for children.

Efforts to advance and protect children's rights have created a legal framework around social work practice in child welfare. Elements of this framework include: child abuse and neglect reporting laws through which proactive mechanisms for community monitoring of parental behaviors have been expanded and the legal mechanisms for responding to parental misbehaviors have been enlarged; increased use of judicial review to facilitate the movement of children out of foster care into permanent family homes; and new statutes to facilitate the adoption of children by expanding the grounds for termination of parental rights, providing adoption subsidies, and easing the restrictions against interstate adoption of children.

The growing interface between social work and the law, including increased formality of juvenile court hearings, can be expected to affect day-to-day practice in many ways.

Workers are expected to use court standards for evidence to guide them in gathering factual data and in reporting data to the court.

Grounds for any recommendation to the court and for casework decisions will be specified in an objective fashion.

Workers will submit written case plans to the court specifying the goals and objectives to be realized in working with a family and stating the means of realizing these goals.

Evidence suggests that the population of children served by the child welfare agencies is older than in the past as a result of: the general movement to deinstitutionalization; the requirement that states cease to place status offenders in the same facilities with youngsters adjudicated as delinquents; the willingness of parents to turn their hard-to-handle children over to the courts and to public social service agencies; and the tendency of public schools to suspend troublesome youth.

Child welfare agencies are not well equipped to serve an older population.

There is a shortage of foster homes in general and foster homes to meet the special needs of the older child.

To meet the needs of these young people, we can expect to see an increase in the use of community based group care facilities, an increase in training for foster parents, and professionalization of the foster parent role.

Social work practice in child welfare is undergoing a transition which should, in time, result in more clearly articulated guidelines for decision making and case planning, reducing the ambiguity that has characterized practice. This should increase each child's chances to be raised in a permenent family home.

NOTES

1. Carol M. Rose, *Some Emerging Issues in Legal Liability of Children's Agencies* (New York: Child Welfare League of America, 1978), p. 3.

2. Gilbert Y. Steiner, *The Children's Cause* (Washington, D.C.: The Brookings Institution, 1976), p. 130.

3. For a review of the advocacy movement, see Steiner, ibid.

4. Steiner, *Children's Cause*, p. 173.

5. J. L. Paul, "Advocacy and the Advocate," in James L. Paul, G. Ronald Neufeld, and John W. Pelosi (eds.) *Child Advocacy Within the System* (Syracuse, N.Y.: Syracuse University Press, 1977), pp. 139–40.

6. H. Rodham, "Children Under the Law," in *Harvard Educational Review*, Reprint Series No. 9 (1974), p. 3.

7. Ibid., pp. 8–9.

8. Ibid., p. 2.

9. This case involved the right of students to engage in nondisruptive, symbolic speech by wearing antiwar armbands. See, Donald Brieland and John Lemmon, *Social Work and the Law* (St. Paul, Minn.: West Publishing Co., 1977), pp. 679–85.

10. Rose, *Emerging Legal Issues*, pp. 4–5.

11. Ibid., p. 4.

12. Brieland, *Social Work and the Law*, p. 802.

13. Ibid., p. 154.

14. Ann Fagan Ginger, *The Law, The Supreme Court and the People's Rights* (Woodbury, N.Y.: Barron's Educational Series, Inc., 1973), p. 366.

15. Rodham, "Children Under the Law," pp. 13–14; Brieland, *Social Work and the Law*, pp. 154, 59.

16. *Children's Rights Report*, Vol. 1, No. 5 (New York: Juvenile Rights Project of the American Civil Liberties Union Foundation, February 1977), p. 2.

17. Rose, *Emerging Issues*, pp. 5–6, 8.

18. *Legal Issues in Foster Care* (Raleigh, N.C.: National Association of Attorneys General, Committee on the Office of Attorney General, 1976), ch. 3.

19. *Children's Rights Report*, Vol. 1, No. 4 (New York: Juvenile Rights Project of the American Civil Liberties Union Foundation, December 1976–January 1977), pp. 4–5.

20. For a review of this aspect of the Children's Rights Movement, see: Beatrice Gross and Ronald Gross (eds.), *The Children's Rights Movement: Overcoming the Oppression of Young People* (Garden City, N.Y.: Anchor Press/Doubleday, 1977).

21. Rodham, "Children Under the Law," p. 10.

22. *Standards for Adoption Services* (New York: Child Welfare League of America, 1973 revised), p. 5.

23. C. Bell and W. J. Mlyniec, "Preparing for a Neglect Proceeding: A Guide for the Social Worker," *Public Welfare*, Vol. 32, No. 4 (1974), pp. 26–37.

24. Institute of Judicial Administration, American Bar Association, Juvenile Justice Standards Project, *Standards Relating to Juvenile Records and Information Systems—Tentative Draft* (Cambridge, Mass.: Ballinger Publishing Co., 1977), p. 71.

25. Committee on Finance, United States Senate, *Adoption Assistance and Child Welfare Act of 1979*, 96th Congress, 1st session (1979) U.S. Government Printing Office, Washington, D.C., pp. 69–70.

26. Roberta Gottesman, *Bench Book: Post-Dispositional Periodic Review* (Washington, D.C.: unpublished manuscript, 1979), pp. 54–55.

27. Steiner, *Children's Cause*, ch. 5, p. 130.

28. *Report of the Panel on Youth of the President's Science Advisory Committee: Youth, Transition to Adulthood* (Chicago: The University of Chicago Press, 1970), p. 41.

29. K. T. Wiltse, "Current Issues and New Directions in Foster Care," in *Child Welfare Strategy in the Coming Years* (Washington, D.C.: U.S. Dept. of Health, Education and Welfare, Children's Bureau, DHEW publication No. (OHDS) 78-30158, 1978), p. 70.

30. Ann W. Shyne and Anita G. Schroeder, *National Study of Social Services to Children and Their Families* (prepared by Westat Inc., for the U.S. Dept. of Health, Education and Welfare, DHEW publication No. (OHDS) 78-30150), p. 28.

31. L. Polivka, P. Eccles and E. T. Miller, "Removal of Status Offenders from the Juvenile Justice System: The Florida Experience," *Child Welfare*, Vol. LVII, No. 3 (March 1979), pp. 177–86. The full extent to which public child welfare agencies are being used as "diversion programs" is not clear. Group care facilities, run under the auspices of probation departments, are an alternative form of diversion. See: *AB 3121 Impact Evaluation Attention Home Program Evaluation* (Fresno, Cal.: Research Unit Fresno County Probation Dept., January 1978).

32. R. C. Sari, "Adolescent Status Offenders—A National Problem," in *Child Welfare Strategy*, p. 301; *National Study on Selected Issues of Social Services to Children and Their Families: Summary of Information Needs* (Washington, D.C.: U.S. Dept. of Health, Education and Welfare, Children's Bureau, D.H.E.W. publication No. [OHDS] 77-30107, 1977), p. 10.

33. Cited in Sari, ibid., p. 301.

34. *Social Indicators of Equality of Minorities and Women* (Washington, D.C.: The United States Commission on Civil Rights, 1978), p. 34.

35. *National Study on Selected Issues*, p. 10; Alan R. Gruber, *Children in Foster Care, Destitute, Neglected . . . Betrayed* (New York: Human Sciences Press, 1978), pp. 183–85.

36. Sari, "Adolescent Status Offenders," p. 289.

37. This type of planning would focus on helping a youngster identify career goals and on identifying the means of attaining requisite skills or educational experiences required to realize career goals. Endeavoring to help a youngster learn the "ropes" of independent living, such as how to locate apartments, how to budget money, and so forth, would be a part of such planning.

Index